Dropshipping Shopify 2021 and Amazon FBA 2021

Learn the Best Strategies to Earn $45,000/Month PROFIT Using a #1 Proven E-commerce Online System to Create a Passive Income Machine with a Low Budget

John Wright

TABLE OF CONTENTS
Dropshipping Shopify 2021

TABLE OF CONTENTS
Amazon FBA 2021

Dropshipping Shopify 2021

Create your E-commerce Empire earning at least $30.000/month - The Ultimate Step-by-Step Guide to Build Your Passive Income Fortune Even Starting with a Low budget

By

John Wright

INTRODUCTION

Dropshipping is a method of shipping and delivery of retail orders in which the store does not need to have the products it sells in the warehouse. Instead, it buys them from a third party, e.g., the store purchases a drug and gets it delivered straight to the consumer. As a consequence, the retailer never sees the drug or manipulates it.

The biggest difference between dropshipping and conventional retail models is that the inventory is not owned or held by the seller. The merchant then purchases products from a third party (usually a wholesaler or manufacturer) who completes the orders as required.

Still do not know exactly what Dropshipping is and how it works, or what its advantages are for digital business? Don't worry, because in this eBook, you will discover what this powerful sales technique is all about and why more and more users are opting for it to start their Internet businesses.

Contrary to how things were only a couple of years ago, anyone who wants to set up an online shop can now go to a Dropshipping company instead of using their goods or warehouses to service their customers.

Therefore, given the popularity that this concept has reached today and how relatively easy it is to have a business of buying and selling products completely online, I think you should know and understand better what it is, what it is for, and how this technique works.

In this way, without having to invest in the purchase of your large stock, you can also sell different items or products in your business that you do not physically own.

In practice, for example, if you are the one who decides to start this type of business, you would be responsible for a Dropshipping e-commerce business, where you would sell products from a third party, called: « Dropshipper. »

CHAPTER 1

THE WINNING MINDSET

The language that many people are speaking suggests that when they come face to face with an opportunity of any kind, they don't expect to win, especially in online business. Therefore, by default, they are preparing to lose.

1. Having "The Winning Mindset." Your mind is your most powerful weapon

Here is an example of what we hear when we talk to our friends and customers who have just bought a product that we have recommended:

"Well, let's see what this product does for me. The last course I took did not achieve any results for me, I hope I am not getting into the same situation again, so I don't keep wasting time."

Does this sound like someone willing to do whatever it takes to make the course he's taking this time work for him? Or does this suggest that this person is not expecting any results other than those obtained in the previous course?

Keep in mind something very important; the way you speak to yourself is a simple manifestation of how your mind works and the belief system that you have installed. The words that come out of you, have to be thought. You may be aware of that or perhaps they are unconscious programs that you have installed that continue to give you the same results over and over again without you realizing it.

So ask yourself, how do you speak to yourself? Is it positive, or is it negative?

Does every direction you look seem to point to failure or success?

2. The Mirror Test to get to know us better

Let's do the mirror test, but first, here's another question for you: what do you see when you look in the mirror? Do you see any imperfection, worry, or failure? Or is what you see the greatness in you?

What do you hear yourself say? Do you rebuke yourself with comments like "I'm fat" or "I'm getting old"? Or do you stand up, with your back straight, and say to yourself, "I look really good" or "I am really good"?

I think that the mirror reflects much more than what your eyes can see. If you listened to the thoughts that were going through your head when you looked in the mirror, you would see that many of these thoughts reflect what you think of yourself and what are the limiting beliefs that you have. What you just saw is a reflection of your soul.

So we challenge you, the next time you are in front of a mirror, and you begin to hear that inner voice of yours and what it tells you... if you do, we know that you will be surprised by what you will hear.

Here are several questions you can ask yourself so that you can gradually grasp what you say to yourself and improve yourself.

What kind of words do you say about yourself in your mind? What are the thoughts that run through your head when you are looking in the mirror? Are they positive, or are they negative? Where did these thoughts come from? Is it really what you see, or are these opinions and influences from outside that you make yours?

3. Change Comes After Pain - We move away from pain and closer to pleasure.

Remember: people don't change until they experience enormous pain with things as they currently are. Only then, when we can't take it anymore, we say, "Hey, enough is enough." Only then do we begin to look for new ways of thinking, feeling, and acting to take action towards what we want.

Only at that moment do we stop making excuses that only paralyze us and stop us on our way to success and protect us from past experiences of pain. We will not go through that anymore if we decide to look for something better for ourselves to achieve our dreams.

4. You can't MAKE MONEY and make excuses at the same time

No matter what is happening in your world, you have to have a winning attitude, an entrepreneurial mindset and decision about what you want to create for your life, that is, you are responsible for yourself and what you want to achieve.

Leave the excuses for your old self, decide to change once and for all, and go for what you want.

At a point in our lives, we experience a lot of regret for not doing the things we wanted, but at the same time, we have a huge desire not to have to endure this pain more in life and start living the life we deserved.

But instead of wanting to make the necessary changes, we begin to deal with pain in a different way.

We start using excuses that we think are going to prevent us from experiencing more pain, but the opposite happens to us; we start to feel more unsuccessful than we previously felt.

That is why we advise you that it is much easier to stop coming up with new excuses for why you cannot do it, and once and for all take action, grab the bull by the horns and start to achieve the things you want.

So what is your excuse?

- "I can't give up a fixed salary."
- "Invest? You want me to lose all my money, don't you?"
- "I have no money to invest."
- "I've tried that before. It will never work."
- "I am not smart enough."
- "My husband would never go for it."
- "My wife would never understand it."
- "What will my friends say if I fail again?"

- "I am young. I still have time."
- "It is too late for me."
- "I cannot do this."
- "I was not born with a computer connected to my umbilical cord."
- "It is easier for the younger generation than it is for me."

Now we want you to go back and read the excuses we mentioned above. There is something in particular about these excuses that we want you to pay attention to. Each of these excuses gives you a reason to put obstacles in your mind that will only keep you from taking action because you are afraid of experiencing any regret that you had in the past.

Also, we use those excuses to blame someone else for our failures instead of taking responsibility for ourselves because we don't want to feel bad about not taking action.

If we have ever experienced any kind of pain or negative experience from past failures, our minds will immediately begin to look for ways to prevent us from feeling that pain again when faced with similar situations.

We don't like to feel pain.

We are creatures who always seek to do something for the pleasure it generates, and we stay away from activities that lead to pain. For this reason, many times, we tend to avoid taking risks as these thoughts get stronger, and we begin to hesitate and avoid taking action so as not to feel pain from past experiences reoccurring or the pain of starting an activity that will take time and effort.

It is these types of negative thoughts that keep us from taking risks and starting our own business in the first place.

THE BEST TECHNIQUES FOR SUCCESSFUL GOAL SETTING

Achieving the highest productivity, evolution, and growth of an organization's business largely depends on knowing how to set corporate goals. It is undeniable that if the goals are set correctly, then they will become a challenge that will not allow relaxation in the company, and that will require constant management and innovation to achieve them.

If a company wants to be productive and achieve success in the market, it must be able to establish the goals it wants to achieve. Goals help drive the business, and its constant monitoring and updating are the engine to avoid stagnation or disorientation of the processes in the organization.

Sometimes people avoid setting goals for fear of failing along the way. This is a serious mistake that organizations cannot afford to make since, without fixed goals, there is no direction for employees to follow. That confusion will hinder the development of the company.

The mistakes and successes that are made during the process to achieve those goals are the basis for improving each day and achieving the desired levels of productivity and competitiveness.

For this reason, we are going to discuss three tips to set goals that drive the evolution and growth of the organization. Let's get right into it:

1. Work as a team:

Teamwork is the basis for conquering the highest levels of productivity and efficiency in an organization. It helps to ensure that each member of the group reaches his best performance to feel supported by the company and work towards a common benefit.

In this same way, to establish goals, the opinions of various members of the organization should be taken into account, be they managers or department heads, and not a single person. This allows for the expansion of the spectrum of opinion and help, to combine different points of view to reach agreements that consolidate concrete and realistic goals.

Without a doubt, a motivated and aligned work team advances better and faster in achieving corporate objectives and is much more capable of reversing the adversities that arise.

2. Establish specific points:

The goals must be supported by figures and specific dates and not ramble between words that want to improve the situation, but do not actually lead anywhere. Goal setting should be specific and challenging with a time limit and a particular goal.

For example, a specific goal could be: within 60 days, the production of a certain product should be increased by 50%. An unclear goal would be: increase production to improve sales; the second is not setting any target value or explaining how it is intended to improve sales by simply increasing production.

It is about establishing concrete and realistic challenges that can be achieved in a specific timeframe, and that can be measured and followed up to know if they are being met or not. Thereby, establishing whether the processes are developing, or must be changed or consolidated to achieve the goals.

3. Turn goals into challenges:

Goals must always lead the organization to achieve new levels of impact in the market. Setting goals that are too low or too easy to achieve is an error that can translate into a lack of competitiveness or a lack of motivation for the team of collaborators.

The goals must bring changes and new efforts in the management and development of work to achieve a higher level of demand in the company. The objective is that the goals force the team to give their best effort, to improve themselves continually, and to grow day by day without setting caps that stop the development of the organization.

As we can see, goals are the common thread that moves the organization. They should become the element that leads it to achieve its highest levels of productivity and competitiveness.

Specific, realistic goals, achievable in a time limit, that have the participation of the work team and that become real challenges, are the key to an organization in constant evolution and growth in the market.

INVEST TIME AND ENERGY

Often we invest time and money in things that give us immediate satisfaction; however, in some cases, they do not generate anything. Only long-term problems.

So let's see why it is so important to spend time, energy, and attention on ourselves instead of dispersing them in projects that lead nowhere. Then, we'll discover how to accumulate things important to our personal growth.

Investing in ourselves is the best strategy we have to improve the quality of our lives, our work, and our relationships.

When we talk about investment, we intend to face immediate spending, not always in economic terms, but also in terms of energy, time, and resources, intending to obtain a permanent and lasting benefit in the future.

Try to think about it: if you invest time and energy in your training, what benefits could you get?

HOW TO MANAGE YOUR PASSIVE INCOME FORTUNE

"Being rich is not a matter of intelligence; it is a matter of habits."

Normally, we do not have this established knowledge and habits since we have never had any subject on money management neither in school, nor in the institute, nor higher studies. And it should be a fundamental subject for the world in which we live. Therefore, you must know that to master money you need to know how to manage it.

Poor people usually say phrases like "managing money restricts your freedom" or "I don't have enough money to manage." These phrases are incorrect. First of all, managing your money is not going to restrict your freedom; on the contrary, it is going to create your financial freedom. Not having to depend on a job is true freedom. And secondly, manage your money, and you will have more money. Don't wait until you have money to manage your money. For example, would it make sense for a person who wants to lose weight to say that they will start exercising and dieting when they lose 5 kilos? Well, it's the same concept here.

Many people believe that it takes a lot of money to be able to invest. What they don't know is that habit is more important than quantities. You need to create a habit to be able to manage your money correctly and have money to invest, to save, for leisure, etc.

Next, we are going to look at a simple money management system to start creating the habit we are looking for. This system consists of creating six bank accounts, either in the same bank or in different banks. Always keep in mind to open these accounts in banks free of commissions and expenses.

Each of the accounts will have the following purposes:

Account no. 1: Financial freedom account. In this account, we must deposit 10% of our income every month. The purpose of this account is to create financial assets, as these financial assets will create new income. These can be property, stocks, bonds, businesses...

Account no. 2: Long-term savings account. Here, we must deposit 10% of our income. The purpose of this account is that we always have liquidity. This will be like a life preserver to deal with any contingency situation. It is important that if this money is invested, it must be in products of maximum liquidity, that is, that we can make liquids in days. Liquidity prevails over profitability.

Account no. 3: Personal development and training account. Here, we must deposit 10% of our income. This account is for courses, books, seminars, conferences, and any type of education that allows us to grow as a person. We must remember that our money will grow as much as we do.

Account no. 4: Basic needs account. We must allocate 55% of our income to it. This account is for any daily need, that is, food, rent, electricity, water ... etc.

Account no. 5: Leisure account. We must deposit 10% of our income in it. This is the most fun account. Use it to give yourself the luxury of ordering a dish you have long wanted in a certain restaurant, renting a boat, taking a trip, booking a 5-star hotel ...

Account no. 6: Donations account. Here, we must deposit 5% of our income. This amount is relative, depending on the money you earn. That is, if you have to allocate a little less because 55% of the income may not be enough for basic needs. You can allocate a little less, and go up as your income increases. From my point of view, I recommend that it is never more than 10%. We will use this account to help others. You can donate to a church, to an NGO, or you simply donate. For example, buying food for someone you know needs it. In this world, to receive, you have to give, and very few things give as much happiness as helping others. You have to try it.

This system has two basic rules:

Pay yourself first. That is, as the money enters, you must manage it to the different accounts. This rule is what will create the habit in you. As time goes by, you will realize that managing money will become an automatic action.

There is no minimum quantity. If you have to start with a dollar or a euro, it doesn't matter. If you still do not have a salary or an asset that generates a sufficient amount of money, you can start with six envelopes or six piggy banks instead of creating six bank accounts until you have a minimum amount acceptable by your bank.

5 TIPS ON HOW TO SAVE THE MONEY FOR YOUR E-COMMERCE EMPIRE

The crisis has led many owners in e-commerce to tighten their belts to make the best of the end of the month. It is about saving money in almost everything, getting the best rates or the most forceful offers without having to give up the most basic and necessary habits on the part of the consumers. This can be achieved by carrying out a sensible and rational cost-containment policy. So this way, it leads to reaching the last days of each month with more money in the current account than in other exercises.

Applying a whole series of proposals aimed at saving, the user will notice that at the end of each month, he will have in his current account a minimum of 500 to 1,000 euros more. He can dedicate this to saving or for some unforeseen circumstances that may occur with this saving strategy as basic as it is special, with the only requirement to be disciplined in its application in e-commerce management.

Logistics lives a golden age, thanks to e-commerce, to the point that according to the Informative DBK Sector Observatory, electronic commerce drives 5.6% of the sales of companies of this type. Experts estimate that logistics costs represent around 25% of total e-commerce expenses, and companies are looking for ways to reduce them.

Trusted Shops, Europe's leading quality label for online stores, has produced a short guide with four practical tips to keep e-commerce sales from skyrocketing. The firm, created in 1999 and based in Cologne, has certified more than 25,000 online businesses in Europe.

1. Do not abuse free shipping costs

The ideal world of consumers is to have free deliveries and returns, and many are the stores that offer it, abusing the voracious competition that exists in the sector. We are currently seeing how large e-commerce players are ceasing to offer free shipping. The expense for a company to offer this is very high, even more, when it comes to retailers and not large corporations. The advice here is not to offer or permanently abuse free shipping. It's okay to do some temporary promotion to incentivize sales, but doing it permanently would increase costs exponentially.

2. Help the customer make the right decision

Charging the customer for returns is not a good idea if you want to incentivize purchases, because they can leave the cart if they see that they will be charged. However, doing so never triggers logistics costs and encourages the customer to buy. The advice is to include good photographs, models that resemble the regular customer who buys in your online store, 3D product presentation, videos, and even virtual reality help. Another good strategy is User Generated Content (UGC), which is nothing more than encouraging customers to post their shopping experience on social media and to post product reviews, thereby helping customers help each other and save potential returns.

3. An optimal organization system

With it, you will save time and money. The speed of delivery is one of the top priorities of any online store. Still, sometimes it is difficult to ensure next day delivery without having an accurate understanding of the product stock. To achieve this, it is advisable to have an optimal organization system that even predicts demand. For example, the ERP (Enterprise Resolution Planning) system that allows the storage of data in a central base, facilitating the understanding of the figures and the relationship between processes.

4. Always be transparent with the client

Keep in mind that the customer is always willing to wait or even pay more if you know how to deal with him. Incorporating a chat helps a lot to solve doubts, and even a well-managed questions and answers section can make a big difference compared to competitors. The objective, in addition to achieving sales, is to create positive messages among consumers, and this can only be achieved by being very clear with them.

5. Promote savings in logistics

With the above-mentioned factors, it cannot be said that the logistics savings model of an online company is exhausted. Not much less. On the contrary, it can also develop in the control of transport costs as one of the items that can weigh down our finances even more than simple shipments. In this sense, it is necessary to use the calculator and show the savings ratio that we can contemplate from this very basic strategy in this class of companies (online companies).

While on the other hand, another of the most relevant aspects that we must contemplate from these moments is the one that has to do with the best management of orders. It can be a strategy that rarely fails to meet these objectives in saving the company, with a reduction in costs that can take up to a little more than 20% on the amount disbursed.

In this sense, no doubt, having products grouped with the logic of our activity gives us the necessary personnel to prepare orders. It does not cost much trouble to carry it out or boost it, and on the contrary, it can offer us many advantages compared to other saving formats, even more powerful. Surely it will be a job that will be very worthwhile, and of course, you will not regret having carried it out at those times. It is, after all, one of the keys that you have ahead to save money in e-commerce.

CHAPTER 2

DROPSHIPPING 101

If you have been thinking about starting an online store for a long time or you are looking for some formula for doing business on the Internet, you may be interested in knowing this system.

Dropshipping is a way of selling through the Internet, in a very non-traditional way and that, as you will see in this chapter, does not require too much investment and has very few risks.

As you know, the internet is a world full of opportunities, but to succeed with an e-commerce business, as it happens with all traditional buying and selling businesses, normally, you must make an initial investment to acquire the most important factor: the product that is sold in your store.

However, here this link in the chain (investment in products) does not have the same role if you use the sales technique of dropshipping.

But first of all, I would like to define this term and explain exactly what it consists of.

What is Dropshipping?

In its literal translation from English, it means "shipping triangulation." The denominations can well know this term, also Anglo-Saxon of "dropship" or "drop shipment."

Therefore, we can define it as:

Dropshipping is an online sales model that allows you to buy products individually from a supplier so that they are the ones who send the products directly to the end customer.

Instead of purchasing a large amount of inventory, you partner with the wholesale manufacturer, also called "Dropshipper," by agreement or prior negotiation.

This method has been revolutionizing the traditional logistics mode of operation for some years now, since the online store should only be in charge of carrying out purely bureaucratic functions, such as managing orders, collections, customer service and possible interested parties.

What does Dropshipping consist of?

Normally, the process works as follows:

- Suppose you are the e-commerce entrepreneur (retailer).
- You create your website and publish the products of your online store there, from which a customer places an order and pays for that item.
- Then, you inform the manufacturer of this order, who directly sends the products from his warehouse to the final consumer, with the signs or badges of your store (retailer), or even without visible badges.

In this way, the manufacturer only charges for the "net" cost of the product, adding a dropshipper commission to its final price.

Therefore, you would remain as a simple intermediary, and your benefits would lie in the sum of the commissions you manage to earn for all your sales.

PROS OF USING THE DROPSHIPPING METHOD

These are the factors that support using the dropshipping technique if you have a business idea:

1. Start-up costs

Investing in inventory is one of the biggest spending items when establishing an online business.

However, this formula avoids this problem, eliminating the risk of spending money on items that may never be sold.

2. Items can be offered almost instantly

Usually, when a retailer wants to start selling a product, they have to wait until they have received it so that they can post it on their website.

With this sales model, when you decide you want an item on the website, you can start advertising almost immediately.

3. A broader catalog can be offered

Having the ability to offer a broader range of products is always something that a digital business should aspire to, and with this technique, it is possible.

With Dropshipping, there is no need to worry about the different colors or sizes to have in stock or where they will be stored.

They are simply published on the website, and the provider takes care of everything else, once the dropshipper has placed the order.

4. New products are tested without risk

When adding new products to the catalog, the risk of not selling them is left in the background with dropshipping.

Having to guess what customers want is often difficult for any business, so being able to test without making a real investment is always a competitive advantage.

This, without a doubt, can increase the conversions of your e-commerce business, when seeing the recurring user who continuously offers new products.

5. Time is saved in organizing efforts

Organizing the stock and preparing it for delivery can be a time-consuming nightmare.

Using a third party in this process of shipping items saves handling, labeling, packaging, shipping, and other time and money expenses.

This leaves the dropshipper extra time to focus on other complementary tasks of his website, such as creating a corporate blog, where valuable content is provided for the potential clients of your brand.

6. It is not necessary to have inventory

One of the drawbacks of selling any item is worrying about storing inventory, keeping track of it, that is, keeping traceability, and even spending part of the money to pay related taxes.

With dropshipping, this does not happen, since the manufacturer or wholesaler bears all these logistics costs.

7. Storage

You don't need a warehouse or any other space large enough to house all the products that are part of your online store.

This, likewise, will be borne by the manufacturing company.

CONS OF USING DROPSHIPPING

Nonetheless, this sales technique also has its drawbacks. Below are detailed some of the most important ones so that you can avoid fairly typical beginner mistakes when starting an online project based on this technique:

1. Scams

You have to be careful with the suppliers and get all the necessary information about them before making payments for the ordered products.

My advice is, before agreeing to this method of shipping, always meet personally, if possible, with the person in charge or team responsible for this supplier company.

2. Lack of quality control

Product output could be lower than originally planned and may not suit that suggested on the Site.

So it's important to maintain firm control over the quality, control the rate of returns, and other issues with customers, as they will blame the business and not the supplier if they are not satisfied with the item they have finally received.

3. Confusing fee structures

If you choose the wrong company, you can end it without making a profit, or you could lose money. There can be so many payments that it is difficult to keep track of our money, even if we make sales ourselves.

4. High shipping rates for customers

If items from more than one supplier are included on the dropshipper's website, the customer may have to pay very high shipping costs when ordering a large number of items.

The reason for this extra cost is that they will come from different points. This may be one of the reasons for abandoning the shopping cart in your store.

In turn, it can discourage future acquisitions and therefore loss of customers over time.

5. Order processing can be difficult

Many companies that use this type of shipment as a sales strategy work with multiple wholesalers.

Each of them imposes different requirements for order processing, billing, and shipping. This can complicate things enormously.

The time between the sale of a product and its shipment can also be longer since there are many previous conversations and actions.

6. Not having all the product information is problematic

Since they never physically handle the products being sold, the person doing dropshipping has no real and clear idea of what they are like.

Many times, the manufacturer does not give enough product descriptions, does not provide exact dimensions, weight, or ease of use.

Lack of data leaves noticeable gaps in the website, and this is not good for the company, because scarce information or the lack of it, can discourage consumers who could become potential customers.

7. Availability

The availability of a product is not always known until an end customer buys it.

This can be enormously frustrating for consumers, who have the impression that they have purchased a product, only to discover that it was not exactly what they expected (or how they expected).

8. Automation

To eliminate the problem, as mentioned earlier, an automated system that regularly updates stock availability throughout the day is preferable.

It is also recommended to ask the supplier to send an email or make a phone call if a certain product is out of stock.

9. Customer service

With this system, there is less responsibility for shipping, but also much less control over the customer experience.

There is no way to ensure that a product has arrived on time and is only known when a customer calls to complain or ask.

At that time, moreover, the problem resolution process slows down, as customer support staff will not have the necessary information on hand, and the query or complaint will have to go through a third-party provider before the matter can be addressed.

10. Competition

Finding great products means that there will generally be broad competition from other retailers in the sector.

The margins of dropshipping products can be quite low in these cases, because many manufacturers charge a price for the service that makes it very difficult to maneuver, to impose themselves on other competing companies.

11. Profitability

Ten years ago, this sales technique was much more profitable.

Average profitability has been reduced quite a bit, with the growth of stores like Amazon and the greater competitiveness in general in the e-commerce sector.

Therefore, it is recommended that, if you want to succeed with a model like this, you have a very powerful and original proposal.

On the other hand, you should offer as much information as possible with the products, while selling accessories and, if possible, complement the offer with some items in stock.

12. Profit margins

Profit margins vary greatly, depending on the products

being sold. For high-end electronics, the margins are small and are usually around 5-10%.

But for low-priced accessories, margins are often close to 100%.

However, on average, gross shipping margins are usually in the range of 10% to 15%.

Examples of wholesale companies specialized in Dropshipping

Having seen the advantages and disadvantages of embarking on this online sales environment, and before concluding this chapter, I would like to give you some examples of companies that have been succeeding in this sector for some years and betting on this method:

BigBuy

It is a Spanish wholesale company, which has made a name for itself in this sector.

It mainly distributes products related to original business gifts, such as gourmet kitchen products, household and electronic cleaning and small appliances, perfumery and cosmetics, and health and beauty products, among others.

MiniIntheBox

This is another large dropshipper wholesaler, which distributes electronic products, based on orders from online stores around the world.

It has been operating since 2010, and its growth has not decreased since then, given the rise of technology, which has, as you know, millions of followers today.

AliExpress

Who doesn't know this Asian dropshipping giant?

From footwear, clothing, electronic products, and even DIY items, AliExpress has been at the forefront in this sector since 2012, when it started operating and selling products wholesale for online stores throughout the world.

The benefits and potential problems of dropshipping are varied. Therefore, if you are thinking of using this sales technique in your online store, you should reflect on all these factors.

Reflect on its pros and cons before deciding to start a business with this Dropshipping system and, if necessary, first consult the experience of someone you know who has already tried it.

Obstacles that often arise can be resolved through careful planning and good coordination between vendors and suppliers.

Once you know what dropshipping is and what its advantages and disadvantages are, conclusions can be drawn.

It is very important to do your research beforehand, to avoid most of the disadvantages that arise.

With previous research, information, and planning work, you can put aside the pitfalls and reap the benefits of using Dropshipping.

Without a doubt, it is quite a viable business opportunity that can help you work from home, with practically no infrastructure or investment.

And above all, the most important thing: it will bring you many benefits!

WHY YOU SHOULD START A DROPSHIPPING BUSINESS IN 2021

Using Dropshipping to enter the world of e-commerce is a good idea. This will allow you to get your hands on it and then move on to stock. Indeed, making stock is the ultimate goal, which will allow you develop your electronic commerce business.

Why do Dropshipping?

1- The investment

The first argument for Dropshipping is a financial investment. You can start your e-business with less investment. That is to say, much less than with an e-commerce site that makes stock. This is not to be overlooked; this is why beginners opt for Dropshipping, and it is a very good idea! Nothing also prevents you from staying in Dropshipping; it is a very good long-term business model. E-traders specialize in Dropshipping and stay in Dropshipping, and they make a very good living!

We do not have all the means to invest large sums in stock, and that is why Dropshipping is a good way to start an online business. It's just crazy to say that you can still be an e-merchant while investing a few thousand euros. Also, this investment can save you large sums. You can create a profitable online business.

2- No stock

Having no stock is a great advantage. It means that we have no inventory management. It's beneficial because there's no financial risk. We don't have to say to ourselves: "Is it going to sell?" or "I hope my stock will sell." With Dropshipping, if a product does not sell, it does not matter—we move to another product until we find the right product. The advantage is that we can test without investing in the stock.

Not keeping stock also makes it possible to have a more substantial product catalog for your e-commerce business. On the one hand, it fills your e-commerce site; on the other hand, you can find more products that will enrich you.

Your product catalog gets to be quite large and diverse, which makes it easy to find good products that will sell by the hundreds. Coupled with good web marketing on social networks and a good natural referencing, you will easily be able to live on your commercial site. You also take care of the integration on your online site, which is an advantage and, above all, a huge time saver!

3- Test, test, test...

The key to success lies in the test. If you do not go through a test phase, do not be surprised by your results! It's primordial. This will serve to highlight two or three different products. It is these products that will make your turnover. The other products you can leave on your online sales site. This will build customer trust, and it costs you nothing to leave them.

Dropshipping allows you to test as many products as you want. That's what's great about it. You can add products every day to test them and find the winning products. If you have inventory from the start you will be spending money on quantities without knowing whether they will sell well. It's always the same principle, and Dropshipping is the solution to start. Become a Dropshipper and become an annuitant thanks to your commercial activity.

Why deprive yourself of this? Frankly, there are no reasons. Low cost, possibility to test different products, this business model has it all.

4- Perfect for a beginner

Dropshipping is great to put a foot in the electronic commerce business. Indeed it is still complicated, and it is necessary to follow the training, but it is very well suited for beginners. It's important to get your hands on it as they say and develop knowledge in e-commerce and digital marketing.

Take Dropshipping as a required pass to grow and move on to stock. It's like a laboratory that tests, and after finding what it needs, it starts to market it. It's the same except that during your tests, you sell at the same time. Pretty interesting, isn't it?

So if you want to get started in the wonderful world of e-commerce, start with Dropshipping. But beware, just because it is suitable for beginners doesn't mean you should go in headlong. Not at all! Take the time to train and change your mindset; this is the most important part to succeed with your e-shop.

If you have the ambition to create a big company or start-up, you will have a taste of what awaits you. And yes, despite what we can see on the net, being an entrepreneur is not easy. It is a huge workload, but it should not discourage you because you can become an annuitant.

It is very interesting in the sense that you will have to become a boss if your activity grows. Indeed you will be obliged to have a team to manage your digital commerce in B2B. You will have to adapt to the function that a boss must exercise. And this is a very wonderful experience. Over the long term, you will develop more skills for your big digital project.

5- Cash flow business

First of all, what is a cash flow business? A cash flow business is a business that allows you to generate money every month. Dropshipping is the perfect example of a business in cash flow. This type of business is used to generate significant funds to create its ultimate project. This is what I explained to you in the previous paragraph.

When you have enough money to develop your ultimate digital project, the mistake you should not make is to abandon your cash flow business, here, Dropshipping. Why leave a business that works and earns you money even when you sleep? I agree there is no reason. What you can do is delegate it—many entrepreneurs delegate tasks for their digital business. Even the entrepreneur has 24-hour days. Yet the daily tasks that a business requires cannot be done by one person in 24 hours. It must also be taken into account that in 24 hours, it is impossible to work all through.

Remember, this is the start of your success. If you want to develop the competitor of Amazon, no problem, but you need experience and especially the funds necessary to develop this project. Remember that nothing is impossible; it just takes willpower and a good mindset!

6- Faster development

Here we are going to talk about developing a business. In your neighborhood, you may have someone who has a business. You may have noticed that development is not done by snapping your fingers. And even when you finish development, it takes some time before it starts to work.

Regarding Dropshipping, there are fewer elements to set up compared to a "traditional" e-commerce site that makes stock. E-commerce must manage its logistics, negotiate with its suppliers, train its team... It is much more complex for a beginner and especially much longer. Please note an e-commerce site is a very good business model but more complicated to set up. Even if Dropshipping is quite complicated, it must still be admitted that it is easier and above all faster.

If you do your job well, you can develop your store in a few weeks. Which is relatively short. There are even e-merchants who shop in one day. It's still amazing. Also, if you are really good and above all well trained you will earn your first euros soon after the launch of the shop.

6 Tips And Mistake To Avoid For Beginners

After choosing dropshipping, you need to make sure from the start that you have a solid strategy. And that means avoiding these common mistakes.

1. Lack of research when selecting the provider

The success of your online trade depends on the selection of your dropshipping partner. This represents the direct interface to your customer so that the performance and reliability of your partner has a direct impact on customer satisfaction. Under no circumstances do you want to run the risk of customers receiving damaged goods or not receiving any goods at all.

Extensive research into the respective strengths and weaknesses of a provider should, therefore, be the first step in the dropshipping business. Practice shows, however, that many dealers invest too little time in a critical examination of the quality of the supplier.

2. Underestimation of workload

As a dropshipper, you have less work to do than conventional online trading. No separate warehouse is required, and you do not have to worry about the multi-step order processing yourself.

This is exactly why this business model is so popular with many online retailers. However, one should not underestimate the work that is still connected with this business model—be it maintaining the supplier pool, marketing offers, or looking after customers.

Tip: It is important, especially at the beginning of dropshipping, to make a realistic idea of the workload. Communication and processing with your suppliers can often be time-consuming.

This is remedied by the digitization of these processes, which largely automate orders with electronic data exchange between your supplier and your shop. Automation and connection of the partner in dropshipping can be made easily using an ERP system. With IT-supported processes, you benefit not only from up-to-date data, but also a lot of automation around shipping management (price updates, tracking information for your customers, creation of return labels, etc.).

3. Expect your products to sell themselves

As mentioned above, dropshipping automatically puts you in a competitive space because others are selling exactly what you are. It is too easy to believe that you can set up dropshipping for your business and then have an instant moneymaker in your hands.

The opposite is true—if you do dropshipping, you have to invest all the time you save on shipping and fulfillment in marketing and SEO. These are the elements that will drive traffic to your business and increase your sales if you are a direct seller. Since you cannot control fulfillment or packaging with dropshipping, you always want to focus on quality customer service and offer customers a positive experience with the parts of the buying process that you can control.

4. Relying on a supplier too much or not testing suppliers

If you rely on a supplier without backup, you can be prepared for logistical problems. What if they raise their prices so much that you can no longer afford it? Or go out of business? Or just decide not to work with you anymore? Even if the scenarios are less drastic, they may not be in stock for a product and have no idea when they will be back in stock. Always have a replacement supplier available to contact if your supplier does not work for a particular order. You want to spot quality issues before they become a problem.

5. Stress about shipping costs

Handling shipping costs can be problematic even if you ship all orders from one place.

Shipping from more than one warehouse or through multiple suppliers can be a nightmare. What if an order consists of two different warehouses or three different suppliers?

Take a step back and look at the big picture instead of worrying about shipping to multiple locations for each individual order. What are you trying to achieve? Exact shipping costs? Or more sales, satisfied customers, and recurring business? If you use more energy on shipping costs with every order, you no longer have energy to spend on creating a better shopping experience, expanding your business, marketing, and so on.

So what should you do instead? Take a look at past orders and use them to calculate a flat shipping fee. Or maybe a tiered rate based on the cart value. Will it narrow your profit margin? Yes, for some orders. But you will prevail against others, and if you set your flat rate correctly, the shipping costs will even out over time. In addition, the conversion rates are demonstrably increased by flat rate and free shipping. One of the main reasons customers leave their shopping carts is shipping costs. A flat rate shipping fee eliminates confusion and seemingly "hidden" fees that appear at the checkout.

6. Returns rate

With the dropshipping concept, you, as an online retailer, are freed from many complex tasks relating to storage and shipping. Returns from your customers are often excluded. If there is a high return volume, this means more work and increased costs for you as a dealer. First, try to outsource the returns processing to your dropshipping provider. If this is not up for debate, your goals of the agreement should be as little effort and cost as possible.

Tip: Investigate the possible causes of the returns and optimize the description and the image of the products offered in the shop. Separate yourself from items that are often returned. Both measures can ensure a quick and significant reduction in your return rate.

As you can see, dropshipping is not an all-in-one solution, but it's a great way to open or scale an e-commerce store. At every stage of your business, you need to step back and assess whether dropshipping makes sense for your business or not.

How To Start With A Small Budget

Unlike traditional commerce businesses that require a large initial investment—several thousand euros from creation to management—dropshipping requires only a minimal investment to get started.

That said, like any business, online or not, dropshipping can become expensive if not addressed and managed properly...

For example, management fees and the cost of plugins and e-commerce applications can quickly increase your expenses and reduce your profits significantly.

To get started in dropshipping at a lower cost, you must have a concrete idea of how you will build your business and manage your e-commerce store.

1. Find a niche

The first step to launching an online business cheaply is to find a niche. This is valid for any field: training, coaching, or online business.

Why? To become an expert in your field and apply real added value to your brand or your expertise.

Your niche must exploit something that you are passionate about so as not to get bored and abandon your project too soon. Choosing something close to your heart is essential.

Finding your niche allows you to target a particular audience with which you will find it easier to sell your products. By analyzing your audience and your potential customers, you are able to respond exactly to their problems with your shop.

So you generate a profit more quickly—then you can reinvest—and you build a real brand image for your shop!

2. Think about the products to sell

If you start in a dropshipping shop tucked away, you will surely have a multitude of products of all kinds in your catalog, and it is a good thing. However, you will need to find your first products that will make your shop take off.

To achieve this, it is important once again to understand your audience and find products that respond to the problems that your visitors encounter. It is more important that these products will be your bestsellers!

For example, if you are launching a store selling horse products, carefully study people interested in horse riding. You can do this through Google searches, Facebook groups, and forums.

This is the right approach to take to find products that will answer the problems of your potential customers.

Now, to find your product for sale, several dropshipping possibilities are available to you:

- AliExpress, which is a very interesting gateway to start in dropshipping—but be careful with the products you sell, some are not recommended, such as electronics or oils/creams.
- Bigbuy or Spocket to work with European suppliers and thus reduce delivery time while offering better quality products.
- WholeSale2B or other similar alternatives for selling luxury goods at several hundreds or even thousands of euros.

It is also necessary to define your margins well to avoid unpleasant surprises when you do your accounts. They must be able to generate a good profit for you by including all management and delivery costs.

Why is this step essential? If your product responds to a specific problem of your audience, it will be easier to sell it and retain your customers.

3. Use the right traffic acquisition solution

One of the essential components for the proper functioning of an online business is traffic. Indeed, bringing qualified traffic to your dropshipping shop allows you to make sales.

Some solutions to promote your products are very expensive, and that is the case with Facebook Ads making it unthinkable to use if you have a tight budget. Like Google Ads, I do not even recommend any form of such advertising campaigns.

No, what is necessary if you have a small budget to invest, it is to use conventional methods to make people talk about your products. Of course, they take time, but in the long run, you will get traffic all year round, without spending a single euro on getting it.

Among these methods, here are the best ones to gain free traffic:

- SEO, which is, without a doubt, the most effective method in the long term. Generating traffic from search engines has a lot of benefits, like better conversion rates.
- Developing your notoriety on social networks is also a great way to create a community and attract traffic. For that, Instagram and Pinterest are very good alternatives to Facebook.

- Speaking of Facebook, you can very easily find groups in your niche to promote your brand, your products, and all your advice. Remember the keyword: become an expert in your field.

You have a very small budget, so you will have to work to get what you want, and all these methods are not exhaustive. You can indeed make the word-of-mouth work by setting up an e-commerce affiliate program.

4) Choose your sales platform carefully

Once you have a niche, starting materials, and an idea of how you're going to generate traffic, you have to put it all in place. But how?

You have to choose where you are going to sell your products. The advice I give you here is mainly oriented for an online store because it allows you to create your brand, and you have great freedom in your decisions. That said, you can sell your products very well on eBay or Amazon, the advice is always good, but the techniques are different.

To get started in dropshipping, the best platform to date remains Shopify, which offers you all the marketing functionalities to create a shop in your image.

Both are offered at the same price, i.e., €27 per month. The investment remains ridiculous because you can start selling without a problem with free professional themes for your shop.

Additional applications will expand the possibilities of your dropshipping store often with additional costs. However, wait to make the figure to invest in these extensions.

And now it's up to you!

There you have it: With a little planning, preparation, and a thoughtful strategy, it is possible to set up and operate a dropshipping shop with few means.

If you follow the steps above, you will start to see profits pour in very quickly, making your strict budget concerns a problem solved.

FREQUENTLY ASKED QUESTIONS WHEN YOU ARE STARTING OUT

What is dropshipping?

Dropshipping is an online sales method for an e-trader to sell products stored at a supplier responsible for delivery.

How does dropshipping work?

The operation of dropshipping is relatively simple. We create a shop where we will sell the products of a supplier. When a visitor places an order in our shop, we send this order to the supplier who takes care of the delivery of the product.

Start and train in dropshipping

How to get started and start dropshipping?

To get started in e-commerce, you have to start by learning and training. For this, there are many free or paid resources: books, training, videos on YouTube, forums, social networks...

How to train and learn dropshipping?

To train in dropshipping, the most important thing is to apply what you learn. The theory is useful, but not enough. I, therefore, recommend that you test as many factors as possible in the hope of obtaining results.

How to do dropshipping?

It is difficult to answer this question in a few words. To do dropshipping, you need to have an online store, a niche, a product, and know-how to bring visitors to your website. There are several ways to do dropshipping depending on the suppliers and marketplaces used (AliExpress, Amazon, eBay), CMS (Shopify, WordPress), or marketing methods.

How to find a supplier?

To find a supplier, you must already have an idea of the niche or product you want to sell. Then, you can search for a wholesaler according to several criteria: location, reputation, delivery times, etc.

Is dropshipping a scam?

Dropshipping is a legal practice and not a scam, as some media suggest. On the other hand, it may be that dropshippers who do their job badly are scammers.

CHAPTER 3

WHAT IS A NICHE?

By definition, a niche market is a very targeted market and often restricts access to a passion that has sales potential. For starters, vegans are a niche market when food is just one sector or group. It is important to distinguish the niche and ultra-niche markets to successfully understand their future customers and target just with the right product. This is where individual entrepreneurs make a huge amount of profit.

If you sell everyday products that everyone consumes, you are not in a niche market. For example, selling chocolate, cars, or furniture is not a niche market at all. Such goods can be found in your city without any doubts, and you don't need the internet to find your joy.

However, there are sub-categories of these categories. The more you dig inside, the more you will get a smaller market. The point here is to find and sell products that few people can afford. And better if it's a genuine hobby (like using the ukulele in music, for example). People can waste a lot of time on interests, so as compared with a smaller market, you will get decent margins.

Take the example of chocolate. Almost everyone loves chocolate. However, there is dark, white, milk, and many other forms of chocolate. This is not yet a niche. But if we did well, we would know that the knowledge about this chocolate is really important. For example, if it comes from fair and organic trade, it is good chocolate, and not everyone is immune to it. Also, whether the chocolate is mixed with original foods such as goji berries or other berries is another factor. Selling chocolate isn't a niche market, but selling organic chocolate from fair trade and comprising of a berry mix, each time you don't find it in big trade (exit blueberry or chili), you may keep it. We are in a market where chocolate and diet lovers who are concerned with more healthy eating may be involved. We then arrive at a niche market we've been building from a regional sector. If we drive the addiction, even more, we can only rely on the dark and protein candy, so we enter the ultra-niche of gourmet athletes who only eat raw and try a balanced diet to improve their strength after a competition.

RESEARCH IS KEY TO YOUR SUCCESS

In the SEO community, we often hear the phrase "content is king." Indeed, your workhorse must be content. But not just content for the sake of it, it must also be quality.

You must have interesting target keywords, and that is what brings traffic. Yes, it is.

But what do you do when you have a website whose theme is a niche with little research?

If you keep a blog on a specific subject and you quickly go around the subject, it will be difficult to attract more visitors.

I will not hide from you that it is quite complicated to manage this situation!

It is said that it is very important to have competition, this shows that there is an established market. When you have no competition, it is because people are not aware of your cause. It takes a lot of work, and many companies fail.

Working in an area where there is more demand than supply is ideal.

Back to our sheep: niches with low research volume. To be honest, this is not going to be easy.

The problems of low research volume niches

I already talked about it a little above, but there are two major problems with low research volume niches.

Lack of research on the subject

Having a lot of visits to a website whose theme is little discussed will be difficult.

When tackling a subject that interests only a few people, it will be difficult to attract more people than the amount of research done. If you talk about lace fabric from the 1940s, for example, you're going to have a lot fewer people than if you talk about football.

It can also happen that it is a seasonal theme, such as air conditioners and heating.

Are your keywords or niche too specific?

We're not going to beat around the bush: having specific keywords is more interesting than having generic keywords, here are the reasons:

- Less competition
- Easier to reach the top position
- More likely to have traffic

However, much more content is needed when targeting specific keywords than with generic keywords. You also need to be certain that your keywords will be searched enough; otherwise no one will come to your site.

The question to ask is, therefore, whether the niche is too specific or the keywords?

If you are talking about allergies, it is unlikely that you will have a lot of traffic coming from that keyword. Your niche is too specific. You may have to review your niche and the way you present it.

If your keywords are made up of several words, it will be difficult to know exactly how many searches are done per month. Then, it will be necessary to carry out the good keyword research even before writing your content.

The first question to ask yourself is, "What does my reader or client want?"

We will see now how to proceed if you think that your current method is bad and needs to be changed.

Make your keywords more specific

When your keyword is in a fairly specific niche, it is difficult to find expressions that are sought. The first reflex to that would be to find a more generic keyword.

Imagine that you have as a keyword "lace towel." This cannot be found on Yooda Insight. The first reflex is, therefore, to use "fabric" or "cloth" instead.

The ideal is to go to Google Keyword Planner, where you can put several keywords at once, in the "Get trends and data on search volume" section. This will help you better define the specificity of your keywords.

This is where you can compare all of your keywords and find out how specific they should be.

Also, think of the long-tail keywords.

If you work, for example, with uber suggest for your keyword research, you can export the list of words obtained and import them into Google keyword planner to have a search idea according to each word. It will surely ignore some errors, but the result will be there.

Make your keywords more generic

If you are already in a niche and are reading this chapter, this is probably your case.

Your keywords are not attracting enough people, and you need to make them more general to attract people to your site.

Start by finding one or more generic keywords, and for that, there is no miracle method, we will have to think a little. Even one is already a good thing.

Once this or these keywords are found, I invite you to select more generic keywords on Yooda Insight or simply Google Keyword Planner.

It will suffice to choose the words whose competition is not the strongest with a fairly high search rate.

You are also free to choose a more competitive keyword if you want to measure yourself against the competition.

Why not the two of them?

Check that your SEO strategy is in order

Your keywords may not be the only reason your SEO is not taking off. Sometimes, in SEO, the little beast is not where you expect it to be!

It will, therefore, be necessary to review your SEO strategy and check each box off the checklist:

- Have you checked that the links pointing to your site are good?
- Is your internal network optimized? No broken links (error 404)?
- Is your content of good quality and original?
- Are you not blocking your site from search engines?
- Are the meta robots tags (noindex/nofollow) or the robots.txt file not playing tricks on you?

- Have you checked that there is no penalty on Google Search console?
- Has your site not been hacked?
- Is it duplicate content?
- The title tag, H1 title, meta description, site content?

All these points are extremely important for your site because it may be a stupid error that you cannot find, and that is right before your eyes.

Search engines are intractable.

The technical side of your site should not be overlooked

There are two points to take into account in terms of the technical side of your site. Indeed, an extremely well search engine optimized site is useless if it is not suitable for mobile and does not load well.

Adapt your site to each device

The first point to take into account is whether your site is displayed correctly on each device.

For a while, it was customary to have two identical sites—one for computers and another for mobiles. The business was not practical since it was necessary to update both when we wanted to make a change.

We often saw URLs like m.monsite.fr, which was done via an automatic redirection.

Nowadays, technology has evolved, and we have been talking about responsive design technology for several years. A site that adapts to all devices, whether it's phones, tablets, computers, portable consoles, or even TVs.

If your site runs on a CMS, I recommend that you choose a suitable theme that is responsive design. They generally cost around sixty euros but are used for the entire life of your site.

For those who have a handmade site, there are Media Queries in CSS3 so that your content adapts to the screen.

The loading time of your site

The loading time is extremely important:

- There are solutions to increase your loading time.
- The first thing to do is to assess the extent of the damage using gtmetrix.

For the second step, you will have to optimize the weight of your images by making them smaller (at least to correct size) and by compressing them. You will lose a little bit in quality, but if done right, you will not lose enough for it to be noticeable. I recommend short pixel on WordPress or the compressor site for this.

The 3rd stage will be playing on the code to lighten and store your cached content. For this, we will minify the code, remove each unnecessary character to make it shorter, and compress it in gzip format. Regarding caching, to put it simply, it's like saving your site information so that loading is faster.

No panic software does it for you. On WordPress, the easiest way is to take a plugin like the fastest cache (free) or WP rocket (paid). For those who have a site coded by hand, I suggest you contact a developer or an agency, as the task is not simple for a person who has not mastered the code.

Having a niche site with low search volume is not an easy task. However, SEO is for all sites, and there are obvious solutions. You don't necessarily have to have a big site to get good results.

You don't need to have years of SEO experience to build a site either.

Patience and a little motivation are the keys to success.

How To Recognize A Profitable Niche

As a new trader, you need to find products to sell and services to offer. The products on your shelves and those listed on your e-commerce site shape your brand image.

The goal is to find products suited to your activity that will appeal to your audience, and that will sell easily. By studying your niche market, you will be able to ensure that your potential products/services will interest your target customers. What products or services best meet their needs? What added value will a specific product provide to your customers? These are just some of the questions to ask as part of the product selection process for sale.

Your success will depend on the quality of the research conducted; the main purpose of this research is to enable you to find a product that perfectly meets the needs of a niche market. This is called product-market correspondence. The choice of products with high profitability potential is, therefore, crucial for both online stores and physical stores.

But what do we mean by product-market correspondence and how to assess it? We detail the concept in this section to allow you to take advantage of it as part of your online store sales activity.

What is product-market correspondence?

Product-market correspondence is a concept for assessing how well a product meets the needs of a market, or simply the profitability potential of what you offer.

Even without knowing this concept, most retailers instinctively try to find the right product-market match based on their audience. In essence, they try to find out what consumers want, offer products that are highly likely to interest them and do the necessary to create an attractive value proposition to capture a larger market share.

Whether you want to change your brand image, change your product selection, or have just started your business, finding products with high profitability potential is often a complex task.

Ask yourself a few questions before starting the decision-making process, including, "What products do I like, buy, and find useful to me?" and "Does the sale of this product/service excite me?"

Your interest in a product is likely shared by other consumers, indicating that there is demand. Also, you will be more excited about selling a product you are passionate about, and your customers will notice it.

Even if trendy products can be sold faster, or encourage a new audience to take an interest in your brand, it would be difficult to build a lasting brand by exclusively selling the flavor of the month. It often turns out to be easier to build a coherent brand by mainly selling timeless products and a few trendy products on appropriate occasions.

Even if it is more practical to choose products first before building a sales activity centered on the offers considered, it is always possible—in the case of an existing business—to replace the products already on sale and to ensure that your business adapts to the changes made.

How to find what to sell: identify opportunities

From products that you appreciate and want consumers to discover, to products that meet a demand ignored by your competitors, finding the right product-market correspondence often involves identifying a business opportunity. We have identified eight types of opportunities:

Discover keyword opportunities: Start with keyword research related to your niche and your audience.

Build an interesting and captivating brand: Create a unique and interesting brand to sell your products.

Identify and resolve a consumer pain point.

Follow your passion: Inject your passions and interests into your business and your product selection.

Identify an untapped market opportunity: Are you interested in some products? Analyze your potential competitors to find out if they offer similar items, or if you could be the first seller to market them.

Use your expertise and experience.

Take advantage of trends early: Are you planning to sell trendy products? Make sure you have them in-store or list them on your e-commerce site as soon as possible.

Most retailers offer both trendy and classic products to keep consumers satisfied at all levels—providing them with the items they need and the products they would like to buy out of envy.

Study your customers to choose the right products

To be able to choose your niche and focus on an opportunity that can benefit your business, you need to know your audience.

If you do not know your customers, it will be difficult

for you to find a good product-market match. By gaining in-depth knowledge of the problems encountered by your customers, you will be able to understand them better, gain their trust, and strengthen your credibility.

You can find out what interests your audience by identifying successful offers from industry leaders, organizing focus groups or surveys to seek the advice of target customers about the products you would like to sell, and learning more about the interests of your audience.

Even if customers frequently buy everyday products, they are also willing to invest their money in products/services that solve a problem, or that fascinate them. Thorough knowledge of your audience is key to building long-term customer loyalty.

Knowing your audience is also crucial, since at the end of the day, once a good product-market match has been achieved, your customers will recognize the value of your product and will be ready to promote it among those around them. Satisfied customers will become loyal promoters of your brand and spread the message. The word of mouth recommendations indicate that it is a good match-market product and your offer provides superior value to your customers.

Repositioning an existing product: the art of finding the right market

Is your existing product not attracting customer interest? If they don't buy it, how should you react?

Maybe it doesn't meet their needs—or it just doesn't meet the right needs. In this case, you could promote your product in another market where it will be better received to stimulate sales.

Here are some questions to ask yourself:

- Is your current market saturated? Do you compete with several competitors who prevent you from having a competitive advantage in your niche?
- Is your product different enough from competing products? Is your value proposition clear enough?
- Could your product meet needs in a high-end market, where customers are willing to pay more and buy more?
- Or is it the opposite—would it be better to target more price-sensitive consumers?

It is also possible to change the team working on a product, to rename or promote a product in a new way, or to use many other tactics until you find a good product-market match.

Align products with your brand

Once the products you intend to sell are selected, it will be important to align your offers with your existing brand. Otherwise, you will need to create a new brand that better reflects the items in question.

Whether you sell in-person in stores, at markets, at trade shows, or during festivals, creating a brand identity will prove essential.

Customers are trying to find out if your product/service will suit their needs. Therefore, it would be wise to inject their needs into the history of your brand.

Also, integrating the history of your product into your brand image helps present a consistent and neat identity to your audience, helping customers to remember your product offering better.

The history of your brand, the cause it supports, and the product itself merge to form a single story. Most customers who buy products from a particular brand know their history—that's what excites them and keeps them repeating their purchases.

Product-market match: measuring success

Launch your product smoothly and follow the sales indicators.

After identifying the products that best match your sales activity, launch the product smoothly, and analyze customer reaction. Start with a test: place a small order, then set a deadline and sales targets.

Once 3/4 of the products ordered are sold, analyze the time it took to sell them, the rate of return of items, and the quantity of customers who returned to make additional purchases.

Even if the key performance indicators are different for each brand, be sure to prioritize the time it took to sell the stock of the new product fully. If most of your sales are made online, you could afford to store the new products for longer periods—an approach to avoid store sales, however. After all, physical storefronts must constantly showcase new arrivals.

Review your POS system data

The point of sale system (POS) data will allow you to track your sales and know whether to adjust your strategy during the test phase.

Test Shopify's POS system: Need a POS system to better track sales data? Try the Shopify POS system.

Follow customer reviews and recommendations

Once customers start buying your product, follow their returns closely. Do they leave ratings on your website, social pages, or customer experience sharing sites like Yelp? Do they encounter difficulties when using the product? Are their needs fully met?

In addition to reviews, analyze how often they share information about your product or brand. If they recommend your shop to those around them, it is a vote of confidence and a sign indicating an excellent product-market match.

In addition to monitoring customer conversations online, have them share their testimonials. Layout comment cards near the cash counter, insert links to surveys in receipts or send emails to customers to find out if they would recommend your product. This feedback will be very useful for you to refine your positioning in the market (and will provide you with excellent ideas on how to promote the product).

What to sell: rely on product-market correspondence

to move forward.

Have you had difficulty finding the right product-market match in your retail business? Have you already successfully implemented strategies that have allowed you to identify what to sell?

Use Google Trends And Google Research For Your Niche

Do you know what Google Trends is and how it can help your business?

What is Google Trends?

In 2006, with the name of Insights for Search (ideas/insights for surveys), the tool now known as Google Trends emerged to offer information about how users search for information in YouTube's Google search engines.

In principle, this tool was considered very static since its updates were not frequent, which meant that the data displayed there was outdated. However, over time and with its new updates, Google Trends became a general data source for all audiences.

It is possible, for example, to find information about the wishes and attitudes of users. This is because the tool manages to capture this type of data according to surveys carried out by people on Google.

Also, it is possible to understand the search habits of users according to the countries in which a certain term is being investigated and to compare the volume of searches for that word during the year and in different regions of the world.

Google Trends is not an average SEO tool. For those entrepreneurs who are dedicated to electronic commerce or for those who provide services in the information industry, knowing the trends in a certain business niche becomes a strategic tool.

Here I share tips on how to use this tool from the giant, Google, efficiently and how that can help optimize your business.

Use Google Trends to find business niches

Thanks to the intelligent use of this tool, you will be able to find new business niches or update the niche that you currently use to do business. Through Google Trends, you can see increases or decreases in search volumes on topics in your niche.

Find relevant product categories that are related

A great advantage that you can find in Google Trends is that you can search and cross-correlate to detect interactions that cannot be seen with the naked eye.

Use the platform for keyword research

The searches you configure in Google Trends will be the source of dozens of keywords that will serve to name your product categories. This platform gives you a lot of clues about the words that your target audience uses the most.

You can collect data on seasonal trends

This is especially important for brands that use e-commerce strategies. With Google Trends, it can show you spikes and dips in different time ranges, which can give you better clues when making decisions for your next digital marketing campaign.

With Google Trends you can identify sources to create fresh content

Content marketing is helping major online retailers gain more traffic to increase brand awareness and gain more customers than ever. Thanks to the information provided by this tool on a certain niche, you can create content that provides better solutions.

The platform helps you find current and segmented trends

On the Google Trends home page, you'll find a section for trending searches. Trend searches are the hottest topics of the moment. You can search for daily trend searches, real-time search trends, and country search. The more current the trend, the more current your content should be.

Analysis of your competition with Google Trends

At Google Trends, you can even monitor your competitors and see how well they are performing against your brand. Define what elements of your competition are affecting you and use mechanisms that allow you to innovate. With Google Trends, you can control up to 5 search terms from your competition.

Google Trends strengthens your SEO strategy

The main contribution of Google Trends towards SEO strategy is to provide information against searches. This system counts the number of times in which a word or phrase was typed in the Google search engine during a time in the geographical area that we are interested in analyzing. With the information from Trends, you feed your overwhelming titles and content.

You can calibrate your content marketing strategy with Trends

It also allows knowing if the topics that we are going to publish are of interest to our target audience, allowing planning of our content marketing strategy to a great extent and generating a positive response from the public.

Other advantages of incorporating Google Trends in your digital toolbox

- It is free, so you will not have to invest in this development.
- It is intuitive to use and does not require strenuous training to operate it.
- Filters allow you to get anywhere in the world.

Have you already used this tool in your business? Do you think it can be of benefit to your digital strategy?

HOW TO EXPLOIT NICHE MARKETING?

Remember that the niche is the term used in marketing to refer to a segment of potential consumers of a product or service within the total market. The components of this segment have characteristics and needs in common.

Niche marketing recognizes segmentation to market a new business opportunity, arising from unmet needs of consumers with specific needs, which are then exploited economically. The current challenge of digital marketing is hyper-segmentation, that is, offering personalized products suitable for each specific sector. Data shows that targeted ads are twice as effective as non-targeted ads.

It is extremely important to limit our market niche, since if it is too broad, it will encompass a group of people that is too heterogeneous, making it difficult to find common needs that we can solve with our offer. The smaller the niche, the better your marketing strategy and, consequently, the more your business will work.

Niche Marketing Benefits

Specializing in a specific market niche will allow you:

- Loyalty to your consumers, who will appreciate your efforts to solve their most specific needs.
- To be able to charge a higher price for a personalized product, higher than if you offered a generic service.
- Explain your product better to your customers, with which your marketing campaign will be more effective because the message will be clearer, and you will generate more empathy with your audience and it allows you to

differentiate yourself from the rest.

- Not to compete with big businesses or brands that are only interested in big markets.
- Reach a wider audience thanks to the internet, which is capable of overcoming geographic barriers. The Internet will allow a small niche to become a large niche.
- Reach a specific audience that is usually more prepared to buy a specific product than people looking for generic things who are not very clear about what they want or need.

How To Exploit Niche Marketing?

Find your specific audience: What interests does the audience you want to target have? Who is this audience? What do they like, and what do they not like? Where do they meet on the internet? Identify what motivates the purchase of a product, it will help you locate communities that share the same values, and it will also help you determine how they relate to each other and what other brands do to attract them.

Identify your problems and solve them: The digital environment allows you to discover with some ease the audience's perception of a product or service. To know the problems that companies have with their users, it is enough to inquire into existing platforms: forums, communities, social networks, blogs. Analyze testimonials and reviews of products and services to identify which of them are missing and which are not being offered by other companies at present.

Calculate the demand for your niche: The demand for a product or service in the market will help you determine the profitability of your niche. To calculate the demand, you can use two different tools:

- Google trends: a free Google tool that allows you to know the level of searches for a specific keyword in a specific period, and enables you to know the variations in that level of searches over time. This information will allow us to know if there is a growing interest in a specific term if that interest has varied over the years, etc.

- Google correlate: a complement to Google trends that provides you with information about keywords related to the keywords you enter and indicates the number of searches they have in a certain period.

Study the competition: knowing who serves our same market niche reduces the possibility of making mistakes similar to those made by other companies when seducing new audiences. Analyze their weaknesses and strengths, and differentiate yourself from them from the first moment so that customers see that you offer new things. To do this, use Google AdWords, a Google keyword tool that will allow you to know the number of monthly searches that a word has, the competition that exists to position itself for that term among the users of Google ads, and the suggested bid for advertisers. This information will allow you to know the interest there is in a specific topic, the level of competition and the profitability (the higher the suggested bid, the more profitable the product will be).

You can also use Amazon or eBay to find out if the products you are interested in offering are currently being sold. Find products with at least 100 reviews.

Be unique: put yourself in the shoes of consumers, be empathetic, and find some differential element that sets you apart from the competition. Find your own sub-niche that makes you even more specific. Find a source of traffic that consumers aren't tapping into. To get visits, you can use SEO, AdWords, social networks, forums, blogs ...

Plan a digital marketing strategy and put it to the test. Once you have specified the objective target and are aware of how the competition is operating, it is time to develop a digital marketing strategy that enhances the information collected and allows you to make the online audience profitable. That is to say: it is about designing a project that aligns with the needs of the users, proposes new products or services to them that respond to their demands, and presents them differently. Afterward, it will be necessary to analyze if the messages, frequency, and channels used in this plan are correct, and to correct and refine the strategy according to the needs of consumers.

As you can see, it is better to be the main supplier of a specific product in a small market, than to be a small competitor in a large and highly competitive market. In niche marketing, the important thing is that you can offer a differential value, improve the offer that exists in the market, and differentiate yourself by offering a specific product of higher quality.

And you, have you already thought about what you can offer that makes you different?

SELECT THE RIGHT PRODUCT IN DROPSHIPPING

Would you like to have an online store but do not know what to sell? Do you think it is difficult to choose products for your e-commerce business? Here's how you can select the ideal products to sell in your online store.

Thanks to the rise of the e-commerce sector, there is an increasing variety of products to sell that are very accessible, and every day there is more demand for all kinds of products.

From very general products such as books to ultra-specific products such as minimalist wallets or purses, there is no shortage of suppliers and customers for each type of product.

Start selling easily

Unless you have a lot of experience with online stores, even with physical stores, we always recommend creating an online store with dropshipping, at least to start with.

Can you imagine being able to sell the products you want without having a warehouse? That is dropshipping.

To minimize the risk of starting to sell, it is usually interesting to have distributors who are in charge of the entire logistics process. This way, you don't have to start with very high investment, and you can concentrate more on selling.

Luckily, many distributors have been climbing into the dropshipping trend until it has become a solid business.

1. Choose your first possible products to sell

In this phase of "paper and pen," I recommend you write down the products that interest you the most or even that you are passionate about.

You can also list those that you know well because you use them often.

It will always be easier for you to sell a product that interests you a lot and that you know how to share its benefits, than a product that theoretically sells well but does not interest you in the least.

2. Do a supply and demand study

On your way to creating a virtual store, at this point, your research is triple:

- Search for dropshipping providers that sell the products on your list
- Find other stores that already sell these products
- Find out if there are customers who buy these products

The first point is the easiest and fastest. A few Google searches will help you see if there are providers or not. Cross off your list products for which you cannot find suppliers.

The second point is still easy, although it may take longer because it is recommended that you investigate each page of your future competition. Write down prices and conditions ... of each store you find.

The third point is the most difficult, and we can only make hypotheses according to the number of stores that sell the products if some pages or forums talk about the products, the number of searches that are carried out in Google, etc.

You can also poll your contacts to see if it is a product that they would be interested in buying online.

From all the products that remain on your list, choose the one you prefer, or several, if necessary, for the following steps.

3. Design your business model

This step is necessary for any type of business and consists of defining the foundations of your business.

Once you have one or several finalist products, you should think about how to build your business around them.

4. To sell !!

Having chosen your products and designed your business model, the next steps will be to set up your online store, take visits to the web, and start selling.

To set up the store, there are various platforms, and we also recommend reducing costs and time using an MVP (Minimum Viable Product). This technique consists of making a prototype of your store that has everything you need to start selling and nothing else. You will have time to improve the design, add more pages, filters, etc.

With the store up and running, all that remains is to get visits either through advertising, SEO, or social networks...

And according to the statistics you are getting, it will be time to review some of the previous points to improve your online store or continue improving it little by little.

CHAPTER 4

FIND A SUPPLIER

Before searching for suppliers, it is important to know how to differentiate legitimate wholesale suppliers from retail stores posing as wholesale suppliers. A real wholesaler buys directly from the manufacturer and will generally be able to offer you a much better price.

How to spot fake dropshipping wholesalers

Depending on where you are looking, you are likely to encounter a large number of "fake" wholesalers. Unfortunately, legitimate wholesalers don't have great marketing skills and tend to be harder to find. As a result, non-genuine wholesalers (simple brokers) appear more frequently in your searches, so you should be cautious.

The following strategies will help you determine the credibility of a bulk supplier:

They Want Ongoing Commissions: True wholesalers do not charge their customers a monthly fee for the privilege of doing business with them and placing orders. If a provider asks you to pay a membership or monthly fee for the service, it is most likely not legitimate.

It is important to also differentiate between providers and provider directories. Wholesale supplier directories (a topic we will explore further below) are organized by product or market type, which have been carefully researched to ensure their legitimacy. Most directories will charge a commission, either one-time or continuous, so you shouldn't take this as a sign that the directory is illegitimate.

Sell To The Public: To obtain the prices of a genuine wholesaler, you must request a wholesale account, prove that it is a legitimate business, and be approved before you can place your first order. Any wholesale seller that sells goods at "wholesale cost" to the general public is a manufacturer that provides items at high rates.

But here are a few legal dropshipping payments you can find:

Order Fees: Many dropshippers will charge an order fee that can range from $2 to $5 or more, depending on the size and complexity of the items to be shipped. This is an industry-standard as the cost of packing and shipping individual orders is much higher than the cost of shipping in bulk.

Minimum Order Size: Some wholesalers will have a minimum initial order size, which is the minimum quantity you must purchase on your first order. They do this to filter out merchants who are "just looking." Those that will waste your time with questions and small orders but will not become important customers.

This could cause problems if you are using dropshipping. For example, what to do if a manufacturer has a budget of $500 per order, but your average order size is $100? You don't want $500 of merchandise pre-ordered only for the pleasure of opening a dropshipping account.

In this case, agreeing to pay the supplier $500 in advance is easier to open a credit account with them to pay for potential orders. This helps you to meet the minimum payment requested by the retailer (you are already investing at least $500) without needing to put a single big order or getting customer orders to back it up.

Finding Wholesale Suppliers

Now that you can tell a fraud from a legitimate wholesale supplier, it's time to start looking for your suppliers. You can use different strategies, some more effective than others. The methods listed below are listed in order of effectiveness and preference, with our preferred methods at the top of the list:

Contact the manufacturer

This is our favorite method of finding legal wholesale vendors with ease. Contact the manufacturer if you know the product(s) you wish to market and ask for a list of their wholesale distributors. Then you should call those wholesalers to see if they are selling dropshipping and ask them about the account opening procedure.

Since most wholesalers deal with goods from a range of suppliers, this strategy would allow you to stock up in the niche you are investigating on several products.

You will easily find the most relevant wholesalers in that market after having made a few calls to the major suppliers in the niche.

Search on Google

Using Google to find quality providers may seem obvious, but there are some rules to keep in mind:

- **You Must Perform A Broad Search:** Wholesalers are very bad in terms of marketing and promotion, and will not appear among the first results for searches such as "wholesale suppliers for product X." This means that you will probably have to search MANY results, possibly hundreds.
- **Don't Judge By The Website:** Wholesalers are also famous for having poorly designed '90s-style websites. So while a good quality website may indicate that it is a good provider in some cases, many legitimate wholesalers have appalling landing pages. Don't be scared of bad design.
- **Use Many Modifiers:** Wholesalers aren't doing extensive SEO to make sure you find their websites, so you'll need to try multiple search queries. Don't just put "supplier of [product]." Try using modifiers such as "distributor", "reseller", "wholesale", "warehouse", and "supplier".

Place an order with supplier samples

Once you have chosen your two or three main suppliers to do business, it is important to ask them for samples of their products. Test the quality of the service, the delivery times, the packaging, and all the questions related to the supplier that you may have so that you are completely satisfied with having chosen that supplier. Requesting samples from a dropshipping provider is an essential part of the selection of providers since it will allow you to know how it will be for your customers to buy on your online store.

Place an order from the competition

If you're having a tough time finding a supplier, you can still use the Asking trick of the market. Here's how it works: locate your rival using dropshipping, and place a small order with the service. Google the return address as you open the box, to figure out who made the original shipment. For certain instances, the provider you can reach would be a bank.

And if you were unable to find a supplier using the approaches as mentioned above, there could be a legitimate reason for this (i.e., the demand is very small, a supplier doesn't have to be justified enough, etc.). So bear in mind this strategy, but don't trust yourself.

Attend a trade show

A commercial exhibition will allow you to get in touch with all the main manufacturers and wholesalers in the niche. It's a great way to network and research products and suppliers, all in one place. This would only work if the market and goods have already been picked, so this is not feasible for all. But if you have the time and resources to enter, engaging with the manufacturers and vendors on the market is a really good way to do.

Directories

One of the most common questions for aspiring e-commerce entrepreneurs is: Should I pay for a provider directory?

A supplier directory is a supplier database that has been organized by market, niche, or product. Many directories employ some form of the investigative process to ensure that the providers listed are genuine wholesalers. Many are run by for-profit companies that charge a fee for directory access.

Although membership directories can be useful, especially for brainstorming, they are not necessary. If you already know the product you want to sell or the niche, you should be able to find the main suppliers in the market by searching a bit and using the techniques described earlier. Often, you most likely don't have to access the list again until you start your company unless you decide to locate vendors for other things.

Having clarified that, vendor directories are a convenient and quick way to search through a large number of vendors in one place and are great for getting ideas for products to sell or niches. If you are short on time and are willing to spend money, they can be a very useful tool.

There are many different provider directories, and an in-depth review of all of them is beyond the scope of this guide. Instead, we've highlighted some of the best-known online provider directories. Keep in mind that we do not sponsor any of these directories; we are simply giving you some options.

Oberlo

- Established in 2015
- Thousands of wholesalers and more than 10 million products
- Automates the dropshipping process
- Price: Starter plan free

Oberlo allows you to easily import dropshipping products into your store and send them directly to your customers—with just a few clicks.

With Oberlo, you can import hundreds of products to your e-commerce store in just a few minutes, and once an order is received, send it directly to your customer. Oberlo enables you to automate the administration of your products and orders, allowing you to spend more time growing your business.

Worldwide Brands

Quick facts:

- Established in 1999
- Thousands of wholesalers
- Over 10 million
- Price: $299 for a lifetime membership

Worldwide Brands is one of the suppliers' oldest most well-recognized directories. This directory states in its ads that it requires only vendors who conform with a series of guidelines to guarantee the wholesaler's integrity and consistency.

When you want a premium catalog for life, and you feel confident making a single big payment, Worldwide Brands is a secure choice.

SaleHoo

Quick facts:

- Established in 2005
- More than 8,000 suppliers
- Price: $67 a year

The SaleHoo provider directory lists over 8,000 wholesale and dropshipping providers and is dedicated to merchants on eBay and Amazon.

Although we have never used SaleHoo to stock up on products, its $67 annual price is one of the most attractive among provider directories and includes a 60-day money-back guarantee. If you're comfortable paying for an annual membership or only need to use the directory temporarily, SaleHoo is worth checking out.

Doba

Quick facts:

- Established in 2002
- 165 suppliers
- More than 1.5 million products
- Price: $60 per month

The Doba app incorporates drop shippers instead of only naming providers (that's why it only has 165 providers), allowing you to order multiple deposits using its unified GUI. Membership also provides a Push-to-Marketplace service, which can simplify the eBay listing process.

Doba's centralized system is more convenient than the other directories, and we presume that's why its $60/month rate is so much higher than others. If convenience is very important to you, and you can find the products you want from these suppliers, the price of the Doba interface is justified.

However, if you can identify good providers yourself and don't mind working directly with them, you can save about $700 a year. If there are only a few key providers in your niche, reducing the number of parties you need to coordinate with, this may be your best option.

Wholesale central

Quick facts:

- Established in 1996
- 400 providers
- 740,000 products
- Price: free

Unlike several other directories, Wholesale Central's quest for providers is free as they charge providers a fee to be included and even view advertisements on the web. They also claim to research and evaluate all providers to ensure their legitimacy and that they are trustworthy.

It's hard to criticize something free, and there's no problem searching the Wholesale Central listings, but you'll need a little more judgment. Some of the suppliers we found appeared to be retailers selling to the public at "wholesale" prices (something a supplier would not do if they were offering true wholesale prices). So while we are sure there are genuine wholesalers listed, it is in your best interest to do a bit more research on suppliers.

Well, now you have found several solid providers and are ready to move on, brilliant! But before you start contacting companies, you want to be well prepared.

You Must Have Legal Status: As we mentioned before, most legitimate wholesalers will ask you for proof that it is a legal business by allowing you to apply for an account. Many wholesalers only disclose their prices to approved customers, so you must have your business legally established before seeing the type of prices they will offer you.

In summary: Make sure your business is legally constituted before contacting suppliers. If you are only looking for answers to some basic questions ("Do they dropship?", "Do they work with the X brand?"), you will not need to submit any documentation. But do not expect to launch your business if it is not well established.

Understand How Others See You: Wholesalers are constantly bombarded by people with big business plans who drive them crazy with questions, waste a lot of time, and then don't place an order. So if you are launching a business, keep in mind that many providers will not make any additional effort to help you.

Many will have no problem opening a dropshipping account for you if that's what they're offering. But don't ask for discounts or have your sales reps on the phone for hours before you've made a single sale. This will create a bad reputation for you very quickly and damage your relationship with the provider.

If you need to make special requests (such as trying to convince a supplier to do dropshipping when they don't normally do so), you must first establish your credibility. Be definitive when you talk about your business plans ("we are going to launch the site on January 20") instead of using expressions of insecurity ("I am thinking of perhaps launching a business sometime in the future"). And be sure to share your past career successes, especially those related to sales and marketing, which will help you in your new venture.

You need to persuade suppliers that as you become popular and start buying a number, the hassle of meeting their specific demands will pay off in the long run.

Don't Be Scared Of The Phone: One of people's greatest worries when it comes to services is just picking up the phone and making the call. For many, the idea of doing it is paralyzing. For certain inquiries, you'll be able to send texts, but you'll need to pick up the phone more frequently to get the answers you need.

The positive thing is that it's not as horrific as it sounds. Wholesalers are used to receiving calls from beginning entrepreneurs. Someone friendly will likely attend you and have no problem answering your questions. Here is a tip that will help you; just write your questions in advance. It's amazing how much easier it will be for you to make the call when you already have a list of written questions to ask.

How to find good suppliers

Like most things in life, not all providers are created equal. In the world of dropshipping, where suppliers are a critical part of the order preparation process, it is even more important to make sure you work with the best suppliers.

Excellent providers tend to have several of these six attributes in common:

- **Experienced Staff And Industry Focus:** The best suppliers have well-trained sales representatives who know the industry and its product lines. Being able to call a representative and have all your questions answered is invaluable, especially if you are launching a store in a niche that is not entirely familiar to you.

- **Dedicated Customer Service Representatives:** Good dropshippers should assign you a sales representative who is responsible for your issues. Dealing with wholesalers who do not assign a specific representative is very unpleasant. It takes much longer to resolve problems, and one generally has to complain about them taking care of something. Having a single provider-side contact who is responsible for solving your problems is important.

- **Committed To Technology:** Although there are many vendors with outdated websites, working with a vendor who understands the benefits of technology is a pleasure. Apps such as real-inventory, a robust web store, flexible data transfer, and searchable online order history are a complete privilege for online retailers and all that will further streamline the operations.

- **Take Orders By Email:** This may seem like a minor matter, but having to call to place each order (or place it manually on the website) makes the ordering process take much longer.

- **Centralized Location:** If you're in a big country like the United States, having a centrally placed dropshipper is advantageous, because deliveries can be shipped in 2 to 3 business days in around 90 percent of the country. When the supplier is located on one of the coasts, it can take more than a week to send the orders through the territory. Centrally located providers allow you to consistently promise faster deliveries, and potentially save you money on shipping rates.

- **Ordered And Effective**: Certain suppliers have professional personnel and excellent processes to promote a secure and error-free operation when processing orders. Others will make mistakes every three to four requests and make you want to rip your hair out. The point is, it's hard to know how competent a provider is without first using them.

Although it won't give you a global idea, placing a few small orders can help you probe the field and see how the supplier operates. You will see:

- How they handle the order process.
- How fast orders go out.
- How fast the tracking information and invoice are sent to you.
- The quality of the packaging when the item arrives.

Suppliers to avoid

It is difficult to know which providers to choose, but there are some indications that a provider should be avoided at all costs. Aside from bad reviews, negative comments, and overly cheap products, other factors can indicate that a dropshipping provider is a bad provider.

If the dropshipping provider insists on charging you monthly or ongoing fees to do business with them, it's a bad sign. Being asked for monthly fees could mean that a provider is part of a directory rather than a single provider.

It is normal for pre-order fees to increase slightly based on the size or complexity of an order, or to decrease with a bulk order. By researching, you will discover suppliers that charge higher than normal pre-order fees, from which it is best to stay away.

The minimum order size is another thing to keep in mind when choosing a dropshipping provider. Most of the time, a vendor is willing to charge the minimum order fee and fulfill orders as they come in. This means that if the minimum order size of a supplier is 200, you must pay 200 units in advance, but the supplier will send the products individually, as you sell them in your online store. Avoid providers who refuse to do this, as it means they usually work only with wholesale orders.

Options to pay providers

The vast majority of providers accept payments in one of two ways:

- **Credit card**

When you are just starting, most providers will ask you to pay by credit card. Once your business is established to be successful, paying with credit cards is still the best option. Not only are they convenient (they eliminate the need to write checks regularly), but they can also earn LOTS of reward points and traveler miles. Since you are buying a product for a customer who has already paid for it on your website, you can accumulate a high volume of purchases through your credit card without incurring out-of-pocket costs.

- **Net terms**

The other common way to pay vendors is with "net installments" on the invoice. This simply means that you have a certain number of days to pay the vendor for the items you have purchased. So if you have 30-day net installments, you can pay after 30 days to your supplier (by check or bank funds) for the products purchased.

Generally, a provider will ask you for credit references before offering you net payment terms because it is the same as lending you money. This is common practice, so don't be alarmed if you need to submit documentation when you pay with net deadlines.

RIGHT PRICING

Online business type dropshipping has lived its peak thanks to the ease of management compared to other business models: not having to manage the stock, avoid devaluation of the products, etc. The headland creating an e-commerce dropshipping allows the online store to focus on the promotion and marketing actions necessary to promote the products in its catalog and thus achieve maximum benefits. And in this sense, it is important to develop a pricing strategy adapted to the characteristics of e-commerce and the products it sells.

The first thing to take into account is the different categories to which the products in the catalog belong. Checking the state of the sector and the market in which they are going to move is key to knowing what the sales volume of each product is and the profit margin that can be applied.

Once verified, the next step will be to analyze the total cost of selling a product. A dropshipping business is characterized by requesting the product from the manufacturer once the end customer has requested it, so in the cost of sale, it is necessary to include the different steps of shipping, receiving, returns, and everything related to the maintenance of the platform online.

With the analysis of the costs that e-commerce will imply, it is time to outline the pricing strategy that is going to be executed. An idea to consider is to add a fixed percentage as the profit margin on the calculated cost of sale. In this way, it is possible to ensure a minimum profit with each transaction. The riskier ones also choose to add this margin to each price unit, so that the profit increases. However, it is necessary to check how the final prices fit with the prices offered by the competition so as not to lose sales precisely due to the price factor.

On the other hand, drop shipping prices can be guided by the PVPR recommended by each manufacturer or seller. In this way, e-commerce can ensure that it is offering an attractive price to its potential customers and even offer interesting discounts on the PVPR to improve the conversion while continuing to make profits.

As for the tricks to take into account to make e-commerce prices more attractive, the rounding off in large numbers and the hook of '0.99' in lower prices stand out. In some cases, e-commerce dropshipping chooses to offer higher prices than the competition and include certain discounts that generate customer acceptance. However, it must be remembered that users also use tools to monitor the price of the products that interest them, making it increasingly difficult to ignore this type of action. Furthermore, these bad practices are increasingly undervalued by the online community, posing a high risk to brand image.

In any case, once the pricing strategy of the dropshipping store is going to be established, it is essential to keep it updated by reviewing the changes that may occur in market conditions. A dynamic pricing tool can become a key ally to carry out this task in a comfortable, global, and effective way.

CHAPTER 5

HOW TO START DROPSHIPPING WITH SHOPIFY

Online commerce and virtual stores are increasingly undermining the internet, this being the best method to start and make money today. That is why the word "e-commerce" (which refers to the web pages that provide this virtual store creation service) has become so popular today, being searched by both connoisseurs and novices in the field.

Among all the platforms where you can do e-commerce today, there is one that is giving a lot to talk about and whose name is none other than Shopify. Could it be the best platform to make my virtual store? If so, how can I best use it, and what is this platform really about?

What is Shopify exactly

As previously inferred, Shopify is a platform to create online stores that currently stays with the tutelage in this particular area of commerce. It was founded in 2006 by Canadian, Tobias Lütke, and currently has more than 600,000 online stores, thus helping various companies process more than 40 billion sales.

The main characteristic of this platform is that it turns out to be very simple and intuitive to use, thus allowing the creation of a complete online store in very few steps. This system allows you to organize products, accept various forms of payment, customize the store's design, and many more.

If you do not have much knowledge on web pages and still want to create your virtual store, then go to Shopify which is capable of giving you the help you need, all without wasting time so that you are able to focus on other more important aspects of your business. Opting for Shopify is a good option!

The detailed operation of Shopify

How Shopify works is very simple: you only have to go on the official Shopify page and register.

To be more specific, the steps to use Shopify correctly are as follows:

- Enter the platform and create your account on it, following the steps suggested by the website.
- Choose a domain that is to your liking and choose the template that the same system will ask you for. There are several models from which you can choose!
- Now select the functions you want your website to have as e-commerce to finally add all those products that you want to start selling online.

There is nothing easier than making a virtual store with Shopify, making its operation one of the most intuitive in the virtual store creation market.

As for its control panel, it is worth mentioning that this is one of the most complete you can find, allowing you to add products, create discount coupons, check the latest reports that your business has generated and even integrated into your blog. Other functionalities include the following:

- Insert images, descriptions, and titles in each of the products that you add to your virtual store. In this way, you will not have to have the best plugins to optimize images in WordPress.
- Manage and create product inventories.
- Accept payments in different currencies and different ways, including payments on management platforms such as PayPal.
- Manage your team's accesses by granting different levels of permissions to administrators.
- Set up customer accounts that are registered on your platform. In this way, customers can access a private area from which they can manage their data.
- Create web pages and blogs that are not necessarily oriented to the virtual store.
- Carry out an exhaustive follow-up of both your clients and their orders, respectively.
- Create and generate discount codes capable of improving your sales while generating a good reputation on the internet.

Advantages and disadvantages of Shopify

If how Shopify works is not enough to learn to use this extraordinary platform to make digital stores, then perhaps you can make this decision considering its advantages and disadvantages:

Advantages of Shopify:

You do not need any computer knowledge to use this online page to create your store. Its simplicity when creating virtual stores positions it just as an excellent and quick to use web page.

You can personalize and redesign your virtual store with total freedom, being able to also create your design with CSS and HTML if you want much more independence.

It allows you total freedom of payment, having more than 70 currencies for international payments, which allows you to sell locally to other countries.

The tax system that Shopify manages is fully automatic, so you don't have to worry about anything when it comes to this topic.

You can easily integrate your virtual store made in Shopify with other sites such as Dropshipping, with applications in charge of making this work a reality.

You can place the number of products that suit you.

You have unlimited bandwidth so that it is not problematic to have to pay according to the traffic of your store.

Disadvantages of Shopify:

Unfortunately, this virtual application has a price to be used fully, which you will have to assume every month once you start publishing your products. The most basic plan you have is equivalent to 26 euros, which is somewhat expensive for most.

Apart from having to pay a kind of subscription or right to use the platform, it also keeps a percentage of each transaction you make, charging a commission that is applied to each product you sell.

Nothing can be perfect in this life, although when talking about virtual stores, there is no doubt that Shopify is the closest thing. Therefore, if you want to do things well and easily, opt for this platform to create your virtual store and start profiting at any moment.

CHAPTER 6

CREATE AN E-COMMERCE SITE WITH SHOPIFY

When we talk about creating an e-commerce site, we immediately have two or three references in mind. Shopify is one of them, alongside Prestashop, Magento, or Woocommerce. Shopify is a hosted e-commerce CMS, unlike Magento and Prestashop (even if the latter has recently offered a Cloud offer). Entering the e-commerce CMS market in 2004, Shopify quickly established itself as a significant player in the online store creation sector with more than 200,000 active users to date.

With an ergonomic and intuitive creation interface, you can create a Shopify site, edit it, and put it online simply and quickly. Shopify has chosen to address users who do not require special technical skills. The emphasis is on ease of use and ergonomics. Shopify offers a wide choice of features and themes to create and develop its online store. It is, therefore, a very popular solution for media specialists in website creation.

If you are embarking on the creation of your first e-commerce site, you will surely need a little help to understand the software. In this resource, we detail the different steps to create a Shopify site.

Step 1 - Setting up your Shopify account

These steps are sufficiently detailed to enable you to get started in the realization of your first e-commerce site, without the need for particular technical skills.

i.   Register On Shopify

Signing up on Shopify is quick and easy. On the Shopify home page, you can create your site in a few clicks. Just enter an email address (which will be the reference address to connect to the editing interface of your e-commerce site).

ii.   Adding personal information

Once your email address has been entered, Shopify asks you to enter your personal information on the "Few more details" page. Classically, you must enter your first and last name, address, city, postal code, etc.

Then, in the second part of the "Few more details" section, Shopify asks you to say a little more about the status of your project. Two pieces of information are requested:

- Do you already sell products?
- How much income did your activity have in the last year?

To validate this information after entering it, click on "Enter my store."

iii. The beginning of the configuration of your e-commerce site

Once this personal information has been entered, you will land on the home screen of your administrator area. It is from this online portal that you can directly create and personalize your e-commerce site (personalize the appearance, add products, configure the payment and delivery system, etc.).

iv. Choose the theme of your Shopify e-commerce site

Choosing the theme for your e-commerce site is a crucial step. Your theme is the identity of the site of your brand. Be sure to select a theme that you like (yes, it is important) and by your e-commerce site creation project. Shopify offers its themes via an interface. Also, Shopify guarantees that the themes are certified by the designers, a guarantee of quality.

Each theme is proposed with a list of modifications that you can make without ever having to enter the theme code. Premium themes obviously offer more possibilities in terms of modifications, but you can completely be satisfied with a free theme, sufficient for a small project, or the creation of an e-commerce site that is not very complex.

However, if you would like to make significant changes to your theme, you will need to modify the site's HTML and CSS code. For this type of modification, do not panic if you do not have skills in these languages, Shopify has an international network of design agencies (called "Shopify Experts") that you can contact so that they modify your site.

1. The Shopify theme browser

The Shopify theme browser is available from your administrator portal or directly by going to themes.shopify.com. It exposes more than 150 different themes. As mentioned above, there are free or paid (premium) themes. We can filter the themes according to the type of activity as well as recency and price criteria. For example, in the "Electronics" category, the Jumpstart and Palo Alto themes are more suited to Tech-oriented activities, innovative products, etc.

2. The functionality of a Shopify theme

Once you have chosen the theme you like, you can get more details by clicking on the theme directly from the browser. Thus, you will get elements of precision on the theme, such as the fact that it is responsive, suitable for mobile use, as well as opinions of other users of the same theme by scrolling the page.

3. Viewing the rendering of your theme

You can even delve into the theme with the demo tool available for each Shopify theme. The navigation on the different pages of the demo allows you to get a good idea of the possibilities of the site both in terms of the arrangement of elements as navigation and animations. We can also test the rendering of the theme on a web browser or mobile. To make the right choice, it is important to know the trends in terms of design and ergonomics on e-commerce sites currently.

If the theme has several appearances, you can switch from one to the other by clicking on another style.

A little advice

The choice of theme is crucial to the success of your e-commerce project. It is not recommended that you choose a visually poor theme, with the sole aim of saving a few dozen euros. Indeed, a quality template will always be a profitable investment.

4. Final validation of the choice of theme for your e-commerce site

To install the theme, it's very simple. Just click on "Install Theme" on the theme details page when it is a free theme or on "Buy theme" if it is a premium theme. Shopify will then request a confirmation. Then click on "Publish as my shop's theme" to install the selected theme on your Shopify online store.

As a reminder, the choice of theme is not final. By this, we mean that it is not because we have chosen a theme that we can never change it. You will then have the opportunity to go back to your initial choice and choose another theme more suited to the evolution of your activity.

5. Finalization of the initial configuration

Finally, a page is displayed with a "Go to your Theme Manager" button. It is by going to this page that you can modify the appearance of your theme. Your theme manager will show you the most recently installed theme (and uninstall the oldest ones).

Change The Appearance Of Your Theme

On most of the themes offered by Shopify, you have the possibility of modifying the appearance of your online store. So rest assured, your site will not look like thousands of others!

In your administration interface, you will find the section which allows you to modify the appearance of your theme in the menu on the left, entitled "Themes." The interface will automatically display the theme used by your Shopify site. You can see several buttons that appear at the top right:

- The three little dots, "...": this button allows you to make basic changes such as changing the name of the theme, editing HTML/CSS language, downloading the theme file or even duplicating the theme (very useful when you want to make big changes to the theme, and you want to have a backup of the initial theme for security).
- The eye: this second button simply allows you to view the rendering of your theme. A new window opens and displays the site of your shop.
- "Customize Theme": this button is important. It allows you to access the settings of your theme in front (direct viewing). This section is very interesting when you want to perform quick tests of choice of colors and typography, for example, but also edit the footer/header, logos,

menu, etc. In all cases, it is an interface that must be tested to familiarize yourself with the Shopify site editor and to know all of the features offered.

Some themes even offer the possibility of customizing the positioning of the elements (image produced on the right/left, center the elements, or align them on the left/right, etc.).

A little advice

Do not start modifying the HTML/CSS of your site if you do not have the required skills, and risk modifying certain elements without being able to go back. That said, you can always copy the file you want to modify and save it on an external document to carry out your tests and have a backup pole in case of mishandling. It is by making mistakes that we learn, so it is always better to have a backup!

Step 2 - Building your e-commerce site with Shopify

An e-commerce site without products is not an e-commerce site. Here we will explain how to add products to your Shopify online store.

Add products to your e-commerce site

To add products to your Shopify online store, go to the "Products" interface from the left menu (the logo takes the form of a product label). On this page appears a blue button, "Add a product." Click on it to add a new product to your store.

Once in the interface, you must now fill in the different fields (the product title and description, images, price, etc.). On the right side of the editor, the "Visibility" category allows you to choose whether the product will be published automatically on the site after validation or if you want to publish it at a specific future date.

Below, there is an important section called "Organization" in which you can assign the product to a category as well as a brand. If this is your first product, you can enter a category in the "Product Type" field, such as a T-shirt. Thus, you will assign the product to this category, and at the same time, you will create the new T-Shirt category (without having to go to the category creation section). The process is the same for the "Vendor" field (brand of product for sale). Further down, the search field allows you to place the product in a collection (previously created), as well as to assign different tags to the product (e.g. #cotton, #noir, #vintage, etc.).

Once the characteristics of your product are filled, you can save it by clicking on the blue "Save Product" button located at the top left of the interface.

If you have not yet created your product collections, don't worry, you can very well create all of your products, and then assign several products to a collection from the "Products" interface by selecting the products and clicking on "Bulk actions"> "Add to collection."

Configure product collections on your e-commerce site

To create a Shopify site in the rules of the art, it is necessary to determine collections of products. A collection is a common repository for several products in your Shopify store. For example, for a clothing store, you can decide to create collections according to the type of person to whom your products are addressed (Man/Woman/Child), families of products (Pants, T-Shirts, Underwear, etc. .), the color or size of the item, or the seasonality of the products (Summer, Winter, etc.).

Products can appear in more than one product category. As a reminder, generally, the categories that you have determined appear on the home page of your site and in the navigation menu. This is an essential step to better guide your future customers without having to click several times to find a product category. A word of advice, try to minimize the number of clicks between the home page and a product.

Automatic or manual collections

When you add a new product collection to your Shopify site, you can decide how the products will be included in these categories.

- Manual addition: You must add and remove products manually in a category.

- Automatic addition: you can define conditions to include products in this or that category automatically.

A little advice

Before you start putting your products online, it is better to have defined the different categories of products and collections beforehand. You can do this work from an Excel file, for example, to group, combine, and categorize your products. It is a significant time saving method since it will save you from modifying products already put online if you suddenly decide to create a new category.

Create pages and add content to your Shopify online store

Creating pages and adding content is not a feature highlighted by Shopify. To add pages to your Shopify e-commerce site, go to the "Online store"> "Pages" section and click on the "Add Page" button. After defining the name of your page, as well as its content, you can save your page by clicking on "Save." The operation is the same as adding a blog post.

Once the page has been created, you can choose to include it in the main navigation menu from the "Navigation" section. The menu of your e-commerce site is very important, and it is the main gateway to your products. It must be clear and sufficiently detailed to facilitate the search process for your users. You can get inspired by consulting this analysis of menu trends in e-commerce. You must then add an item in the "Menu items" sub-section and assign the new page created to the new menu object. To define a tree structure on your site, you can choose to link your page to a "Web address" in the "links" section and define the path of your page. For example, if a catalog page is created, we will define "Web address" then in the right field "collections/all."

Assign discounts to products on your Shopify site

If you wish to make your customers benefit from promotions, the entire management is carried out from the "Discounts" section. You can then add a reduction by clicking on the "Add discount" button.

Once in the editor of the promotion codes, click on "Generate code" so that Shopify chooses a code that will have to be entered by your visitors if they wish to obtain the promotional discount. You can decide what form this reduction will take: Fixed discount in €, reduction percentage, or even free delivery. You then decide on the value of the reduction, as well as its field of action (in other words, which products will be subject to this reduction). You can apply the reduction to all of your products, a single collection, or even a single product.

Also, you must decide whether this reduction can be used an infinite number of times or configure a usage limit.

A little advice

Emailing represents 50% of the income of e-commerce, and it must be integrated as soon as possible. Sendinblue offers, in particular, a specific Shopify plugin to facilitate email collection, basket restart, and other features. A great way to get started in email marketing.

Step 3 - Manage the payment methods of your Shopify e-commerce site

Configure payment methods

The payment gateway of Shopify (or payment interface) allows you to receive payments made by your customers via your e-commerce site. The two important things to consider are the price and the commission rate. We can add to the elements to take into account the functionality of each means of payment (because all means of payment are not equal).

Commissions charged during transactions

When you opt for the commission system, some payment systems will take a small percentage of the transaction or a fixed amount in exchange for using their payment service. To assess this type of payment system, you must take into account the number of sales you anticipate making.

The different types of payment cards

You need to know the different types of cards accepted by your payment gateway. All gateways accept VISA and Mastercard. The PayPal solution, which has become very popular for online transactions, is also available.

Orders made outside your e-commerce site

Some of the payment gateways will receive payment on their server via one of their forms. This means that in this case, the customer will be redirected to a page outside your site (from the payment page) to enter their bank details and confirm their order. However, they will be redirected to your order confirmation page once the transaction has been completed. In other words, it gives you a little more control over the payment process. About your confirmation page, Shopify only allows you to change the CSS of the page.

The commissions charged by the payment gateways are added to the commissions charged by Shopify. Depending on the pricing formula for which you have chosen, the number of commissions charged changes. Transaction costs decline. The more premium your subscription, the lower the fees charged:

- Basic Shopify: 2.0%
- Shopify: 1.0%
- Advanced Shopify: 0.5%

A little advice

It is, therefore, important to remember that depending on the number of sales you plan to make, it may be more advantageous to opt for a lower formula, even if the fees charged are higher. Indeed, if you anticipate 100 sales in the first year, the "Basic Shopify" solution, cheaper, remains the preferable solution.

Step 4 - Configuration of the elements to remember before moving on to the launch of your e-commerce site

Before moving on to putting your site online (patience, patience), you still have a few things to add, notably information relating to your business, the delivery method, and the tax system applied to your products.

Enter general information about your company

In your administrator interface, you can add details of your company from the "Settings"> "General" section. It is preferable to fill in all of the fields in the three headings:

- "Store details": the name of your store as well as the email addresses.
- "Store address": everything is in the title, fill in your details.
- "Standards and formats": definition of time zone, the currency used, etc.

Manage the taxes applied to the products of your online store

In the same section, "Settings"> "Taxes," you must define how taxes are applied to your products. The box "All taxes are included in my prices" is checked, which means that the sale price displayed on your products contains the tax. For example, if you sell pants for 100 € and this box is checked, this means that the price excluding tax (for a French online store) will be $100/(1 + 0.2) = 83$ €, so an amount of taxes of around 17 € (20% of the total sale price).

You can check on a product sheet that this tax system is properly applied. By going to a product sheet, you must then ensure that in the bottom section, the "Charge taxes on this product" box is checked.

Choose a delivery method

Delivery management is done from the "Settings"> "Shipping" section. Normally, having entered your address when creating your Shopify e-commerce site, the fields in the "Shipping origin" sub-section are pre-filled. If you want to change the address for sending commands, you must edit this field by clicking on "Edit Address". Below, information regarding the delivery amount appears. Depending on the area and the weight of the products sent, the amount of delivery varies significantly. This amount is divided into two: "Domestic" (France, for example) and "Rest of world" (for a shipment outside of France).

Test your order process

Nothing worse than realizing afterwards that your payment process is not working properly. To verify that there is no problem, you can do a test very simply using the Bogus Gateway:

- From the administrator interface, go to the "Payments" section.
- Click on the "Select a Credit Card Gateway" drop-down menu in the "Accept credit cards" sub-section.
- Select "Bogus Gateway" in "Other" to perform a test.

- Click on "Activate" then on your online store.
- Place an order in the same way as a customer would have done.

Once on the payment validation interface (Checkout), you must enter the following details (instead of actual bank details):

Credit card number: each of these numbers simulates a different scenario.

1: simulation of a successful transaction

2: simulation of a failed transaction

3: simulate an exception (generating a message indicating that an error has occurred on the payment gateway)

CVV (verification code located on the back of your card): enter a random 3-digit number (Ex: 333).

Expiration date: Enter a date later at random.

You can also test a transaction with your actual bank details:

- Select the payment gateway you want to test in the "Payments" section.
- Purchase on your store by entering your real bank details in the payment validation interface.
- Once the payment is validated, be sure to cancel the transaction immediately, to reimburse yourself, and avoid paying the transaction fees.

- Finally, check that the payment has been entered into the payment interface.

Performing this test is completely free. Make sure you have canceled your order directly after confirming payment.

Step 5 - Putting your Shopify e-commerce site online

Choose a domain name.

To put your Shopify e-commerce site online, you need a domain name. Two solutions are then available to you.

Buy a domain name via Shopify

With this option, the purchased domain name will be automatically linked to your online store. This is the simplest and fastest solution, especially if you do not have technical knowledge in terms of website hosting. For the purchase of a domain name, it takes between $13 and $54 per year.

A little advice

If this is your first website creation, it is better to buy your domain name directly on Shopify, this will save you from having to transfer a domain name bought elsewhere, which requires time, and it's not that simple!

Buy a domain name external to Shopify

You can also decide to buy a domain name through a third-party provider. Think of providers like GoDaddy,

IWantMyName, or Gandi. This solution is certainly much less expensive (from $0.99 for the domain name), but you will have to redirect your DNS record yourself, which can be scary at first, admittedly. Here's a step-by-step process on how to put your Shopify e-commerce site online with a domain name acquired from a third-party provider.

Add a new domain in Shopify

In the Shopify administrator interface, go to the "Online Store"> "Domains" section and add an existing domain by clicking on the white button at the top right "Add existing domain."

Shopify add an existing domain

Update your DNS server

You must then register the domain name previously purchased from a third-party provider and make certain modifications to your DNS records:

- Replace the @ or the main record with the following IP address: 23.227.38.32
- Add or replace www CNAME with monmagasin.myshopify.com (i.e., the link of your Shopify store without the HTTP)
- Delete host passwords
- Without performing this step, no one will be able to access your site, even once online

Configure your default domain

From the "Online Store"> "Domains" section, select your domain name from the drop-down menu. It is also necessary to ensure that all traffic will be redirected to this area by checking the box. This is a crucial step in terms of SEO because it will give importance to the domain selected by default.

Add other domain names

You can repeat the operation several times, depending on the number of domains you want to add. All domains will redirect to your main domain ("Set as primary"). Please note that the number of domains you have has no impact on SEO.

With all of these explanations, you can build elaborate Shopify e-commerce sites. The interface is intuitive, the categories simple and the features very well thought out. By training for a few hours, you will be able to create a complete and perfectly personalized site according to your needs. You can also go a little further by seeking to double the conversion of your product sheets.

CHAPTER 7

HOW TO START DROPSHIPPING WITH AMAZON AND EBAY

Dropshipping on eBay

Like Amazon, eBay is one of the leading marketplaces worldwide. This American company, born in 1995, has already been a simple auction platform for years.

Hundreds of thousands of sellers and buyers come together every day on eBay to market products from all over the world.

According to information published by the company itself, in 2017 alone, the eBay marketplace accumulated nearly 170 million active users. In this study published by eBay last year, we compare the users of its platform with the total population of different European countries, to highlight the magnitude of its figures.

This data—and many more things that we will cover in this section—show the strength of this marketplace on a global scale. This is why so many people are considering selling on eBay and, if possible, doing it through dropshipping.

Advantages and disadvantages of dropshipping on eBay

Like any sales channel, dropshipping on eBay has advantages and disadvantages. So let's look at these:

Benefits of dropshipping on eBay

Very high user traffic: As stated earlier, eBay is very well positioned in the minds of your potential customers. This is why by selling on eBay, we use this force and the hundreds of thousands of daily users who go to the site to search for products.

Good reputation with the consumer: Users trust platforms like eBay or Amazon more than a company you just discovered. By selling on eBay, you can use this good reputation to your advantage to sell more.

Good positioning and promotion: Positioning e-commerce on Google is difficult (if you tried, you would know). Plus, it's not the only job you have to do if you want to sell. You'll also need to use the SEM, work on your social networking accounts, place your items online on Google Shopping, set up retargeting ... Many individual activities, which take a great deal of time and expertise. Through selling on eBay, however, you take advantage of all of this marketplace's influence to advertise your goods.

Advanced user experience: eBay is a platform that is over 20 years old and has some of the most qualified professionals on its team. By selling on eBay, you will provide your customers with a user experience (fast web browsing, ease of payment, etc.), which is very complicated to have with an e-commerce business.

Disadvantages of dropshipping on eBay

Strong competition: Like you, there are many people who have seen these benefits and want to take advantage of them. So yes, there is competition. But in truth, today, any online sales channel is very exposed to competition.

Depend on eBay requirements: His house, his rules. By selling on the eBay marketplace, you will have to adapt to what they ask you. With e-commerce, you have the last word, but here, no. If eBay wants to block or limit your account (for whatever reason), you can do nothing.

You'll have to pay commissions: Selling on eBay is not free, of course. You will have to pay a sales fee, and a fixed monthly expense will be added if you have a Business Boutique. However, if you sell plenty, those prices are very manageable.

How to start dropshipping on eBay

To start selling on eBay, you must first have a professional account on this platform. If you already have an account but don't need it, attempt to recover it. Blocking a new account is not unusual for eBay as it assumes that a customer is repeating his information:

- **Regular Business Account:** If you continue selling for a standard account, you would have to pay a charge for each ad you publish after-sales separately. You'll also be charging a fee for everything you deliver. That could be a reasonable option if you want to add a limited amount of advertising.
- **eBay Store:** There are three different eBay Stores; Basic, Advanced, or Premium. Each has

a fixed monthly cost (which ranges from €19.5 to €149.5) and, depending on which you choose, will be able to post a series of ads for free. If you exceed this maximum number of free ads, you will be charged an additional fee. It is interesting to calculate how much you are trying to sell per month and calculate the profitability of each.

How to choose a supplier

When you do dropshipping on eBay, the supplier you choose is essential. In reality, it is important to practice dropshipping with any platform. In essence, you already have your e-commerce, you sell on marketplaces, or through social networks; dropshipping is a strategy in which the supplier takes undeniable importance.

So, if you want to do dropshipping on eBay, follow these several tips for choosing a supplier:

Choose a supplier who is used to working with eBay

Each marketplace has its own rules. Whether it's Amazon, eBay, or whatever, you will have to adapt to a few rules. It is, therefore, better that your supplier knows them in advance and is ready to give you an answer.

Ask yourself what synchronization options you have

When doing dropshipping on eBay, you will have to

synchronize your account with your supplier's catalog. There are various ways to do that, and every provider provides some of them. The keyway is via CSV files, but some suppliers provide automated frameworks that enable integration to be done far more easily. It might also be useful to do so with an API, but that presupposes that you have some programming experience (or ask someone who has it).

Once you have created your account, chosen your supplier, and synchronized the catalog, you will need to review the costs and your margins.

Costs and margins when you do dropshipping on eBay

As you probably already know, the difference between your PVP and the selling price at which you purchase the drug from the manufacturer is your profit margin when doing dropshipping. For example: if you buy earphones at your dropshipping supplier for 5 euros and sell them for 10, your profit will be the 5 euro-difference.

As we said earlier, when selling on eBay, there are certain fees that you need to take into account. This is not unique to eBay. All marketplaces establish a series of commissions, be it a monthly price, a sales commission, or any other system for making profits.

To note:

Depending on the country in which you sell, eBay fixes certain tariffs.

- Prices for sellers in Spain
- Prices for sellers in France
- Prices for sellers in the United Kingdom
- Prices for sellers in Italy
- Prices for sellers in Germany

Don't have time to read? Here are the conclusions

Doing dropshipping on eBay is a very good option for making profits with online sales. In this chapter, we have presented some main aspects to take into account when you sell on this marketplace.

Here is a summary:

There are many advantages to doing dropshipping on eBay. This marketplace has very high buyer traffic, it has a great reputation, and it will be much easier for you to reach potential customers.

On the other hand, there are also disadvantages: The rivalry is intense, you will have to conform to the conditions put on you, and you will have to pay to print your advertising as well as a sales fee, as in any marketplace.

You can sell using a default business account or an eBay store. This or that alternative would suit you, based on the amount of advertising you want to run and what you are trying to market. Take into account eBay commissions for each type of account, or you may end up incurring losses.

The dropshipping supplier you choose is essential for success on eBay. If your supplier is not ready to meet your needs, the end consumer will be affected. Consider looking for a supplier who allows you to synchronize their catalog with your account easily.

DROPSHIPPING ON AMAZON

Dropshipping is one of the most used businesses today because it does not require a large investment. It has the purpose of selling products without the need for expensive shipping or inventory; basically, the user is in charge of setting the prices for the products and attract customers to the website while the supplier is in charge of shipping, manufacturing, and inventory. We can find several examples of this type of business, although the most widely used and known are Mercado Libe and Amazon.

Benefits Of Dropshipping On Amazon

The first thing we will notice is that there is no storage cost. Apart from not having to worry about taking inventory of your virtual storefront, you also do not have to spend a lot of time on the logistics of storage, since as a supplier, when selling a product, you need to send it directly to Amazon. There, they are the ones in charge or send it to the destination, no matter where it is.

As it has the advantage of being a well-known website, there is a lot of ground to have contact with many people, so you have many more sales opportunities. You have to keep in mind that every time you sell a product and have it at a good and reasonable price, you will be creating a good reputation which is one of the first characteristics that new visitors and experienced buyers are looking for. Therefore, if you want to create a large terrain and sales, it is recommended that you start with this option since it is very easy and advantageous.

As for advertising, Amazon offers you many advantages to being a novice seller. We have to take into account that Amazon itself has its virtual traffic, that is, its daily visitors, and that is why making your products more striking is significant.

Disadvantages Of Dropshipping On Amazon

One of the policies that Amazon has created is not to allow resellers on the website. To explain it better, if you want to resell any product, Amazon allows it but using a special program called FBA created by Amazon itself. If it is not used, this site does not allow the purchase of any product or the wholesale purchase of something on offer and reselling it by the same means.

How Does This Web Portal Work?

Amazon is one of the most popular sales sites out there today which grew in popularity because it allows visitors to easily register and sell their products regardless of whether they are wholesalers or retailers. Best of all is that even the most famous physically registered coffers can also sell their products through this page and thus make their products more accessible worldwide.

This site works through a program called FBA, which stores all the products that you register in a kind of showcase and sends them directly to your customers. However, it must be borne in mind that not all the products that you register can be registered. There are certain parameters to be able to sell on this type of site.

Step By Step: How To Dropship on Amazon

- First, you must create an account on Amazon; you must confirm in which country you want to sell since it is a worldwide platform.
- Enter the country where you or your company is located, including its legal name and what type of company it is.
- Then Amazon will present you with an information sheet that you must fill out with all your data or that of the company.

After creating the account and entering all the corresponding data, you must synchronize it with your supplier's catalog. This step is very important because this will help all the data to be presented correctly, data that will be viewed by the client who searches for said product, not only about price but also about product description, quality, location, and any other information that is of interest to buyers.

For this, Amazon offers you three synchronization options that will help you a lot. CSV is an application that Amazon offers you, which is downloaded to your pc, and then you upload it to your account. At the same time, it synchronizes all the data that is needed; there is a CSV for the cost of the product, another for the location, and another for the product description. As Amazon has its CSV designed, you must make sure that yours is linked to that of the web portal. Therefore, it is recommended that your provider provide it to you. Otherwise, you have to design something that is not highly recommended.

API is another option, but its disadvantage is that you need to know about programming to be able to use it since it is more automated. If you don't know how to do it, you will have to hire programmer, which will require more expenses.

SYNCHRONIZATION WITH AUTOMATIC TOOLS is another option offered by some of the pages. When you create your account and synchronize it with the website, it automatically allows you to synchronize all the data that the page asks for without the need to do so separately:

- After synchronization, you must establish the cost for the use of this platform, which can be a monthly payment or a payment for each sale that is made. This will depend on the volume of sales obtained.
- The shipment of the products will depend on the urgency that the buyers have, that is why it offers you options to establish how urgently you want shipments that normally last 4-5 days, or urgently 24-48 hours.

Amazon is a very popular company thanks to the good reputation of its platform. Therefore it is very demanding because it needs to maintain it. As a result, you have to offer good products to be a good seller and have a wide clientele.

CHAPTER 8

HOW TO DEMOLISH THE COMPETITION

Differentiating a product or service in a mature market requires a good strategy. But it will only be effective if you design effective communication and you can rethink it if your competitors imitate you.

Innovation

When the product life cycle is getting shorter, the company that achieves an innovative advantage will enjoy the reward of being first. Marketing studies conclude that innovative products are 33% more profitable. But innovation also has its weak points: New products that are very rudimentary or ahead of demand, high development costs, difficulty in competing, and the appearance of imitators who offer lower prices and continuous product improvement.

Quality

Quality level refers to the ability to meet consumer expectations. Depending on the product, quality is identified with durability, reliability, safety, etc. To differentiate yourself in this sense, you must manufacture "the best product" or, at least, a product or service superior to the existing ones. Companies that have higher quality products are more profitable because they can charge higher prices, and their customers are more loyal. However, after a certain point, an increase in quality means a decrease in performance. The secret is to choose a level of quality appropriate for customers and superior to that of competitors.

Value Added

A product can be offered with some additional features that complement its basic function. There are many different possibilities in this regard, as it has been shown that almost everything can be added to a product: detergent with disinfectant, toothpaste with the elixir, moisturizer with caviar, shower gel with honey ... But whoever chooses this Strategy must find out what is worth adding to the product, calculating the value that this additional feature will have for the consumer as opposed to the cost that it will represent for the company.

Design

Fifteen years ago, companies competed through prices, and today they do it through quality, and tomorrow they will do it through design. Design is the most difficult feature to copy, and consumers are willing to pay a premium for a different and attractive product. The company that intends to influence design must know that it affects the aesthetic appearance, but also the functionality. A well-designed product should be easy to use and easy on the eyes.

Container

The packaging is an element of extraordinary relevance since it constitutes the consumer's first contact with the product and actively influences the purchase decision. It is especially important in high-end objects, that is, elitist and that take maximum care of the design, such as jewelry or watches, and in beauty products, such as perfumes or cosmetics. But it can also become an effective weapon of differentiation if it is specially taken care of in consumer products, in which the packaging is not usually given importance.

SERVICE

Another form of differentiation is to provide additional services when purchasing the product. They facilitate the purchase and use of the product, and the consumer gets guarantees as added value. Good service builds customer loyalty and makes it less price sensitive. The downside to choosing this form of differentiation is that it is easily imitable. Custom and delivery facilities, installation and maintenance, personalized attention during and after the sale, guarantees, attention to complaints, and money-back are the services most valued by customers.

Advertising

To create a message, attractive, rational, or emotional concepts can be used. Rational ads affect quality, profit, or price, and emotional ads use positive or negative emotions. Fear, joy, disgust, shame, love, and humor are concepts used to make a different advertisement. However, although these ads manage to attract more attention from the viewer, they can make it difficult to understand, provoke rejection and hide the product, not forgetting that ads like these can go out of style more easily.

Image

Public relations comprises a series of activities dedicated above all to promote the image of a company and its products. They differ from advertising in that the company does not pay for space or time in the media, but for a group of people to develop ideas, circulate them for free and lead events such as product presentations or sponsorship of sociocultural activities.

Atmosphere

An important tool to differentiate yourself is the physical space in which the company produces or sells its products. The furniture and its distribution, the architecture, the materials, and the colors used are of great importance, especially if it is retail trade. For a store to be at a competitive advantage, the environment must be prepared almost as if it were a theater stage, so going to buy is, above all, an experience.

Personnel

The company can differentiate itself from the competition by having better-trained people among its workers. The most qualified person should be competent, courteous, convey credibility and confidence, and be responsive. The company may also choose to have an employee with some characteristics or skills different from the rest.

Symbols

The image of a company is enhanced and differentiated from the rest with the use of symbols that represent some aspect of the company and that remain in the consumer's mind. The symbol can consist of an object, a pet, a color, or even a person.

Name

The company chooses to name its products away from the line set by its competitors. This requires making crucial decisions regarding the brand, ensuring that the name of the products is suggestive, as well as easy to recognize and remember.

High Price

Price is associated with considerations such as quality, value, or social status. Therefore, the consumer may opt for the most expensive product since he wants to afford the luxury of displaying a symbol of social success. Experts have repeatedly stated that most skincare cosmetics contain identical ingredients. However, the high prices of certain brands continue to convince the consumer that they are acquiring the best product.

Low Price

There is a current trend among consumers, a group that includes so-called "precision buyers." These people have lost interest in luxury brands that charge a premium for their products and opt for cheaper products, provided they are of acceptable quality.

Offering a product that is cheaper than the competition can be a good differentiation strategy, provided that the consumer does not perceive it as being of poor quality.

Channels

The company can also break with tradition in the selection of channels, choosing means to distribute its products different from the usual ones. You can sell your products in exclusive establishments, create your stores to distribute them or opt for the Internet or direct sales. It is also worth noting the franchise as an expansion strategy. With this system—if well designed—it is ensured that both the image and the quality of the offeror customer service are the same in each store in the chain.

CHAPTER 9

HOW TO PROMOTE YOUR BRAND AND YOUR PRODUCTS

Although we are in the 21st-century, more than ten years after the meteoric rise of social networks in our lifestyles, the question of how to promote your brand on social networks is still an issue. Why? One of the main reasons is that social media is still one of the main acquisition levers on the web, which is also accessible to all marketing budgets. Contrary to many popular beliefs, Facebook still retains its interest in promoting a brand, in particular, to generate traffic. YouTube is still present and generates traffic; Instagram and Twitter complete the list in terms of visibility and conversations. We could add Snapchat, which may also be of interest. The costs have certainly increased. We will focus on the methodology and strategy to apply to properly promote your brand, but also generate traffic on your website.

Promoting your brand on social media: Methodology and application

Despite the ease of advertising on social networks, it cannot be improvised. On the contrary, you need to have a global vision of your brand on its market, as well as the ecosystem that allows you to be visible to the people you want to reach. This involves defining the acquisition channels for your brand. Concretely, what are the steps to reach my goal of sales, lead generation, or basement? Once we have these phases on paper, we can then proceed to activation. But let's see in more detail these different stages.

1 - To promote your brand on social networks, you must correctly define the acquisition phases

From experience and without reinventing the model, the marketing phases are divided into four major acquisition phases. These can potentially be structured in sub-phases, but it depends on your market and on your business model. Here, we are interested in the four main ones, which are:

- Phase 1: awareness,

- Phase 2: the conviction that we can call "recruitment" on social networks,

- Phase 3: conversions: purchase, contacts, subscription, etc.

- Phase 4: loyalty and upsell.

If there is one thing to remember at this stage, it is that it will be difficult to complete any of these phases without having completed the previous one. Concretely, it will be complicated to sell your product or service (phase 3) if your brand is not known at all (phase 1). Just as it is with the loyalty/upsell phase; the phase cannot be completed if the person did not buy... It seems logical, but it is not uncommon to see brand managers think the opposite.

Let's go into detail each of the acquisition phases on social networks by specifying the event that triggers it, marketing objectives, channels or supports, planning, and KPIs to measure performance and know whether or not these phases are completed. The document template below can be used to ask each of the acquisition steps. The document can serve as a repository internally or with providers. Here is how it is structured:

- A summary to support the context,
- The event that launches the campaign on the networks to increase awareness,
- The main marketing objectives (they must be encrypted),
- The channels/media, i.e., The social networks used,
- The calendar: from when to when is the campaign activated?
- KPIs to measure performance and know if the phase is completed.

Awareness, commonly called "awareness."

The first marketing "stone" that will serve as the foundation for the building is the awareness phase. It corresponds to an objective of notoriety. For this, social networks are extremely efficient with reasonable costs and interesting statistical details.

Which gives us:

- Summary/context: a summary of the points set out below,
- The triggering event: the announcement of a product, a service, creation of a new brand...,
- The main marketing objectives: spread my message to x people located in France, etc. Recruit so many people on Facebook...,
- Channels media: Facebook? Instagram? YouTube? ...,

- The calendar: from which day to which day,
- The KPIs: impressions, reach, repetition (very important), video views (if this is the case), social interactions, recruitment, expenses.

When we talk about "promoting your brand on networks," we often stop only at this phase. If we cannot ignore it, it represents only a quarter of our social media marketing plan...

The "conviction" or recruitment phase

One might wonder why the awareness phase does not join the recruitment phase ... In my opinion, it is important to separate the objectives of these two phases. Wanting to fulfill a visibility objective, which is only a passive action on the part of our audience, to a recruitment objective on social accounts (i.e. an engaging activity) can be complicated. I'm not saying that by promoting your brand or your product on Instagram, nobody will follow your account in return. Still, the interactions will not be direct because the placements and formats of advertisements may not be correlated with recruitment.

Like the awareness step, it is good to put your strategy on paper with the same template: summary/context, quantified marketing objectives, social platforms, planning, and KPIs.

The awareness phase made it possible to test the target audiences, to see how much it cost and what type of profile governed the best. By combining the data, we can define one, two, or even three targets to be recruited according to their market and budget. This so-called conviction phase is very important, because the more qualified the recruitment, the more the performance will be visible in the following phases.

The conversion phase (s)

The crucial step for any business, because it directly generates your turnover or prospects that can be transformed later in some cases. The conversion phase applies, in theory, and practice, the good insights from the previous two steps. At this stage, we know the audience, the social networks that suit the objectives as well as the effective advertising placements.

This phase must, therefore, reactivate the targets recruited in stages 1 and 2, but also extend the reach by reaching new audiences only if the marketing budget allows it. It is necessary at this stage, to privilege a repeated diffusion of the advertisements rather than to touch the mass. It is always fun seeing customer cases advertising hundreds of millions of impressions without mentioning the reach (number of people reached). Without this last data set, it is impossible to know the repetition and, therefore, the quality of diffusion. No study objectively suggests which repetition to achieve to ensure good dissemination. I agree that over seven days, it is good to achieve a repetition between 4 and 6.

The loyalty and "upsell" phase

By reaching this phase, you have: made your brand and your products known to 2/3 personalized audiences, recruited an audience pool (your fans, your followers, etc.), activated a conversion campaign, and analyzed the results. Now, we must "close the loop" by retaining the people who have converted. What is meant by "building loyalty" on social networks? It is a question of implementing the loyalty program on the social platforms where your brand is present: transmit your email address to join a "club" regardless of the name (more and more e-commerce sites offer to purchase as a guest, that is, without going through the creation of an account), and subscribe to social accounts to be able to play on the organic scope of its future publications, offer or promote discounts and products.

To achieve this, social networks provide tracking tools that are to be configured and placed on your website. Facebook Pixel for Facebook and Instagram, Twitter Pixel for Twitter, LinkedIn Tag for the professional social platform, and the Global Site Tag for YouTube (and all of Google). Snapchat also offers to place this cookie on your site. The "technical" part finished, these tools will allow you to retarget a typology of visitors to your site: those who have placed an order, who have seen a product, who have subscribed to the newsletter, etc. With the loyalty phase, we will rather be interested in customers and therefore recommend that they follow the Facebook page, the Instagram profile, or even the Twitter account.

In summary, the mistake to avoid at all costs is to want to combine phases 1, 2, and 3 at the same time as the conversion stage, which is what brings the business to life. For this, the following is a good example. Can we in a few seconds: catch someone's eye, make them read/view a message, convince them to follow us, and then encourage them to go to a store so that they buy our product? Knowing that the store may not be efficient in terms of conversion? Wanting to perform these steps, even on a campaign lasting several weeks, is risky. There are products that we consume on a whim, but that does not prevent people from learning about the brand. This is where social evidence comes into play, and phases 1 and 2 helped develop this evidence.

Working your presence on social networks in this way allows you to have a clear and understandable roadmap for everyone working on the subject. One can very well imagine thinking of the 4 phases for a product launch, the creation of a brand, or simply for the web marketing plan for next year. By following this method, you will see that promoting your brand on social networks cannot be improvised and that Facebook, Instagram, and others are not levers to activate from time to time even if the creation of a social ads campaign can be configured in 1/2 weeks (with the creation of content), unlike a personalized display campaign.

CHAPTER 10

HOW TO USE SEO TO SKYROCKET YOUR BUSINESS

If you have an e-commerce business, digital marketing is essential for your success. You need quality products and an adequate platform, but without marketing, your products will not be visible, and you will not make any sales.

Fortunately, there are many effective ways at your disposal to develop your audiences, such as SEO, Facebook/Instagram advertising, content marketing, display advertising, sponsors, influence marketing, and much more.

The challenge is that there are so many different channels that it is difficult, if not impossible, if you are not a marketing expert to know where to start and how to take your marketing to the next level.

If you have set up the basics of SEO on your site and have invested in content marketing with a link strategy to rank better, there are ways to speed up this process and get results even faster.

In this chapter, I want to share with you four advanced strategies for SEO in the world of e-commerce. You can use them to appear more in the search results in your niche. The goal is to build the reputation of your brand as well as increase your traffic and achieve the development objectives of your business.

Here are the four strategies:

- Brand profiles
- Local SEO: the barnacle tactic
- Semi-automatic data entry and network information
- The Content Marketing Funnel (NBED)

How to benefit from brand profiles for SEO and conversions

If you are an e-commerce company, you absolutely must have your platform and your brand. Without your website, you will constantly pay a percentage on your sales to other platforms in exchange for their audience, and you may end up being limited in your growth because their business does not entirely match yours.

But I don't disagree that selling your products on other platforms is doable. Platforms like eBay and Amazon are very successful, mainly because they have huge capital resources and have created a place where other traders can easily sell their products.

If you search on the internet for a brand like GoPro, you will see that their profiles on other websites are very present in the search results. Profiles on platforms such as:

- Twitter
- Youtube
- Amazon

- Instagram
- Facebook

When you have a small business, these channels can be used to lend your web more exposure when someone is looking for your brand. You can also do it as an individual:

This function is also called reputation management. Sometimes an article or an unwanted site appears in your brand's search results, as has happened to GoPro. However, it's still a very effective way to show those who are looking for your brand that you are a reliable company and recognized.

If you are trying to reference ten profiles for terms related to your brand, you will need to dedicate your energy to achieve and succeed.

When trying to get your brand to appear more in search results, you should:

- Vary sites and profiles by making a brand anchor text link to your site when you publish on other platforms or appear in registers.
- Link your most important profiles to your main website to make them valuable.
- Give priority to high-performance websites (use MozBar from Moz to see your domain name authority, which is a performance indicator) and make sure you have complete profiles, unique content with everything you can share (video, etc.).

The final strategy here is, of course, to find websites that allow you to have reviews posted so that the internet users who have done the research trust you with positive and independent reviews.

Local SEO: the barnacle tactic for e-commerce sites

Each niche has a few main companies that hold the majority of the market. However, these companies are not always the most popular, so people are looking for competitors or alternatives.

A good strategy is to have your site referenced when a potential customer is dissatisfied with the big brands and is looking for "competitors" or "alternatives."

Let's say your website is in the business of selling tree seeds. You sell seeds from a tree that is often considered an alternative to maple trees because some people don't like maple trees.

There are at least five sites you can contact to add another tree species to those offered (and link to it) or to have your link published by making it visible to visitors on their sites.

This strategy is similar to Google Autocomplete to find new keywords to target.

Semi-automatic data entry and the information network

When thinking about SEO for your e-commerce site, you should consider as many questions and alternatives as possible that people could type in when researching before purchasing a product.

These are certainly your most important keywords for positioning yourself correctly, as they direct user traffic directly to you, traffic, which you know you can convert. And if conversions increase, they are useful both for positioning yourself and generating traffic via SEO, AdWords, and Facebook/Instagram.

But this is only one piece of the puzzle, nevertheless an important piece, which represents SEO for your e-commerce site. Higher in the funnel of conversions, is your potential customer's research before buying.

This is where you can invest a bit in paid research: create content that answers questions from your potential customers so that they get to know your brand better and are more likely to buy from you.

If you develop your strategy well, you can also use it to collect email addresses so you can continue to communicate with your customers through a well-optimized strategic email marketing campaign.

Here is how the autocomplete SEO strategy works so that you can develop your keyword network.

First, use the following tools to understand Google's suggested search terms and those that could drive traffic to your site:

- Soovle
- UberSuggest
- Longtail Pro
- Keywords Everywhere

When I use UberSuggest to search for "Nike vs." combined with Keywords Everywhere, I get a list of brands that people compare to Nike. If you have a shoe e-commerce site, this can be a great way to inform your users and encourage them to buy from you:

Imagine being able to place your e-commerce site on this list. Competition is low, and user traffic is high. What more?

The objective is to identify all the keywords used by your potential customers when they are in the discovery phase in their search. So when they are ready to buy, they know and consider your brand and are more likely to buy from you.

Take advantage of reviews on other sites to develop your organic traffic

Finally, how to write an article on Trustpilot without talking about reviews? As an e-commerce site, you not only need opinions about your company but also about your products. If you are both a product manufacturer and a seller, you are probably using other platforms to sell your products.

Take the example of the outdoor industry. The North Face is not only a seller, but also a manufacturer of products. If I search for one of their products, like their Thermoball hooded jacket. My search is "thermoball NorthFace," and I find the following results:

- TheNorthFace.com
- Amazon
- Moosejaw

- Sporting Good Dicks
- REI
- Backcountry.com
- Youtube
- SteepAndCheap.com

Notice what The North Face has done.

They built their own space to get opinions, which are then shown in the search results. They, therefore, have their platform, which is necessary for the longevity of the brand.

However, they also sell through other distributors, and they both rely on them to receive reviews but also to actively invite customers to leave reviews on these platforms. If everyone appreciates the jacket, as is the case with Thermoball, even potential customers will be convinced that the product is of high quality and has satisfied consumers.

What should we remember from this?

If you are selling your product, you should also use the other available platforms to reach a larger audience and sell more. In addition to owning your platform and optimizing your website, this can be another great strategy for growing your business, if it is financially viable.

The same applies to your brand since customers may want to buy a product, but ultimately determine their purchasing decisions by the reputation of the brand. In a world dominated by social networks, the work you do to improve and promote your brand directly influences your buyers, and this helps you to retain your customers.

Investing in your brand by collecting customer reviews is one of the best ways to improve your business, regardless of the ranking of your research. The best part is that reviews also help you improve your search rankings and clickthrough rates when star ratings appear in search results.

CHAPTER 11

HOW TO HANDLE SECURITY ISSUES WITH YOUR BUSINESS

Despite a growing sector, the security of online stores still needs to be improved.

As the Internet has developed and in particular, e-commerce, site security and safety have become a major issue when creating a website.

On the one hand, cybercrime has developed a lot and threatens trust, an essential pillar of e-commerce, but on the other hand, security breaches in e-commerce sites have caused financial damage.

Also, the laws have adapted to the Internet, and there is a legal framework to protect Internet users and e-merchants, provided that the latter respect it.

Protection has, therefore, become an essential element to take into account when you are going to create an online store.

Let's see in a few points how to create a secure website. But also how to effectively protect an e-commerce site by starting by defining what is malicious, dangerous, and therefore what to watch out for at the technical level, then at the legal level to have a professional site.

Mobility becomes a norm

The good health of e-commerce is no longer to be proven. After a growth of 13.7% in the 1st quarter, online revenue was estimated at 64 billion euros in 2015. With 14,500 new online stores created during the past year, there are now more than 164,200 e-commerce sites.

With the main players ensuring a mobile presence, mobility has today become a standard. The e-commerce market is estimated at 4 billion euros, with a majority of mobile sites taking over applications.

Security of its e-commerce site: efforts to continue

Actions taken against credit card fraud are bearing fruit. The fraud rate was down in 2013 and represented 0.251% of the number of transactions. Despite this observation, it still remains more than 20 times higher than the fraud rate observed on proximity payments.

French internet users, however, remain sensitive to site security. 85% of them believe that safety is important when choosing a site on which they order.

Security could be improved. 70% of e-merchants would be imprudent about protecting internet users' passwords. Only 14% of them have implemented processes requiring users to complexify their login credentials. However, 45% of sites continue to send clear identifiers and passwords to customers' mailboxes.

E-commerce sites are prime targets for hackers

In retail, 31% of attacks are Directory Traversal, navigation techniques that aim to access protected content. More than 11% of websites using HTTPS have a vulnerability: mixed content, when, in an HTTPS page, resources are loaded in the non-secure version of the protocol.

According to OWASP, in 2013, 97% of web applications remain exposed to known vulnerabilities, which were exploited in 80% of successful attacks in 2015.

Importantly, it takes 197 days for an e-commerce site to detect a deep attack on its information system while it takes 98 in the financial sector. Finally, only 34% of e-commerce sites have implemented incident response procedures.

Google's recommendations for website security

E-commerce relies heavily on the main search engine, Google. The latter specifies the importance of the security of a website in its many recommendations and even devotes a part of the menu of "Search Console," an essential free tool and necessary for any owner of an e-commerce site.

For the leader in search engines, messaging, and browsers, having an insecure site is having a site where a hacker can install malicious code. This can record the actions of visitors' computers, steal the identifiers they use to connect to their online banking services, carry out financial transactions, or even divert them to other sites.

Also note in passing that Google considers as dangerous and insecure any web page proposing to install a deceptive system (the promised advantages are not respected), or which incites the users to do something unnatural, does not state all the details of the offer, destabilizes the user's system, collects or transmits private information without informing the user, or is associated with another program, without the user being informed (see the unwanted software policy).

In some cases, some advertising systems are also considered "malicious," especially since certain hackers have successfully infiltrated display advertising platforms, such as certain tracking or statistics systems.

Note also that this means that anyone who will make a site (showcase site and e-commerce site) likely to present security problems will be reported by Google and probably "devalued" in terms of SEO (natural referencing) as much that he will not have shown "white paw" again. Google is forcing owners of contaminated sites to quarantine them until the problems are resolved.

How to protect your e-commerce site?

Several actions can be taken to protect your e-commerce site.

The ba-ba retains the establishment of an SSL/TLS certificate on all the pages of its e-commerce site. Remember, last July, WiziShop offered to all of its e-merchants to benefit from this SSL certificate to secure their site, reassure their visitors, and even improve their SEO.

Even if your site is secure, you still have to be careful. So:

- Respect good practices from the site development phase.
- Detect and protect the site in real-time (WAF, IDS / IPS...).
- Regularly analyze your site using vulnerability scans.
- Host the application in a certified environment (PSI DSS, HADS, ISO...).
- Set up a password and access management policy.

Here now, in detail, is the implementation of technical and legal security on your e-commerce site.

How to technically secure your website?

In addition to the previous recommendations, the security of e-commerce is common sense.

1. HTTPS

First, an e-commerce site must have an SSL certificate. The https protocol simply refers to the secure version of the usual HTTP. Reserved until now for secure transaction systems, it has become a standard for any site, in particular, e-commerce, because it makes it possible to be certain that the traffic and exchanges of information between Internet users and the site are indeed between them without third party or diversion. On WiziShop, when you are going to create an online sales website, your domain name will be natively in https. The SSL certificate will be directly hosted on the server. You don't need any knowledge.

2. Updates

In 2017, very few e-commerce sites were made from craft code. Most are based on systems like WiziShop, hosts with solid infrastructure, a dedicated, secure server, and resistant database systems (MySQL, Oracle, DB2, etc.).

In particular, to keep a low level of insecurity, these systems are regularly updated, and site maintenance is well managed, but on some e-commerce CMS (Content Management System), these updates may not be automatic.

I advise you to check this regularly, especially in terms of configuration or web hosting contracts, the same way as it is checked on your computer compared to the OS or the main programs you use regularly.

3. Unnecessary access closed

An e-commerce site is, first of all, a computer system which, by its nature, has many open passages and, therefore, a certain vulnerability.

In addition to the back-office with content management, it can be accessed via the database, via FTP, via ssh or other means. It is, of course, necessary to know them, to know if these possibilities are open or closed and if necessary, who has access to them.

Also, the back-office of the site must be secure. Check that the login and password, as well as the connection URL, are not too simple and know also who has access there.

At present, without going through too complicated systems, we can limit all these accesses to the heart of the site, by the IP address with htaccess, for example, according to the techno used (to avoid that anyone can have access to it) or at least set up specific tools to know when someone connects to it.

4. Change your passwords regularly

Very often, the weaknesses of a site come from the passwords used for the accesses to its back-office, for access to the host, or to the service provider, which manages the domain name. Avoid passwords that are too easy, change them every 3 or 6 months, and do not keep them on your phone or computer. A good old notebook is much better.

5. Antivirus

Most web hosts constantly scan the sites they host with antivirus software to save their infrastructure.

Be aware of the frequency of these scans and what steps are taken in case of trouble.

In some cases, the anti-virus will be able to block the whole site or simply a part, put the file in quarantine or delete it.

Whatever the method, the important thing is to be notified as soon as there is a problem because if not, your site can be downgraded and even banned. Not only on search engines but also by suppliers, which will take you away from your turnover, but may even allow a competitor or cybercriminals to replace you.

6. Backup and reinstallation of your site

In the event of a security problem on your website, the best way to provide the service is to be able to put a secure version online quickly. For this, you must very regularly back up your site and have a safe, quick reinstallation procedure.

Some hosts offer all this as an option, but it is also advisable to double these services with an external system, in case.

How to legally secure an e-commerce site?

When we talk about security in e-commerce, we mainly think of the technique but this aspect is far from being the only one. Legal certainty is also very important.

1. Domain name

We must first make sure that the domain name is the property of the company. Sometimes it is indeed a service provider that is the real owner of the domain name. Via the Whois service, always remember to check who the real owner is and do not hesitate to hide the Whois information if the domain name is linked to a particular email address and a mobile phone number.

If the domain name is a brand, then it is prudent to secure the brand by filing with the INPI, especially when a logo is attached to it.

When the e-commerce site is present in several international markets, then it is sometimes good to buy domain names with local endings. Even if this investment can be expensive when you are present in several areas, this can prevent cybersquatters from taking advantage of the name of an e-commerce site and overtime to devalue the brand or to recover customers.

Domain name refers to your website but also emails for your emailing strategy. To secure the whole, it is preferable to deposit the domain name with a provider other than the host. Thus, the mails will be managed by a service provider different from the one who manages the site, and we will not depend on the host if ever we have to change the hosting site quickly.

The domain name is an important element of the intellectual property relating to the site, but it is not the only one.

2. Ownership or right to use the content of the site

The owner of the site is responsible for its content or at least authorized to use it. This means in particular that the texts and images must be able to be used on the e-commerce site without a third party being able to dispute it.

If you are the owner of the texts and images, declare ownership, and make sure they are not used elsewhere. If you use texts and images of a brand, make sure that you have a contract allowing it.

3. Ownership or right to use the container

The container, that is to say, the tree structure of the site, specific structural as well as ergonomic and "design" developments, must also be secured about their property or right of use. The software licenses which can be used for the existence of the site must have been acquired if they do not enter the field of free software. If there have been specific developments made by a company or freelancers, the transfer of ownership must have taken place so that the operator of the e-commerce site not only has the right to use them but is not duplicated or obliged to pay a fee to have the right to continue its activity.

If very specific technical developments with high added value have been made, it is possible to deposit them at the INPI, with a notary or a specialized company, and even to value them in the company's accounts.

4. Legal notices and GTC

Any site must have legal notices, which mainly identify the site owner, the publication manager, as well as the host while providing the means to contact the site managers.

Also, if the e-commerce site is aimed at individuals, it must include CGV (General Conditions of Sale) adapted to the specifics of the sale on the internet, the CGV e-commerce. These specific General Conditions indicate the conditions of sale proper (conditions relating to the transfer of property, logistics, etc.), how a sale takes place via the site, the scale of unit prices, delivery costs, terms of payment, commitments and guarantees of the site, cases of force majeure, customer rights, withdrawal period, conditions and address for possible returns (if it is physical e-commerce).

The e-commerce T & Cs are a real regulation of the site, contrary to popular belief. They protect both the e-merchant and the customer because they allow, in the event of a dispute, to know what was planned and what the customer should know (which must validate the GTC before any purchase). The writing of the CGV must, therefore, be the subject of specific attention and it is not recommended to use models (which by definition are general) or to copy/paste the CGV e-commerce of another site, which, moreover, may be subject to a fine.

It should be noted that a site without CGV e-commerce or legal notices can also be condemned to pay a significant fine.

5. Terms

Cousins of the CGV, the general conditions of use, or CGU, legally frame the reports and conflicts that may arise between the site editor and the visitor. Nothing obliges to have them, but their presence is recommended because they fix:

Legal notices relating to the company or its registered office,

The conditions of access to the site,

The various services and products offered by the site,

The terms relating to the creation of a visitor or customer account,

Intellectual property,

The protection of personal data (very important with the implementation of the GDPR or General Data Protection Regulations),

The publisher's responsibility and its limits,

Responsibility of the visitor,

The duration and evolution of the contract, and

The competent court and the law are applicable in the event of litigation.

They, therefore, also contribute to the legal protection of the site.

6. Payment system

In the vast majority of cases, the online payment solution is managed by a bank or a financial organization that provides or indicates a technical solution that will make payment legally and technically secure. Concretely, during the payment action, the user often leaves the site for that of the payment system.

The bank or financial organization is not limited to providing this payment system. In the vast majority of cases, it goes hand in hand with a VAD (Distance Selling) contract, which legally allows the merchant to do Distance Selling. This area legally encompasses the trading activities of e-commerce sites.

This aspect, which is often overlooked, is very important because this distance selling contract specifies the responsibilities, rights, duties, and remedies of the online merchant.

The protection of an online site is, of course, technical but also includes legal aspects to ensure the intellectual property of its operators and protect it from the inevitable ups and downs of trade, whatever its type. With the growing power and expertise of regulatory bodies, consumer associations, competition (which is often used first to denigrate and annoy), and the threats of cybercrime, an e-commerce site can no longer afford to ignore the basic precautions that guarantee its sustainability.

Computer security is one of the most important aspects of protecting the operational functions of society, since technology, and in particular, computers are now essential for the management of the production phase and the preservation of the data of the network and customers. Very often, however, companies do not feel concerned and wrongly think that the risks are with the neighbor or only on large structures. They maintain an indifferent attitude towards a possible security problem, which can be very dangerous both for the network infrastructure and for the data, sensitive or not, which passes through it. In detail, in this section, we will try to give simple but effective tips to improve IT security in your business.

Use secure passwords

Companies still underestimate the importance of using secure passwords and updating them regularly. Using a password generator is a good start to having meaningless words, if not easily hacked by hacking systems. Where it is also available, we suggest using a two-factor authentication system where possible to increase the level of access security further. Within the company, all users must be minimally aware of IT security.

Have an audit carried out by a specialized company

When it comes to infrastructure security, it is never advisable to take things too lightly. The geographic position, the different suppliers, are chosen, and the mail servers are just some of the components of a single, fallible system. It would be a good procedure for a company specializing in security to carry out an audit to analyze the network and detect any critical point suggesting effective solutions. This audit can be combined with an RGPD compliance audit to comply with the company's regulations in this area. If your resources are limited, carry out an internal audit by using the guides published by ANSSI.

Develop a robust information security program

The threat of cybercrime is concrete and real, and, as already noted, the general security of the network infrastructure should not be overlooked. Therefore, it is relevant to develop a security information program which includes security policies, identification of systems and data, incident response planning, configuration management, training and awareness, disaster recovery, and many other essential elements, such as the company's IT charter.

Secure your professional messaging

Check the sender of the email before downloading attachments or clicking on malicious links. In particular: if the email contains an attachment and the sender is unknown, take no action. If the sender is a collaborator or a known sender, it is still advisable to check the integrity of the shipment. Indeed, if the colleague has the infected inbox, the virus tries to spread by sending the malicious package to other users. Choose an effective e-mail protection solution integrating virus and malware detection mechanisms, like Altospam for businesses or Malwarebytes for individuals.

Train your employees on security protocols

Employees of a company have browsing habits that often make it difficult to correct them. To effectively protect sensitive information in corporate networks, a security awareness and training program is essential to inform all staff of the protocols adopted for data protection. According to the iPhone specialist Pixypia, "it is very important to pay attention to the security of smartphones of company employees." Smartphones often contain work data such as contacts and are left out of the corporate security perimeter.

We also very often forget that the Internet is a public resource. Therefore, confidentiality is not guaranteed, especially for sites in the social media category. If a company's employees use social media such as Facebook and LinkedIn on corporate devices, it is essential to educate them about social media security protocols to maintain cybersecurity. This is the reason why educating your team is essential, as is the use of secure passwords and the implementation of effective email protection of the company. Also, it will be interesting to carry out a security audit of your company and anticipate a loss of data: an emergency procedure to follow can prove to be very useful at this time!

SELECT THE RIGHT PLATFORM THAT IS SECURE

When we have finally decided to set up our online store, the next questions that assail us are, which platform is the most suitable for creating an online business? Is it better to opt for your development? Our response will depend on the type of online business we plan to create.

But, as we know that it is not an easy decision, we are going to review the main platforms so that when creating our e-commerce site, we do it with knowledge of the cause. In this way, deciding the one that best suits our needs will be a piece of cake.

Criteria to consider when making a decision

It is important to keep in mind that there is no better or worse platform to sell online. What we can find is an e-commerce solution that is more adapted to what our business needs.

With this, we do not mean that you set up the cheapest online store on the market, but rather that our future electronic commerce must contain all the functionalities that interest us. For this reason, we have prepared a brief guide with the basic aspects that we must consider when creating our online business:

-What economic resources do we have: we have to be clear if we are going to choose to contract the development of our online store or, on the contrary, we are going to do it ourselves. In this way, we will have clearer the budget that will be needed to carry it all out.

-Technical knowledge: Do we have enough knowledge to get our e-commerce afloat? With this, we are not only referring to setting up the online store, but also, knowing how to manage it and constantly update it.

-Start an online store from scratch or consolidate our business? Choosing a certain platform will depend a lot on the objectives that we have set for ourselves. If, for example, we want to start a project from scratch, we may be more interested in an e-commerce platform where we can test our products, than a custom-designed platform. In this way, we will not have to risk our economic resources, and we will be able to verify if our business is viable.

-The volume of products in our online store: as we well know, setting up an online store with 20 products is not the same as creating one with more than 1,000 references. This will help us to focus more on what we are going to need.

-Know if we are going to have support to attend any type of incident.

Surely, they seem obvious points to us now, but when putting them into practice, if we are not clear enough, we have to put our hands on our heads to avoid the typical headaches and not be constantly changing platforms. Before making a decision, the best thing we can do is assess our needs and possibilities very well.

CHAPTER 12

HOW TO HANDLE YOUR CUSTOMERS AND PROVIDE GOOD CUSTOMER SERVICE

In the 21st-century, the main element of distinction between brands will be Customer Relations, before product quality and price. Companies have often considered customer relations as a source of necessary expenditure, but they are now aware of its importance. 80% of companies assess the customer experience as their priority strategic objective.

However, changing customer expectations and different trends can make mastering this area very complex. Indeed, there are many obstacles to overcome when trying to provide quality customer service.

DIFFICULTIES IN MANAGING CUSTOMER SERVICE ACTIVITY

Business management should be seen as the foundation of your Customer Relationship strategy. This involves using the right tools, processes, and strategies to deal with requests effectively. The main obstacles are, among others:

1. Allocate messages effectively

Without good organization, dealing with large amounts of requests quickly becomes a problem. The messages come from different channels, with different themes, in different languages... Handling them manually would take a lot of time, drive up costs, and ultimately hurt customer satisfaction.

The first step in dealing with these difficulties is to analyze your activity to identify the criteria by which you should redirect messages. This can be done depending on the language or subject, for example.

When you reorganize your teams by skills and not by types of channels on which you are present, this allows you to improve your processing of requests, to break silos and to have a better organization. You will, therefore, be able to redirect messages according to skills and availability automatically. Thus, you will be sure that a request, received by email, chat, or messaging, will be directed to the right agent. It will also help smooth the workload if one channel receives more requests than another. Your resources will thus be optimized, which will allow you to process messages efficiently.

2. Manage peaks of activity

Customer service is often very uneven throughout the day, which often requires you to redirect messages manually. Spikes can also be caused by seasonality (sales, new product launches, the holiday season) or by specific events (technical problems, weather disasters, promotional offers, etc.).

Not all of these peaks can be predicted, but specific methods can help you anticipate them. You have to rely on figures that allow you to identify patterns of peak activity to allocate your resources effectively.

Analyzing the amounts of requests by the time of day and day of the week will give you the insight to predict peaks. For unexpected peaks, refer to tools that allow you to analyze live data and monitor it. For example, a Telecom company that has network problems may give priority to requests related to this subject to ensure that their customers have a rapid response.

Managing peaks effectively is a challenge that companies must see as an opportunity to excel in the area of customer relations to overshadow their competitors.

3. Improve key KPIs

Customer relations departments should closely monitor certain key KPIs such as Average Handling Time and First Contact Resolution. The latter has a significant effect on all other KPIs. In essence, an SQM Community analysis reveals that raising the FCR by 1 percent results in a 1 percent increase in consumer loyalty and a 1 percent decrease in costs.

This indicator can be improved in various ways, for example, by analyzing the cause of repeat requests, ensuring that the customer's problem is resolved at the end of each interaction, and by giving agents better access to information. They can also rely on specific tools (response assistant, spell check, database) to reduce processing time.

DIFFICULTIES IN MANAGING CUSTOMER RELATIONS TEAMS

After you have put the right processes in place to manage your business, you should seek to improve your team management. We often hear about customer satisfaction, but the satisfaction of your agents is another point that should not be overlooked. Successful agents will be more motivated and will provide better responses, which will ultimately have an impact on customer satisfaction. This will also reduce the employee turnover rate, which represents a challenge for contact centers since the average turnover rate is as high as 30-45%.

A MetricNet study confirms that "happy agents equal happy customers": their conclusion highlights a close correlation between satisfied agents and satisfied customers. This study also shows that happy agents lower the turnover rate. How can we help them flourish and be able to benefit from such benefits?

1. Giving autonomy while maintaining control

Finding the right level of autonomy to give your agents is not easy. You don't want them to talk to customers like robots, but you can't let them do whatever they want. To provide excellent customer experience, it is necessary to offer personalized and rich interactions, while maintaining the coherent discourse of the company with quality responses.

It is possible to give your agents a certain degree of autonomy. A perimeter must be set up within which specific initiatives can be taken to empower them and increase their self-esteem. One of these initiatives, for example, may be to be able to grant a refund if he/she deems it necessary. With a well-defined policy and adequate training, you will ensure that reimbursement will only be granted if it is relevant and that it respects your pricing policy.

Another approach to providing greater flexibility is to focus on resources, such as models, to provide contextualized responses to the agents to allow them to provide short and full answers.

2. Free up time for your agents

A large part of your agents' time is wasted on basic and repetitive tasks: seeking customer information on several tools, repeating the same answer to the same question, etc. All this lost time means higher costs for the company and lower satisfaction for agents.

Freeing up time for agents will allow them to focus on higher value-added tasks like upselling. The company will be able to create opportunities to generate profit, and the agents will spend less time on repetitive tasks and will, therefore, feel more valued.

Customers today want to be able to carry out certain actions themselves, which increasingly encourages companies to set up self-care systems. This approach allows customers to perform some basic tasks, such as updating their contact information. This also explains the rise in popularity of chatbots. The microbots, concentrated on a single subject, respond instantly to customers 24/7 and thus free up time for agents.

3. Reduce the need for training

Training agents is another challenge. The use of several tools requires constant training, involves higher costs, less available agents, longer adaptation time, and less time to study products and offers.

To give them the autonomy and contribute to the development of your agents, you have to change your perspective by focusing on the products and identifying which training elements can be reduced. Another objective of customer relations teams must be to reduce the number of tools used.

LACK OF CUSTOMER KNOWLEDGE

72% of customers expect a customer service agent to know their contact details, the product concerned, and their customer service history as soon as they come into contact with a brand for customer support.

1. Use the available data

In the era of big data, companies have an impressive amount of data on their customers. This can include their contact details, interests, profession, etc.... Both organizations retain vast volumes of data but are finding it much more difficult to produce actual customer information from these datasets.

The most critical thing is to define which data form is suitable for your company and your objectives. You will then be able to evaluate this data smartly to strengthen your approach and to get your consumers a great experience.

2. Identify customers

Omni-digital means that customers contact you through different channels on which they have multiple identities. For example, the same person can contact you by email with an address such as jean.dupont@mail.com and contact you a few hours later elsewhere with the username @jean_d. If you do not identify that these two requests come from the same person, this forces you to answer twice to resolve the same problem, which leads to a loss of time and therefore, an increase in costs.

To manage this problem, you must have the right tools that will merge the different social identities and identify the best channel to respond to the client. Rather than getting a perspective compartmentalized by networks, agents have much to learn from a complete understanding of client personalities and their experience of contact. This full view allows agents to get all the information about the customer and avoid solving the same problem more than once.

3. Lack of information for agents

Another recurring problem in customer service is the lack of information. Silos make it difficult to centralize and analyze data. When handling a request, agents may not have easy access to all of the data concerning the said customer, which means that they have to wait or redirect them. According to Forrester, owing to broken networks, outdated user interfaces, or various programs, 42 percent of customer service agents are unable to address issues efficiently. This has an impact on the customers' perception of the service, which results in the loss of upsell opportunities and, therefore, of profit.

To facilitate access to information for agents, it is essential to provide them with a 360° view. This means that they must be able to access both transactional and conversational information when responding to requests. To access these two types of data on a single interface, you must integrate your CRM into your digital customer interaction platform.

4. Obtain customer reviews

Another essential component of knowing your customers is their opinion about your services and products. Getting to know what your customers think of you is a great opportunity to improve your offers. Did you know that 70% of companies delivering the best customer experience use this type of feedback? However, gathering these opinions is a challenge, and many companies do not make an effort.

Social networks are important channels for monitoring customer feedback, but we need to do more than just analyze feedback when there is, we must actively encourage customers to leave comments and share their opinions. This will ensure regular returns that will allow you to produce the best customer experience possible.

It can be as simple as a survey after each interaction. You don't want to ask customers to put in too much effort; surveys should be kept short and easy to complete. For more detailed surveys, it may be helpful to have a reward strategy in place to encourage customers to respond.

THE DIFFICULTY IN DEVELOPING A CUSTOMER RELATIONSHIP ECOSYSTEM

1. Synchronize data

Digital Customer Relations requires the use of a wide range of tools daily: CRM, Digital Customer Interaction Platform, reporting tools, voice solutions, etc. They all gather a large volume of complementary data. When all these tools are independent of each other, the information does not circulate, and this generates obsolete and redundant data silos that cannot be exploited or synchronized.

To cope with this expansion of data, you must be able to synchronize your tools, which remains a great challenge for businesses. When you connect your customer relationship tools on a single interface, it allows you to synchronize data from multiple sources, resulting in improved customer experience.

2. Improve the reliability of the connection to the channels

External channels such as Messenger or Instagram regularly update their APIs. If you connect directly to these channels or use an earlier version, this will cause reception problems, and you may then miss messages or send late responses.

To avoid this kind of situation, which is a source of frustration for customers, companies must rely on partners who constantly keep their connectors up to date, with a team ready to intervene quickly in the event of a problem.

3. Adapting to new Customer Relations channels

Integrating all the newly available channels is an ongoing challenge: it is necessary to adapt to their technical specificities, train teams, etc. Just like Messenger in 2016, other messaging channels will adapt to Customer Relations: WhatsApp, iMessage with Business Chat...

To incorporate these emerging platforms to satisfy the needs of your consumers, you need to focus on a technically agile partner who would be able to implement current developments in the industry.

4. Establish collaboration between chatbots and agents

Chatbots are one of the big trends of the moment in Customer Relations. As we explained, they can be used to provide very simple and specific instant responses to recurring requests. However, a chatbot will never answer all questions. It is thus necessary to provide a device allowing the chatbot to transfer the conversation to an agent who will then be able to answer it. This will prevent the customer experience from deteriorating.

To enforce this strategy, a perimeter unique to chatbots and transparent to customers needs to be established. An open platform will then allow you to set up an agent's support system as required.

Knowing that 82% of customers have turned their backs on a brand after a bad experience, this subject must be a priority for any business. Providing an excellent customer experience is a good way to distinguish yourself from your competitors and inevitably have a positive business. To deal with the obstacles that we have put forward, you must rely on an advanced platform that will help you optimize your activity, adapt to market developments, and connect you to the various tools. Thus, you will be able to adapt to the new expectations of your customers and maintain high-quality customer service.

TIPS AND TOOLS TO SUCCEED!

Entrepreneurs and self-employed, have you finally found clients? The goal, for now, is to keep! In other words, you need to find methods to retain them. For this, the basic rule is to have a lasting relationship with them and install a climate of trust. You can stand out by setting up an effective CRM.

A good loyalty strategy allows your company, among other things, to increase its profits and develop a dominant position vis-à-vis your competitors. Discover the best tips and tools to build customer loyalty.

TIPS

1- Be attentive

Listening is synonymous with respect and trust. Indeed, by listening to your customers and your prospects and by showing empathy, you will be able to adapt better and respond to their requests.

2- Respect your commitments

If you get involved in a project, make sure you keep your word and do your share of the work. It is important to always respect your commitments to your customers. Otherwise, you risk losing them. If you are not able to meet a specific expectation for your client, be honest, tell him! This is always less degrading for your image than promising something you cannot assure.

3- Keep in touch

It is essential to keep in touch with your customers after a sale to show them that you value them. Therefore, he will keep you in mind. Emails, SMSs, phone calls, social networks—lots of tools exist to maintain good communication.

4- Ask for recommendations

It is important to ask your customers to recommend you once the mission is over. The client will represent you and recommend to those around him. These testimonials show the quality of your products or services and allow you to expand your client portfolio.

You can, for example, display these recommendations on your LinkedIn page.

5- Have good customer service

To be available to the customer is to build loyalty! Make it a point of honor to have quality customer service: answer (quickly) their queries and their questions, show them that you are ready to help them, etc.

The tools

1- The loyalty card

It is a tool with double advantages. One for you: collecting valuable information about your client (contact details, purchasing habits, etc.) and one for your client: the more they consume, the more benefits and promotions they gain.

2- E-mailing or email marketing/The newsletter

Simple, easy, low cost to set up, the newsletter or e-mailing are very widespread tools on the web media. They regularly allow you to advise, give, and inform about new promotions, events, and news of your business. So you show the customer that you are there and listening. You thus create a climate of confidence in future sales.

The difference between these two tools is that subscribing to a newsletter is voluntary on the part of the client. The subscriber expects information, not advertising.

3- Sponsorship

Sponsorship is to encourage your customers to talk about your services and products to those around them. Thus, you would get new customers to expand your business base while strengthening the relationship with your current customers. To set up such a tool, encourage your most loyal customers to sponsor their friends and then reward them with discounts, promotions, etc.!

4- The gift/the sample

Your client has just trusted you, thank him! Establish a relationship based on something other than the simple price of the service: a gift. It should make your customer want to send you an email or call you to thank you. These gifts can range from simple goodies with your company logo to a bottle of champagne, chocolates or high-tech gadgets, etc.

5- Social networks

Social networks: an essential means of loyalty these days! By creating your Facebook page, LinkedIn, Twitter, etc. you will be closer to your customers. You can publish and share content, and exclusives to your target audience. Also, you can create contests to retain your customers better.

Now that you have the tips and tools in hand for good loyalty, do not hesitate to use Kiwili, the best management software, to simplify your daily business management.

CHAPTER 13

30,000/MONTH STRATEGY

On the web, there is no shortage of opportunities to earn money. You can make additional income, even making a fortune.

Both are possible. Earning 30,000 euros per month is largely feasible in several ways.

You probably know some of them: e-commerce on different marketplaces such as Amazon, eBay, Rakuten, dropshipping, infoprenariat, affiliation, freelancing...

These are different business models that allow significant gains. So why not €30,000 a month?

First of all, we will develop these multiple possibilities. Then, we will detail the mindset needed to succeed in these different areas.

E-commerce via different marketplaces

E-commerce is simply a business that is done only online. There are many ways to do this. Here we are going to talk about e-commerce with a stock of products in a market that is not yours. You use a market such as that of Amazon, eBay, Rakuten, etc. to sell your products. How does it work?

You choose products to sell, and you buy stock. You then offer them for sale on Amazon, for example, by creating your product sheets. That's it, and your product is online!

You can send your stock to their hangars and let Amazon (it's the same for other marketplaces) manage the logistics.

The advantage in this way of doing e-commerce is that we do not manage orders, delivery, or even after-sales service! Another advantage is that there is no need to create a site or advertise outside of this type of platform, which can cost you dearly at first.

The disadvantage is that you have to advance the budget of the stock before selling it, at the risk that the products do not sell or very slowly. Another disadvantage is that the customers are not yours but those of the platform in question. You cannot contact them to offer them something else.

To remedy this, there is a particular model of e-commerce, which is known as dropshipping.

Dropshipping is a particular business model of e-commerce that consists of selling products without previously purchased stock. That is to say, you are selling a product that you do not own.

The principle is simple: you have created an online store that offers different products. The customer places an order. With the money from this purchase, you, in turn, order the product from your supplier. It is he who will deliver to your customer directly.

This e-commerce model allows you to have no stock and, therefore, significant sums to advance for the products. In the same vein, it leaves time to test the products to see if they sell well before making the stock, or even a brand if you decide to. You can also stay in dropshipping and the gains can be colossal.

Another way to earn 30,000 euros per month on the internet is to sell, yes, but not only physical products. The world population more and more consumes digital products! It is, therefore, a question of doing infoprenariat.

What is infoprenariat?

It's about selling, not a physical product, but information, knowledge.

We all have more or less advanced knowledge in certain fields. This knowledge and personal experiences monetize on the web.

Example: Are you a dog trainer? You can sell training, videos, an eBook, or any digital format for individuals who have a dog and who would like to be educated about pets.

Customers are people who seek to learn, train, and develop further concepts already acquired...

Infoprenariat has this advantage, which makes it possible for everyone to get started in their chosen field. There is no need to have been trained as a trainer or to be a teacher. Another advantage is that you can get started in the infoprenariat on a very small budget.

You don't have to invest a lot of money upfront before it can pay off!

Another possibility to earn 30,000 euros per month on the Internet is the affiliate system.

What is affiliation?

This is a marketing method used by companies to sell more products. How to use this method to earn money?

The principle is simple. A company puts a product on the market. It gives you an affiliate link, which allows you to record the sales made thanks to you. On your side, you promote this product for it. Each sale made from this affiliate link earns you a percentage. You are simply an advertising intermediary for this company, and it pays you for that. It's a win-win!

Advertising can be very expensive for a business and does not guarantee sales! On the other hand, the affiliation has a cost for the company, yes, but this budget is used only after the sale of the product in question is made. This allows for an always positive advertising cash flow for the company and the assurance of being paid for the affiliate.

Affiliation can pay huge dividends by spending only a very short time in the end.

That's not all, the internet still has other opportunities to offer you to earn €30,000 per month! Freelancing is one of them.

What is freelancing?

Being a freelancer means that you are a self-employed person.

Whatever the field, freelancing is there to put your skills and experience at the service of individuals or businesses. It is about the provision of services. All skills, whatever they are, can be converted into cash.

Examples:

Do you speak another language? Offer your translation services to whoever needs it!

Are you a designer? Many people are looking for visuals on the internet, introduce yourself!

The possibilities are limitless!

Freelancing allows you to monetize your skills while working at your own pace.

Digital marketing

For those who have a knowledge base in the management of social networks and site creation, it is also possible to offer these services to increase the internet visibility of physical businesses (craftsman, restaurant, hairdresser, etc.).

A marketing agency has crazy potential these days, because, without the web, traders in the traditional market will find it difficult to develop. They are, therefore, fond of people competent in this field to delegate these tasks.

It is not necessary to start and open an agency, you can simply offer your freelance services first.

Canvassing companies and offering to manage their visibility on the internet and create a site can pay big dividends because they do not necessarily have the skills or even the time to take care of all this.

This is a non-exhaustive panel of the different ways to earn 30,000 euros per month on the internet, but there is one thing to develop and maintain to succeed in all these areas: MINDSET (the state of mind). Without a good mindset, you will not be able to succeed.

What mindset do you need to succeed on the internet?

As all web entrepreneurs will tell you, working on the internet is not complicated, but it is not easy either! Many people believe that money will fall easily, thanks to the internet! There are several factors related to success on the web:

Training: Without knowledge, you will be able to do things, but you will not go far. Training is a key point to success! No matter the method (with a mentor, groups, a coach, training, books ...), as long as you train! Knowledge is essential.

Procrastination: It's an enemy to fight at all costs! You could have all the knowledge in the world, and if you do not take action, nothing will happen by itself. You have to put in place the learned strategies, and apply them without finding excuses; otherwise, there is no point in learning.

Having very clear objectives and a deadline: This allows you to plan and organize yourself. Having a goal to reach is very important in the accomplishment of your actions, even if the path is strewn with pitfalls, you must have the vision of the goal to reach.

Perseverance: Whatever the obstacles encountered, you must continue! Do not give up on achieving your goals! Many people, unfortunately, give up at the first difficulty. It is not easy to work for yourself because no one is watching or forcing you to do anything.

Self-discipline: It is very complicated to tackle a task when you are alone, and you are constantly in doubt. You have to succeed in doing small actions every day so that they become habits and thus add other restrictive small actions...

Surround yourself with the best: Loneliness is a poison for web entrepreneurs. Meeting new people and discussing their doubts and difficulties shows us that you don't have to be alone in difficult times.

As you can see, there is no shortage of opportunities to earn money on the internet and reach a significant level of 30,000 euros per month. You have to find the business model that suits you the most and invest in it as much as possible. The state of mind in which you will work, because IT HAS TO WORK, will lead you, or not, to success.

The Best Techniques Of Cross-Sell And Upsell

Surely you have noticed that in the most popular online stores, e-commerce supergiants such as

Amazon or Rakuten, many related products encourage us to compare and complement our purchase with other items. Indeed they are sales techniques of online commerce known as related products and are designed to sell more in your e-commerce business. Specifically, their mission is none other than to increase the average value and profitability of the shopping cart. Just because you have related products in your online store does not mean that your store will sell. However, they are a fundamental technique for those businesses that are already selling, since they will sell even more.

Up-Selling

The Upselling is a sales technique widespread in electronic commerce where an online store shows similar customer products or more profitable products for your business (need not be more expensive). In other words, we might assume that the shop will seek to convince consumers to buy items with more profit margins or those we choose to get rid of. This is what has long been regarded as "advertising what concerns us." It is important to use the up selling technique before the customer enters the shopping cart. Otherwise, we run the risk of distracting them excessively and losing the sale. Let's put an example so that you can see it much clearer. A customer of an online photo camera store has clicked on a low-end reflex camera in which we have a little profit margin. At this time, in the product sheet, we show you other similar SLR cameras or some that we may have on offer. The objective, as we have already said: always to achieve a possible best sale for our interests.

Cross-Selling

Cross-selling, also known as the multiplier sales, is based on offering the buyer of an online store various products "complementary," i.e., items that can be used to complement the chosen product. Let's say that we have a fashion store and a client has chosen a red plaid shirt for a boy. With cross-selling, in related products, we will show extra items that complement our shirts such as navy blue pants, brown shoes, and wayfarer sunglasses that would give a complete look. This technique is aimed at multiplying sales with the main mission of increasing the amount spent by the customer in the shopping cart.

Cross-selling has to be on the cart display page without being a distraction. Rather the opposite, you have to boost impulse sales of these related products by showing only a buy button, without displaying the product sheet. In addition to being used in the shopping cart view, cross-selling is also used elsewhere. And many first-rate online stores use it days later through email or even on the thank you page of the purchase when it is confirmed that they have successfully placed the order. If we delve into the statistical plane, in the world of results and numbers, we see, according to various platforms specialized in related products and first-line online stores, an improvement in sales of between 15% and 20%.

Although it is true that with up-selling (compare) the conversion is sought and with cross-selling (multiply sales, complementary products), the amount of the purchase and the average number of products per cart is increased, with both an improvement is achieved relevant in your business numbers.

How to configure the related products of my store

It is important to note that the configuration of related products through up-selling and cross-selling in online stores is usually carried out for each product individually, not at the global store level. In this way, the configuration options are more flexible and precise. There are generally two ways to select related products: automatically or manually.

Automatic smart recommendation systems

- **Upselling:** The systems show similar products taking into account the characteristics or attributes of the product, such as categories, labels or tags, brand, etc. In some more advanced cases, algorithms based on user behavior are even used.
- **Cross-selling:** The systems show complementary products based on the shopping experience of other users who have already purchased the same product.

Manual systems (You select the most relevant products yourself)

In the case of Upselling: If we are selling the iPhone 5 and we want to compare this product with others that we sell in our online store, we will select as related products the iPhone 5c, which is more expensive, the Galaxy S4, with which we have more margin and the iPad, which we have 100 in stock and it costs us to sell more. In the case of Cross-selling: If we are selling the iPhone 5, our goal will be for the customer to buy other products that complement the iPhone, such as a case, a screen protector, or headphones.

How To Have A High-Profit Margin

How to improve your profit margin? One aspect that entrepreneurs, and self-employed people must be very clear about is that income is never equal to benefits. The production of any service or product involves a cost, so you must ensure that your profit margin is sufficient not only to cover all the costs of your company but also to help you grow.

In this section, we are going to focus on how to improve the profit margin, something very important that you should never forget if you want your business to be sustainable and profitable.

What is the profit margin?

Before going any further, it would be good to know what the profit margin is. The profit margin is simply the difference between the retail price and the costs of production or acquisition of the product or service.

This is a margin that can be net margin (after-tax) or gross margin (before tax), but in which costs must be taken into account variably (properly linked to the production or acquisition of that unit) and the fixed costs of the company.

Generally, we only talk about profit margin referring to variable costs. Example: If I buy a product from my supplier for 6 euros and sell it for 15 euros, I would get a profit of 9 euros. On the final sale price or final income, it means that I would have a 60% profit, compared to 40% that would be expenses.

If you want a formula to calculate the profit margin, you would only have to divide 9/15 (= 0.60) and 6/15 (0.40) and multiply the result of each by 100.

Now, here you are, only having taken into account the costs of purchasing or manufacturing the product. You must also take into account those fixed costs that are not directly related to that product, but that you also have to bear—for example, labor, marketing, and advertising, electrical spending, etc.

Therefore, keep in mind that very small profit margins will not allow you to assume the fixed costs of your business unless you sell a huge amount of products or services.

How to improve the profit margin

The first thing to improve the profit margin is to know how to calculate it. So before putting these tips into practice, make sure you know how to do it.

Having said that:

1. Be aware of the real prices in your sector

You may be selling at a price well below the market price. This can be adopted as a low-cost business strategy. The problem is that you need to sell a lot to make it profitable. And to sell a lot, you are going to have to invest a lot in advertising and marketing.

Therefore, be clear that selling a lot does not always equal profitability. Your profit margin may be so small that fixed costs make your business unprofitable.

2. Better small than large products

You would be surprised to know that, if we look at the percentages, a company can get a much higher profit margin selling small and cheap products than large and expensive products.

Large, expensive products tend to be more difficult to sell, and may also leave a lower profit margin. On the other hand, a product that you buy for 1 or 2 euros gives you many more possibilities and you can sell it for 5 or 6 euros and it obtains much higher margins.

It is true that with money, you earn less if you sell a large product, but the profit margin can be greater, it supposes less risk, and it is easier to manage for your treasury. You need to sell cheap products, with good margins and easy sales, in addition to expensive products.

3. Don't make mistakes when calculating profit margin

Making mistakes can lead you to have bad numbers. If you use the formula that we have given you before, it is much easier to calculate the profit margin. The problem is that many people put it differently; they calculate the profit margin on the cost price and not on the final sale price.

For example, if I know that a product costs me 6 euros and I want to make a 60% profit, it seems easy. I add to 6 that 60% profit that I want to get, and the matter is finished. But it would be a MISTAKE. That is, it would be wrong to say that $6 + (0.60 * 6) = 6 + 3.60 = 9.60$. If you sell it at 9.60 as a final price, you would not be making a 60% profit.

To get 60% of the profit, you have to buy six and sell 15 to win 9.

4. Beware of discounts

Please note that many unjustified discounts are deducted from your profit margin. In other words, your supplier may not give you a discount, but you give your buyers a discount of 15% of the final sale price.

That means that your final profit margin will be 45% and not 60. But imagine if you only got a 20% margin, if you make such a big discount it means that you would hardly get 5% product profit. It is a business model that has many risks and would hardly be profitable.

5. Control your fixed costs well

Because we insist, don't just look at the merchandise and its costs, or the production costs, or the labor if you sell services. You must take everything into account, including electricity, water, telephone, advertising, taxes, etc.

If your profit margins are very low, it will cost you a lot to keep your business afloat. A good help for you to have a good overview of this situation would be to use a business management program that allows you to visualize income and expenses, as well as the benefits you finally get.

How To Scale Your Online Business

If the proof of concept, i.e., a viable business model, has been accomplished, the next move will be to make more money with less investment. After all, it is no longer possible to do many things which cost a lot of money to set up. Such systems may be streamlined, meaning that certain activities no longer require workers but machines and licenses only. Scaling involves turning a business idea into one that makes it much more competitive. "Scale" means, and derives from, stairs, scaling means growth.

Learn to scale from the online marketer: Ads

Many social media managers who launch a scaling search want to find out about the topic, i.e., how do you do more with little?

Many young online marketing entrepreneurs often launch their first scaling in the affiliate marketing field. Sometimes the basis is a small blog with posts or a landing page (single HTML page with a sales-optimized area). In this section, there is, for example, a test report on topics such as e-cigarettes, the classic coffee machine or the coffee pad test, of course, the same applies to bicycles, e-bikes or the automotive industry. The so-called affiliate links are then stored in the individual blog articles. Every time a user is referenced by the product affiliate link, the blog owner earns between 5 and 20% (usually 10%) on sales. This is how affiliate marketing and scaling work on a small scale.

The young entrepreneur aims to use targeted advertising on social networks to purchase a range that generates enough sales. Every page or advertisement that generates sufficient sales, then becomes a sustainable project for the entrepreneur. The advertisements start with small budgets and, if they perform well, are turned up. Scaling!

Tip! Read more about our agency:

- Facebook marketing
- YouTube marketing
- Instagram marketing
- TikTok Marketing
- Influencer marketing
- Photo/video production
- Speaker/workshops

Effectiveness test on a budget

With a small budget, they now test various advertisements for effectiveness and compare the campaigns with one another. The cost is not too high, because each advertisement is conducted at either only € 20 or € 30 a day. From these results can be calculated, and the most successful advertising campaigns can be found. These campaigns are then provided with the budget of the campaigns that are not running as well. The less effective campaign will be switched off.

All clicks achieved by the reach are then directed to a blog or the specially set up landing page.

Let's summarize the example again: The young developer should have set up a blog with specific analysis and research results of our best practice. These are marketed through individual ads in social networks.

Monitoring, optimization, scaling

After about 50 items, the items are equipped with advertisements. Any single item gets a promotion of ads. Then there are the different commercials inside this promotional strategy that are measured against each other. So, it could be an e-bike shot of one person riding. A second graphic could show the e-bike. A third graph, without a human, could show the e-bike in the garage. Which of these three graphics will get the most purchases and clicks? This would result in 150 different advertisements for all 50 items. After a short period of 2, 3 days, the results can be evaluated. Individual advertisements that convert poorly, which means fewer clicks and fewer sales, are switched off early. After monitoring, it is decided.

Of 150 advertisements, 20 or 30 may still survive. However, these are profitable! Each page or advertising costs around € 50 a day, which, in effect, brings € 70 in affiliate revenue. This results in an average benefit of € 400 to € 600, a monthly income of no volatility of € 15,000. A small blog or a landing page on comparisons and tests became a proof of concept. The functioning business model was then further optimized, budgets were redistributed and thus further expanded. For a single person, a good job.

Check Out:

Revenue Investment (ROI) — Sales measurement and investment estimate — Return on investment is one of the main considerations of company management and, of course, ...

Response Rate: Description, Social Media & Calculate-The Answer Rate determines what is the response rate to a given advertisement. Compared to...

Social Selling - Shopping on Facebook, Instagram, and Youtube - Social Selling deals with the art of generating sellers from social networks. Through creative...

Pins and pinboard: Use Pinterest for free, create, and share pins - pins are the specialty of Pinterest. Just like its name on Twitter to ...

Add More Products To Your Inventory

Taking inventory in your store, both online and physical, is something very common and also recommended for all the advantages it presents and that you will see in this chapter.

I am sure that, for many people who have spent years working in the commerce sector, both electronic and traditional, this term has somewhat negative connotations.

And, if your business has a considerable amount of products, taking inventory will mean a process of endless hours that is somewhat repetitive.

However, in this section, in addition to revealing what an inventory management system is, in case you are one of those who do not know this concept yet, you will know all the advantages of carrying it out periodically.

What is an inventory management system?

An inventory management system is a procedure through which every one of the existing units in stock of each type of product in our business is accounted for, in this particular case, in our e-commerce.

In most cases, it is a process that is carried out once a year, in order to make sure that there is an agreement between the sales made in your store throughout that cycle and the number of remaining products that have been left unsold.

In the digital field, there are already programs or modules (some of which we will see later) that help us make this arduous process much lighter.

However, in Offline businesses, this requires the participation and joint coordination of a large part of the staff.

Why is good inventory management so important?

Once the total of products that were in stock at the end of the year (or the period that you decide to establish) is counted, it is compared with the initial investment that was made to cover the hypothetical clients that would buy them during that period.

Here we would establish the profitability that they had, since, above all, this metric will mark the success or failure of the initial investment made.

The less inventory there is at the time of accounting for the stock, the greater the profitability and this will give us a very important metric or KPI for future investments in this or another type of product.

3 Tips to better manage the inventory of your store

The incorrect corrector management of this flow can mean the good or bad running of your business, both digital and physical.

Hence, once the remaining stock has been made and seen to be effectively disposed of, we must ask ourselves precisely what to do with it.

Take note of these tips with which you can manage it more efficiently from today:

212

1. Stay alert for perishables

Depending on your sector, you may handle products with expiration dates.

In these cases, your alert levels should be maximum, since selling them beyond that interval could lead to not only legal, but reputation and brand image problems.

In these cases, running some type of clearance advertising campaign might come in handy enough to give you a quicker exit.

2. Product storage is stagnant money

You may not have thought that simply keeping a certain amount of "stocked" products from previous seasons would mean a waste of money.

But it certainly is, since having a product stationary and without movement means that you no longer perceive the profits that would have been obtained by having sold it.

Also, in the place of that product, there may be in stock another that you could get more profitability from.

3. Apply the "FIFO" rule

A highly recommended technique in these cases and which is part of the "Lean" philosophy is to apply the FIFO ("First IN, first OUT"), whose initials in Spanish would say "that the first to enter is the first to leave."

According to this, the oldest products, which were the first to enter your business in stock, should be the ones that you should give out in the first place.

In this way, you will avoid problems such as the one mentioned before about the expiration dates, if they applied to your business model.

And in case the expiration was not a handicap, the "fashions" would be another condition since an old-fashioned product is difficult to give a profitable outlet.

Best modules to effectively manage inventory in e-commerce

As I promised at the beginning of this chapter, below, I will show you which are the most effective add-ons in this type of business process.

They will help you and also organize your mind so that you do not find surprises at the end of the year:

1. Inventory Information Module - Impulse Purchase

When automating the operation of your business and tracking the available stock of each product at all times, you must have the "Inventory information - impulse purchase " module.

It manages to put the e-commerce alarms on autopilot so that they notify you every time stock is approaching zero.

In this way, you can always have a series of minimum units inventoried, to supply your customers so that they do not have to wait for you to invest in more stock before receiving theirs.

PrestaShop partner companies have designed these indicators in such a visual way that you will not have to invest more than 5 minutes in it.

It is highly recommended, especially in cases where the volume of your business does not allow you to spend a large amount of time doing this task alone.

2. Knowband Module - Notification Again In Inventory

In case you fall into the error of having run out of stock (precisely why you must use the previous module), and your products continue to be offered on your e-commerce store... you have a problem.

And also, the user experience and, therefore, the usability of your website will decline, since offering something that you do not physically have (unless you are doing Dropshipping) is not very professional.

However, in these cases, you can go to "Knowband - Notification Again In Inventory," which will implement a functionality through which the user can subscribe to news related to this product.

In this way, when it becomes available on our e-commerce store, thanks to this module and email marketing, you will be notified by mail by sending a newsletter, causing you to have to re-enter (hopefully) to finish your initial purchase.

3. Products disabled module without stock

If you have read the great usefulness of the two previous modules about the inventory of your business, this represents a real revolution...

If you did not pay attention to the indicators of the first add-on recommended (or did not even install it on your website), and you ran out of stock and also had no loyalty to the module offering you the possibility of subscribing so that you will be notified when more stock arrives, don't worry.

The "Disabled products without stock" tool is triple security against this unwanted fact of not being able to offer the user what they were looking for in your business.

As I mentioned before, the ideal in cases where you do not have stock would be to manually remove that product temporarily from your e-commerce site, so as not to lead to misunderstandings.

But if this task seems somewhat tedious or a waste of time, PrestaShop has thought of everything with this module, which automatically deactivates those products for which it detects that there is no stock.

Thus, your users will not see them. It's that simple ... and useful!

It's time to take control of the inventory management of your online store if you did not do it when you started your digital venture.

You already know the importance of doing it periodically and what compensates you, both professionally and financially, but as you know, almost no system is infallible.

Therefore, I hope you have taken good note of these modules recommended to you to manage your inventory.

CHAPTER 14

HOW MUCH MONEY DO YOU NEED TO START A DROPSHIPPING BUSINESS?

If you have ever been bitten by the bug of setting up a dropshipping store, you have surely asked yourself that question. And it is possible that you could not have answered it, because the money that you can spend in a dropshipping business is, like everything in this life, very relative.

For starters, forget about the myth that opening a dropshipping store does not require any money because it is completely false. At least, if you intend to have a dropshipping business and earn money with it.

Regardless of whether you want to start a large business with several employees or an online store that allows you independence, the investment you need for a dropshipping business is the same as for any other online store except for one point: you do not need to invest in the stock.

The "happiness" of not having stock

You will read on many blogs or corporate websites that e-commerce stores that operate under dropshipping are intended for small entrepreneurs who cannot invest large sums of money, and this is a great truth. Starting a business without having to invest in the initial stock is a great advantage and a great possibility if you do not have large investments to start. But we must not forget that setting up a dropshipping business is setting up an online store with all the complications that this entails.

In the same way, although it produces happiness not having to deal with inventory, orders from suppliers, updating stocks ... if there is a headache that nobody gets rid of, it is to solve incidents with stock breakages or late deliveries, defective and missing stock. You and your drop shipper will have to deal with these problems since your company is the image of the product. The customer who buys a product is your customer, not the dropshipping business of which you are a customer in this case.

That is why it is very important that in your expense forecast, you consider all these possible returns and incidents that you will have to face. The drop shipper you work with may eventually take care of many of them, but the initial solution always has to be put by the online store without draining the package.

Expenses that nobody frees you of when you have a dropshipping business

But then, what expenses does nobody save me if I decide to start a dropshipping business?

The two most obvious: hosting and domain. Are you thinking about setting up an online store and making money with it with a free domain? We hope not for your sake.

Investing in hosting is a basic thing if you want to provide a quality service to users, avoiding system crashes, and the consequent loss of potential sales. Investing in a good server is essential. If we also have a dropshipping business as a form of self-employment, we have to pay attention to this matter and look for a service provider that helps us to resolve possible incidents in a comfortable, simple way, and that does not involve more complications. The same happens with the platform we use to set up the online store of our dropshipping business.

Then, keep in mind that some drop shippers request either registration fees for working with them or even monthly payments. Others, on the other hand, make a living from selling your products but do not request any additional payment. There are also dropshippers who discount a part of your sales so that if you reach certain percentages, they sell you the product cheaper, increasing your profit or giving you the possibility of lowering your prices.

As you may already know, economic activity cannot be carried out without invoicing it. For this, it is necessary to pay the corresponding self-employed fee and the taxes that apply in each case.

There is another basic expense that should not be missed, such as having a bank account linked to a payment gateway where your customers can make payments for their purchases, as well as a PayPal account or you may even need a credit card corporate. There are many dropshipping businesses that have to make payments to their suppliers through this means.

Other expenses you should have if you want your online business to work

What we have told you so far is fine to start a dropshipping business, but it is possible that you barely get sales, and your business does not advance. For this, you will need to invest a little more money. Up to this point you have created a business, from here what you have to do is generate traffic because without traffic there are no sales, so how do you go about it?

The key is to invest in Online Marketing, from the positioning of the online store in search engines to Google Adwords campaigns with your products, just as any business does today, whether online or not.

Making SEM campaigns, selling through Google Shopping or other Marketplaces is a way to increase traffic on your website, your margins may be reduced, but your sales will also grow significantly.

Other expenses that may arise when setting up a dropshipping business include investing in details that give your company added value, such as a telephone customer service, a content blog that attracts the public, or hiring specialized services of an online marketing agency that increases traffic to your online store.

The good thing about drop shipping businesses is that they are easily scalable, you can serve a client with practically the same infrastructure as 100. Truly, these expenses are quite low:

- Domain
- Hosting
- Returns expenses forecast
- Online store platform
- Freelance registration fee (optional depending on how we organize our company)
- Banking expenses

The important thing is investments because they are the elements that are going to make us earn money. A dropshipping business that only spends but does not invest in itself is a business that is unlikely to prosper.

Benefits Of Dropshipping On Black Friday

Black Friday has become one of the most important dates of the year in terms of sales. Traditionally, on this day in the United States, the starting gun for Christmas shopping is given, since it is celebrated just the day after Thanksgiving night, specifically the fourth Thursday of November.

This tradition has been spreading throughout the world, becoming today a date indicated in the Spanish trade calendar. During the campaign, small and large companies make large discounts on their entire catalog for several days, linking these discounts even to Cyber Monday, which is held the following Monday after Black Friday.

If you are thinking about how to generate more sales on this year's Black Friday—mark November 23 on your calendar—the dropshipping model is a great sales option for this day. Its key is that it allows e-commerce to sell more without incurring storage or shipping costs.

In recent years, the Black Friday phenomenon has been growing, breaking records in 2017 with an increase, according to Netrica, in orders from Desktop of 32.8% compared to 2016.

And although Black Friday is not a matter of a single day, Friday is still the strongest day in terms of sales.

The searches made with the words "Black Friday" and "Cyber Monday" have multiplied by 14 in the last four years, a clear example of the evolution of Black Friday.

Thanks to dropshipping, any e-commerce can expand its product catalog, achieving a greater number of sales without worrying about shipping them.

During the year 2018, there were already many companies starting to use this distribution model, making their stock management cheaper so that they could invest more in other fields such as marketing.

The forecasts are even better since, by taking advantage of the advantages of dropshipping, merchants are expected to have more economic resources to attract new customers and, of course, loyalty to those who already are.

Advantages of dropshipping on Black Friday

Thanks to the dropshipping model, you can enjoy great advantages at times of the year with a large number of sales, such as Black Friday. Below, we highlight some of these benefits.

Do not worry about logistics

As we have mentioned, one of the great advantages of using the dropshipping distribution model on Black Friday is that it does not have to incur effort or expenses related to shipping orders.

Avoid delays in your orders, and your dropshipping provider will be prepared to cover the great avalanche of orders that occur during this time.

Expand your catalog with everything you want

A dropshipping provider can offer you a large number of products, divided by categories, that you can include in your e-commerce business. Even if you do not have stock stored in your store, you can use your dropshipper once you have made the sales, which increases your chances of selling.

Promote the top categories of Black Friday

No matter what sector your e-commerce business belongs to, you can use dropshipping as a complement to your online store to expand your catalog and have the best-selling categories at each time of year.

According to Google, 58% of searches carried out on Black Friday are with the term "technology," so you already know what products you should highlight in your e-commerce during this time. Thanks to the dropshipping model, you can promote the categories with the most sales without worrying about shipments. Focus all your efforts on promoting the best-selling products of the moment in your online store and reaching your potential customers.

If you finally go for the dropshipping model, remember to plan your Black Friday marketing strategy well, as it will help you achieve better results.

7 + 1 Keys That You Should Know Before Starting A Dropshipping Business

Now that you know what dropshipping is and also know how it works, you may be considering starting your own dropshipping business. But wait! Before launching into this new adventure, there are certain things you should know.

Surely you agree if we say that before doing something for the first time, we prepare for it.

If you must speak in public, prepare your speech in advance. You don't want anything to go wrong, and you try to learn what that moment will be like, you study what position to take on stage, what tone to use, where to look ...

The same goes for starting a dropshipping business. Before starting, you must prepare the ground well. What do you want to sell? Can you sell any product? Who will be your dropshipping provider? Solving these questions from the beginning can make a difference, and having a business plan can be essential.

We want to help you make your business a success. That is why we tell you here the seven keys that you should know before starting an online dropshipping business.

Keys to help develop your dropshipping business plan:

1. Choose a good niche

Choosing what to sell is one of the most difficult parts of starting an online dropshipping business. But although it seems that everything is "invented," the key is to try to find innovative products or services or whose sector is not very exploited, and you can "reinvent it."

You can help yourself with tools such as Google Trends, Google Keyword Planner, or Uber suggest. In them, you can search for products and know if they are trending, if many people are looking for them...

Likewise, to find the perfect niche, you should ask yourself the following: who do you want to sell to? Choose your target audience, and little by little, you research on it to find a need to fill. You can research various segments of people to find the right one.

This is one of the most important keys when creating your dropshipping online store. Once you are clear on what to sell and to whom, it is time to find the perfect supplier.

2. Select the best dropshipping provider

Now that you know the type of product you want to offer in your business, it is time to find the right dropshipping provider. Carrying out a good search is necessary to be able to choose a provider in which to place all your trust.

If you can't find the perfect supplier to offer the products you want, it is advisable to do a niche search again.

A supplier for this type of business must meet a series of requirements, such as having a wide variety of products, that is, a wide dropshipping catalog, as well as having good logistics to make shipments promptly and also have their stock for it.

Another important feature, for the future, maybe its radius of action, that is, you may prefer a supplier that ships to all of Europe, in case you decide to expand your market later.

3. The e-commerce platform you use is key

Before building your dropshipping online store, you must choose which platform to use.

For this, you can look at different factors, such as being intuitive both in its back office and in the front office (what users see). This will allow you to run your business more easily and, at the same time, boost purchases.

Having an online store that allows full integration with your dropshipping provider is essential to start a business with these characteristics.

Some dropshipping wholesalers offer complete solutions, with which you only have to worry about publicizing your online store and getting sales once it is launched.

4. Varied forms of payment make the difference

And although it may seem that this point is not important, offering your customers the appropriate forms of payment is key.

Know the market and activate in your online store the payment methods most used by your potential customers.

If you offer more than one form of payment, you will be reaching more users: credit card, bank transfer, or PayPal are the most common, but there are many other forms of payment that are being used successfully today.

5. SEO positioning

Once you have your online store, the time has come to work so that Internet users reach your dropshipping business. SEO positioning is one of the most useful tools.

Focus the contents of your online store on the keywords for which you want to appear in search engines.

Good SEO positioning can be the key to getting the quality traffic that your online store needs to start selling.

6. Opinions to stand out among your competitors

Prepare your online store so that the users who buy from it become your best ambassadors.

Use trusted platforms that verify their opinions and with which it is easy to collect them after the purchase of your customers. Include some opinions on your online store, as well as the trust marks that these platforms offer you.

Keep in mind that a large majority of users enter the

Internet before buying, seeking the opinions of other users.

7. Investment in advertising, your great ally

Yes, to start your dropshipping business online, you are going to need to invest in advertising. Before starting to create your online store, create a line item from your budget for online advertising.

Ads on Google Ads and social networks like Facebook, Instagram, or Twitter are key to start making you known to users.

Reaching your target audience when you start from scratch is complicated, so we advise you to take advantage of the different options that exist in the market to advertise your website.

7 + 1. Don't give up on the first change.

Before starting your dropshipping business, you should know that beginnings are never easy. The first time you speak in public, your voice trembles, you doubt your words, but you don't give up, you keep going, and your speech ends up going well, you overcome the difficulties, and the audience ends up applauding you.

The same can happen with your online store. The first few weeks will be difficult, starting to get traffic will bring you upside down, but don't give up. Consistency is one of the best tools to achieve success.

If you are looking for the right moment, it is now. If you work every day to achieve it and follow these keys, we are sure that you will get a successful dropshipping business.

CHAPTER 15

POSITION YOUR DROPSHIPPING STORE

Dropshipping is one of the increasingly widespread e-commerce models, which is why it is establishing itself as a business path that generates great interest.

But the really important thing is to get traffic to your dropshipping store, and here we have one of the main strategies to take into account even before opening your dropshipping business: working on both content and technical SEO to achieve a good positioning of an e-commerce site on Google.

Why is SEO important to my dropshipping store?

A dropshipping business carries low investment risk, but the benefits are also small. For this reason, it is very important to meet a series of requirements to set up a dropshipping store, and one of the main ones is to work perfectly with the SEO strategy of your e-commerce. The main reason is that in this way, you will be able to stand out from your competitors and your business will have a higher volume of traffic, which translates into achieving the highest profitability for your business.

What do I have to take into account with the SEO strategy of my dropshipping store?

A dropshipping business involves necessary work time; therefore, when working on SEO optimization, several parameters must be taken into account. In this way, these invested hours will be productive and will bring many advantages to your e-commerce business.

No to duplicate content

When importing your supplier's catalog file, it includes descriptions, product names, title, meta title, etc. All drop shipping wholesale customers share unless the product is changed by-product. What problem does it entail for SEO positioning of my dropshipping store?

Duplicate content is highly penalized on Google and, therefore, its direct consequence is that this will not allow your business to have optimal positioning. Therefore, it is key and very important to create your content so that your e-commerce has good positioning. And on what should I base myself to create this content?

Carry out an SEO study and put it into practice in the content

An SEO study has to be carried out to find out what keywords are related to your business that should be included in each description of the items in the store. Keep in mind that you must select those words that have the most searches.

Also, this study of keywords should be implemented in the categories of your e-commerce store. How do you do it? Keywords must be entered in the visible content of this page and the Title and Meta description.

Visible content: It is highly recommended that there is descriptive text on the category pages, and it should be between 400 and 800 words. And, of course, in this text, you have to include the keyword to work to position each category.

Title: It is one of the most important HTML tags since it indicates the title of the URL, and it is one of the main parameters that Google takes into account to determine the positioning. Therefore, it is essential to include the selected keyword to position the page. That is, if, for example, the category I am working on is cosmetic products and the SEO study tells me that "buying cosmetic products" is a word with many searches, it is important to include this term since it fits perfectly to the items that are in this category. The reason is that it is going to position the page and the traffic it will attract fits perfectly with what is offered. So the chances of converting and making profits are very high.

Meta description: This is a short text that Google and other search engines use to describe the page in search results. This must include the keyword that will position that page. Also, the inclusion of a "call to action" to attract the attention of potential customers is recommended. In this way, attention is captured, and it is possible to attract a greater quantity of quality traffic with a high probability that they buy from your dropshipping store. Regarding the length, the text must be a maximum of 160 characters and a minimum of 150.

Keep in mind that most searches are usually done on categories such as furniture, perfumery, kitchenware, etc. These types of searches are those that usually bring traffic to e-commerce.

Do not leave out the URLs

Supervise all URLs so that there are not two different ones that lead to the same product. This can happen when the same items are included in different categories.

Check that there are no URLs generated on pages of different categories with the same products. The reason is that the Google search engine may have problems when choosing the best page to rank.

When will the SEO optimization of my dropshipping business give me results?

SEO optimization of any website is a background job. You have to be patient since the results of good positioning are gradual. So there is no need to despair, if the job is well-done, sales will come.

How To Add Value To Your Dropshipping Store

Okay, I already have my dropshipping store perfectly configured, synchronized with the dropshipping companies with whom I have a contract to put their catalog for sale, and very nice and ready to sell as many products as possible.

Now what?

As you have surely read on many occasions, e-commerce is not a magic formula to earn money quickly and easily, but, like any physical or online business, you have to take care of it, keep it up to date and, above all, offer possibilities to consumers differentiated from other competing online stores, that is, offer added value.

All this sounds very nice on paper and theory, but how can I give it the added value that I am looking for in my dropshipping store? We offer you several possibilities in the form of the following tips!

Trust dropshipping companies that allow you to differentiate yourself through images

We are not saying anything new if we affirm that a large percentage of our daily decisions are based, almost 100%, on the image that is transmitted through the people, products, or experiences that we come across.

For a potential client, it will not be the same to find an online store that transmits quality in its products for sale than another with poorly maintained, pixelated, or outdated images.

As good and attractive as our products are, our potential customers cannot see them live or touch them, so a good image and product photography will be our ally.

Our advice is that you bet on a dropshipping provider that takes care of the image of the products in its catalog, and that also allows the free download and use of banner examples and other types of images so that you can provide your dropshipping store with a unique image style.

Set up a multi-language dropshipping store

There are drop shipping companies that offer their distributors the possibility of setting up a multi-language dropshipping store. We advise you to take advantage of this opportunity since, apart from multiplying your business possibilities, you offer a very important added value when it comes to transmitting confidence and the image of a large and powerful company to your potential clients.

It does not matter that you do not know languages, if you bet on a good dropshipping provider with this service, you will be able to have e-commerce translated natively and perfectly prepared for any demand from your national and foreign clients.

Offer complete customer service

One of the services that consumers value most and best on online stores, just as surely you will have done to choose among all the dropshipping companies out there, is the customer service received. You cannot offer personalized service like the one that can be found in a physical store, but it is very similar.

Put special dedication and attention to ensuring your dropshipping provider perfectly meets the promised delivery times that you indicate on your website. You must also be well informed about its after-sales service and the tools it offers to its distributors when managing different product return policies with any problem.

In any case, the management of direct communication with the client is on your part, so here you have your opportunity to put into practice everything you want to offer.

Transmit transparency and closeness

Quite related to the previous point, although with nuances, transparency, and a sense of closeness are other enormous advantages of an online store over others of its competition.

Don't be afraid to search and find opinions of your clients, especially if your service is correct, on online platforms such as the opinion websites, forums, or social networks, even going further and directly asking for them.

This is invaluable and transparent information that will encourage other potential customers to trust you and purchase products from your dropshipping store.

Make your clients commit to you

This last point is a summary of everything discussed above. One of the most difficult tasks for a company offering products and services is achieving long-term commitment from its customers.

Consumers seek, apart from receiving good service, to complicate life as little as possible, and, when they trust a company, it is difficult for them to separate from it. Even if the prices are somewhat higher than the competition, if this commitment has been achieved, it is not easy to change them either.

So we recommend that you take advantage of this enormous possibility not only through offering good service but also using online customer loyalty tools and strategies. Some of these include product newsletters to report news, promotions, exclusive offers for customers, or product promotion programs, related to the purchase they just made.

These are some tips that you can apply to your dropshipping store now to differentiate yourself from your competition, so what are you waiting for?

What Are The Best Marketplaces For Dropshipping?

Marketplaces such as El Corte Inglés online version, are spaces with high traffic of visits in which to place your products for sale without the need for customers to go through your online store.

There are two types of marketplaces, the generalists, which have products of all kinds, and the specialized ones, which work specifically in one sector. If you decide to use a marketplace and do dropshipping, you have to analyze your market well and know if there are specialized marketplaces in your sector, since you may be interested in participating in one of them.

If you have or want to set up a dropshipping store, selling on marketplaces is a good option that, like everything in this life, has its advantages and disadvantages:

Advantages and disadvantages of marketplaces for dropshipping:

The good:

> Cost savings, especially if you are starting and do not have an established brand yet. Starting to sell in a marketplace can save you money, since they set up the infrastructure and charge you a monthly fee or a percentage of sales.
>
> You do not have to invest in online advertising since the marketplace usually invests by itself so that your site and the searches for your products are well-positioned.

- Synergies with other products. If you have a camera case store, what better than a marketplace where people buy cameras to sell your products?
- Access to a significant volume of traffic. Obtaining traffic to a new e-commerce site is slow and expensive, but placing your products in an area that already has traffic can serve as a good showcase.
- Guarantees, since the anti-fraud systems of these platforms are of high quality, and the transactions are much more secure.

The bad:

- More competition. The bad thing about being in a showcase is that the whole market is precisely competition.
- It does not give freedom. You have to show your products as the marketplace tells you; it does not give rise to creativity or to doing more different things.

- It is almost impossible to make a brand from a marketplace.
- Reduced profit margins since the marketplace keeps a part of them with each sale.
- Web positioning. Part of the digital content you have prepared for your site has to be duplicated, and marketplaces tend to be better positioned so that you can compete with yourself. This is avoided by creating new content for the marketplaces.

Now that we more or less know what is good and bad about dropshipping marketplaces, we are going to list which are the most popular general marketplaces on the market.

CONCLUSION

MARKETPLACES FOR DROPSHIPPING

Amazon

The American company was founded in the USA in 1994, and since then, it has become the largest marketplace worldwide. They function as a huge electronic business platform for all sectors (books, electronics, footwear...).

eBay

eBay started as an auction portal in 1995, although its offer has evolved over the years and is not limited to auctions alone. Although the company has become widespread to the consumer, it is true that on eBay, you can find artisan products and even collectibles that have traditionally brought together a large base of non-professional buyers-sellers who carry out their operations as an auction.

The Buy It Now formula allows the seller to propose a fixed price that the buyer accepts or not, as in any other trade. Also, classified products work like traditional press announcements of buying and selling.

eBay works as a system of intermediation between individuals, but it is a market in which small companies or businesses that have products that are a little more particular or difficult to find fit very well.

AliExpress

The famous Chinese store, owned by Alibaba, serves as both supplier and distributor for any dropshipping store. If you wish, you can easily sell Alibaba products that they send as drop shippers on your website, in the same way, they are also a good marketplace for dropshipping and locating your products. They work in quite a similar way to Amazon.

Also, it should be noted that AliExpress has opened a market place in Spain called "plaza" where it locates its national suppliers, with the advantage that both shipping and customer service are made from Spain. Therefore it is a good time to use AliExpress as a marketplace for dropshipping.

Keep in mind that AliExpress works with bargains. They are the retailers of the Alibaba group and possibly its most popular store for the general public. AliExpress customers are used to bargains that come from China, so if you decide to work with them as a marketplace to do dropshipping, keep in mind that you are going to have to move at very low prices ... you have an idea of selling.

Rakuten

The Japanese company arrived in Spain in 2013, and just three years later, in August 2016, it closed its doors in Spain and the United Kingdom to focus its European efforts on Germany and France. They work around the world with a formula very similar to that of Alibaba. In essence, they do not sell products directly, but instead, they bet on the model of a large online shopping center where other companies sell the product.

Amazon FBA 2021

Learn the Best Strategies to Earn $15.000/Month PROFIT using #1 proven E-commerce Online System to a Successful Private Label Passive Income

John Wright

INTRODUCTION

Talking about Amazon is talking about an innovative and successful business model. To the data we refer: Amazon made record profits in 2018, earning more than ten billion dollars in net income, seven thousand more than the previous year.

Another interesting fact is that the company had hardly registered large profits until 2016. What is the secret? Probably the insistence and belief of its creator in the idea and...in a renewed business model in which everyone can sell products on Amazon. But overall, you will find out more in this eBook.

Over two million people are selling on Amazon. You can sell on Amazon yourself!

Amazon offers several alternatives so that you can sell your products and take advantage of their perks and visibility. The latest big trend is Amazon FBA.

We are going to discuss this trend, try to explain what this new modality consists of and if it is a viable and profitable alternative.

FBA or "Fulfillment By Amazon" is the system that Amazon makes available to its sellers offering the following services:

- They receive your products.
- They store your products.
- They send the products.

- They handle returns.
- They provide customer service.

In other words, the seller will only have to send the products to Amazon, and the eCommerce giant handles the rest. Interesting? From the start, it seems like a solution that greatly simplifies the job for the seller. Let's go deeper into the heart of how Amazon FBA works.

Until now, you know that Amazon will do most of the work, and the seller only has to send the products to Amazon. Thus, it can be said that the seller acts as a supplier of Amazon products.

But before we start discussing the functional methodology of Amazon FBA, let's go to the initial and fundamental step to be part of this system: register as a seller.

CHAPTER 1

THE MINDSET OF A MILLIONAIRE

Do you dream of being rich someday, but are not sure how?

There is a myth that the rich are born with an innate talent to strive for excellence and to think creatively, but that is nonsense, being a millionaire is not just a matter of having millions in a bank account.

Rather, it is about having the mind of a millionaire, to create and maintain wealth, and that anyone can achieve.

Similarly, it is your way of thinking (right or wrong) that will allow or prevent you from becoming a rich person.

Think about this: Why do some people who win a huge amount of money, a lottery, for example, go back to the same point in a couple of years?

It's because they never learned to have a millionaire mindset.

Therefore, the amount of money you have at any given time does not necessarily determine your future financial level. Since it depends more on your way of thinking, it is all a matter of changing your psychological approach towards money, success, and happiness.

When you think about the word "Millionaire," what springs to mind first?

To some, it's a luxurious lifestyle, an eye-catching guy living in a grand mansion, flying in a luxury plane, wearing designer suits, and so on.

Surprisingly, the average millionaires aren't the stereotype created by Hollywood and the media..

Most millionaires, like average citizens, work full time, live in middle-class households and shop at convenience shops.

They don't get carried away by material possessions.

They are driven by being able to make decisions, having the " freedom " to make any decision, for example, being able to quit a job they don't like or send their child to the university of their choice.

The number of millionaires in the world has almost doubled in the last decade, with more and more people getting richer every day, and some millionaires are even becoming billionaires.

Anyone can become a millionaire.

Millionaires have a lot in common with each other than just their bank accounts; everything is their way of thinking.

Although becoming a millionaire itself is not that easy, adopting the right mindset (millionaire mindset) is what can make a difference and get you on the right track.

Improve the quality of your thoughts

What you think is what attracts you.

The nature of the human being is that he can reason, and he can choose his thoughts.

Thoughts become actions, and actions make up your reality.

So, if you consider yourself poor, it is because that was your choice.

You may think that it is not possible to become a millionaire since you do not have enough capital, education, or experience.

But know that most millionaires made themselves, thinking that they were capable of making a lot of money and that they could even earn it while doing what they most enjoy doing.

With their millionaire mentality, they think of multiple ways they can get money, and they don't rest until they do.

Don't expect the Universe to give you money

Don't make the mistake of waiting for the universe to give you riches.

If that had been the case, you would have been born wealthy, but if you are not (yet) wealthy, it just means that wealth is something you can create out of your creativity and hard work.

The first step is, as I have already said, to adopt the millionaire mentality, which generates wealth.

Millionaires know that they have to work harder than others.

They do not expect to be lucky.

They make a plan to make things happen and execute it.

They take a huge "*calculated risk*" and sooner or later reap the rewards.

Chase anything but money

The idea of becoming a millionaire is very appealing to anyone, but most millionaires know that chasing money doesn't get them anywhere.

They all chased "*something*" in their lives, but the money came alone, as a reward.

What would you do if you were already a millionaire? What are your talents? Are you adept at your work and do it excellently?

Understand that money will always come as a result of your effort and dedication.

You must be productive and create quality results for the benefit of others.

Pursue excellence in your work, in your career, in your business or company, or your discipline if you are an artist or athlete, but never chase money; it will come if you do what you like, do your best, and are good at it.

Stop spending money and start investing

If your main goal is to reach a **million dollars**, buy a large mansion and a luxury car, you will not be a millionaire in a long time.

Millionaires know the importance of investing instead of spending.

They earn, they save (that's their habit), and they don't just spend.

They earn to keep their hard-earned money, and they don't touch it to buy expensive items that don't make a profit.

They know that the money saved today can serve a bigger purpose tomorrow.

On the other hand, millionaires reinvest most of the money they earn.

And they use it to create new opportunities to generate new income and become more and more successful.

This is an essential component of a good millionaire mindset.

Continually strive for success

Winning in abundance implies acquiring more and more knowledge about your work, having a strong passion for learning new things, and improving your skills.

This desire to excel must be part of your daily routine.

Millionaires are passionate about **learning** and facing new challenges.

Just as a child gets excited about learning something new, you need to have that passion for excelling no matter what gets in your way: problems, emotional trauma, financial setbacks, or whatever.

Live below your means

This is something you must have read hundreds of times, but it is a golden rule within the millionaire mindset.

But...**why?**

When you've worked hard enough to buy a *Ferrari*, you must believe you deserve it, **right?**

Well, that may sound logical to most, but millionaires don't think that way.

The reason behind this golden rule is that, gradually and unwittingly, a person always begins to spend more money than they earn.

Therefore, true millionaires never spend more than they earn.

It is as simple as that.

An example is when parents give their children a monthly allowance, and that's it.

In this way, both themselves and their children, millionaires, cultivate the habit of "*spending smartly*" and develop the habit of "*saving*."

Just wanting to become a millionaire is not enough.

Millionaires have a different mindset, and most think and live before boasting about the lifestyle that money can bring them.

Some of the things mentioned above are not that difficult to do, but the important thing is to adopt the millionaire mindset and the discipline to stay on the right path of achieving what you want if you want to become a millionaire.

Don't expect money to fall from the sky; take action!

Pursue excellence in what you do.

Stop spending so much and bragging about what you have accomplished, and start investing.

Study and learn from the example of other millionaires.

Tips to succeed in business

There are several reasons why an individual should start their own company. From unemployment to current job dissatisfaction, the desire to be your own boss leads many people to make this decision. Yet inspiration is not enough to make the company efficient.

Many companies die early in such a competitive market due to a lack of financial organization and other knowledge related to business management. What should be done to prevent yet another failed entrepreneur?

How to be successful in business

There is no recipe for success in business, nor has the most professional boss any promise that the company will be successful. When some caution is taken, and proper preparation is undertaken, however, the risks may be minimized.

1. Set and assess your ambitions

Understanding where you want to go and how you are going to work to make that happen is the first step to being successful in business.

The most important questions you will ask yourself include what you want to bring to the industry and whether you can enter the corporate world. This will help you set goals and prepare the next moves.

2. Save some money

The cost of starting a company very much depends on the region. We do share one thing in common, though: establishing a stable base and financial security requires time.

And you need to have resources to guarantee the company's longevity before you hit the break-even stage. If you don't get the most suggested, which is making your own money, go to the financial institutions or invest in venture capital.

3. Having expertise in the area

You need to learn how to handle the company's staff and partners. You need to have the expertise and previous understanding of the business field for this, learning how the market functions within and outside is a crucial move towards success. When you don't have this experience, you should spend some time, like a regular person, working in the field before you feel confident to take your own measures.

4. Creating a solid network of contacts

Also, progress in business relies on a successful network of contacts, because it is not only about what you know, but also who you know.

Connections with effective individuals in the field will provide good therapy. When they are guides, that is, they will follow you and, even better, support you on your journey. Those partnerships will also help you locate successful vendors and partners that are involved in your project.

5. Check the scalability of your product

Companies that are in the initial phase need to be scalable, particularly in the case of startups. But what is scalability, and how to test it? It is a business concept with a high potential to raise sales without increasing costs proportionally.

The demand needs to be established, and its distribution and marketing outlets extended, but with caution so as not to make rash judgments.

The best techniques for successful goal setting

Goal setting is one of the most productive and effective things you can do to be more successful, happy, and fulfill your dreams. Why? Simply because you start by knowing what you want to achieve within a certain time. You realize how important it is to reach certain goals for yourself and to feel fulfilled. The simple fact that you are aware of this will make you more proactive in reaching it.

Goal setting is the first step in turning the invisible into the visible.

It is important that the establishment of goals and objectives is done frequently; I would say that this is something we should learn from school. It is so important to set goals to achieve them because sometimes we are so disconnected from what we want that it is difficult for us to be aware of it. Also, you cannot achieve what you want if you don't even know what you want. Have you asked yourself what you want to achieve in your life or at least what you need right now that makes you feel more satisfied with yourself?

Sometimes we think we have a goal, but it is not clear enough. For example, if you have a goal of losing weight, have you set yourself a smaller, more specific goal such as, "This month I will lose 2 kilos"? If you do not set clear goals, you will hardly know if you have already achieved them or do things that lead you to achieve them.

Goals and objectives are essential to be happy and successful

Being aware of what you want and setting goals for yourself to achieve it helps you create the future you want and helps you become more aware that you are responsible for creating your life. You are in control of changing and creating the life you deserve, and you just have to establish what it is that you want.

Maybe we are used to thinking about what we DO NOT want, but that is neither the simplest nor the most appropriate way to create what you want. Remember, positive thinking gives you the advantage of seeing opportunities where before you saw nothing but obstacles.

That's why setting goals and objectives frequently can help you be more successful, feel satisfied with yourself, and be happier.

The secret to successful goal setting

There are two basic questions for setting goals:

The first question when you are identifying your goals is: What do I want?

Something happens when you say what I want (as if you need it) rather than simply what I want. Desire is the beginning of creating your life and being happy. It is taking away the idea that you need something to be happy, rather what do you want to do with your life, that fills you, and that satisfies you?

The second question is: Why do you want to achieve this goal? What experiences can you have with this objective? How do you want to feel?

Continuing with the previous point, when you focus on **YOUR DESIRE**, on what you want to experience, and start thinking about what you want to feel and how you want to feel, you make it yours. And then you have all the necessary reasons to strive to make it happen.

You may realize that I haven't talked about your type of desires; it doesn't matter what you want, be it physical, money, a trip, or something you want to achieve. Here everything is valid. The advice is to focus on your experience and how you want to feel, and that will change how you feel about achieving your goals.

Define smart goals with the SMART technique

Below I will give you some tips to make your goals accurate and, therefore, achievable, and you can make them come true. The principles that I give you here are using the SMART technique.

The SMART technique is simply an acronym that reminds you of the basic principles so that you keep your goals in mind and keep your direction towards them.

When you think about your goals, make sure they follow the following SMART principles:

Specific: The more specific you are, the better. Following the example above, if you want to lose weight, set how much weight you want to lose. But not only that, if you put an image to that objective, it surely feels much better to want to do it. Something like: I want to lose 5 kilos so that I can fit in my favorite jeans and feel good in them. I am sure that with such an image in your mind, it will be much easier to do things that bring you closer and closer to that goal. Don't forget that a visualization is a great tool that keeps you motivated and focused on your goal.

Measurable: Your goal must be measurable, that precision is what will let you know if you have achieved your goals or not, and it will be clear what you have to do to achieve it if you have not already done so. Concrete goals will keep you on track to achieve them. For example, "I want more money." We all want more money, but it is not a measurable goal. If what you want is to improve your financial situation, then you should analyze your expenses, establish a payment method for your credit cards, save a percentage of your income, and know if you have a way to measure your progress. Besides that, in your goals, you can establish precisely that strategy and keep it up for a while to see real results.

Achievable: If you set goals that you know you cannot achieve or are too big for this particular moment in your life, then from the start you will be sabotaging your progress and your success. When you set a goal that you consider unattainable, you create a feeling that it is impossible to achieve it, so you do not allow it to flow, then you maintain that motivation, which leads us to the next point.

Realistic: Maybe right now, you want something like never working in your life again, or spending 6 hours a day playing golf. Yes, it is possible, but it may not be so easy at the moment. So why don't you start with smaller things that lead to your ultimate desire, and divide that dream into multiple achievable parts that keep you motivated? For example, if you say you want to lose 20 kilos in a month, perhaps that goal is not realistic, it is easier to establish small increases and with this achieve a true result.

Time: You must establish a time limit, if not, you run the risk of not doing anything to achieve it because, in your mind, you do not have time to do it. This, it is most likely that you forget it. You need to set a realistic time to achieve it. As I told you in the previous point, set a time where you feel you can achieve your goal.

Goal Setting Exercise

This exercise will teach you to establish your goals and objectives.

Instructions

Set out 30 minutes of your time without being interrupted to finish the exercise.

Write quickly without stopping.

Permit yourself to dream; you are a child who dreams big and firmly believes that your dreams can come true.

Try to keep your sentences simple, don't try to write in great detail, just quickly write your general idea, and clear enough for you.

Realize that what you are doing right now is what you are capable of achieving and what you want to become. This is your true future; it is time to start creating it.

The main idea is that you have a brainstorm in each

section (I, II, III) for 5 minutes without stopping. Where you will generate a list of goals and things you want to do, have, or be. Once you have your list, assign to them the period in which you want to achieve them; 1, 3, 5, or 10 years. Then, choose three goals for each area (the most important and those that are short-term - 1 year) and for three minutes, write why it is necessary to do it, be it, or have it. And very important, write what you would lose if you don't.

I. Personal Development

a) Write down everything you want to be, have or do in your life, achieve or change within yourself or to a place where you want to go or be. - 5 minutes.

This includes the emotional, mental, social, spiritual, your physical body, and who you won't be.

Some ideas: What do you want to learn? What are your goals in your emotional, mental, and social development? Emotionally, what do you want to experience, or achieve? What are the skills or character traits you would like to develop? What are your spiritual goals? Do you want to improve your physical body, your physical condition? How do you want to relate to other people? Would you like to develop an artistic skill or maybe public speaking? Would you like to learn a new language, play an instrument, or cook? Do you want to have more friends or change your place of residence? Where do you want to travel? What would you like to create?

IMAGINE

b) For each of your goals, establish the time in which you want to achieve them. (1, 3, 5 or 10 years) - 3 minutes

c) From your list, choose the three most important goals for you and write why it is so important to achieve them and what would happen if you do not meet them. 2 minutes for each one (Total 6 minutes)

II. Career, business, or financial goals

a) Write down everything you want to live or be; a matter of work, what career you would like to pursue, your financial goals, or the business you want to have. - 5 minutes

Some ideas: How much would you like to earn monthly or annually? Would you like to invest your money? Would you like to create your own business? Would you like to change your career? Would you like to save for your retirement or your children's school? Would you like to save to go on vacation or to buy something specific? Do you want to get a better position in your working life?

b) For each of your goals, establish the time in which you want to achieve them. (1, 3, 5 or 10 years) - 3 minutes

c) From your list, choose the three most important goals for you and write why it is so important to achieve them and what would happen if you do not meet them. - 5 minutes.

III. Material things

There are no limits, feeling good, and having the things you want is part of your life. Treat yourself to dream and believe that you can get everything you want.

a) Write down everything you want to have or create all the pleasures you would like to give yourself or the adventures you would like to live. - 5 minutes

Some ideas: What would you like to build, create, or buy? Would you like to go to a specific place, an event that you would like to attend? Would you like to write a book, participate in a play, or give a concert? Would you like to travel the world or meet someone important?

b) For each of your goals, establish the time in which you want to achieve them. (1, 3, 5 or 10 years) - 3 minutes

c) From your list, choose the three most important goals for you and write why it is so important to achieve them and what would happen if you do not meet them. - 5 minutes.

Contribution

They say that the best way to maintain true harmony and satisfaction is through contribution to the world.

What did you think of this exercise? Are you ready to set your goals and objectives?

Do not forget that it is recommended to do this exercise ideally three times a year.

Time management

In this section, I will give you some keys and rules to better organize and manage your time, which will help you achieve greater productivity and increase your professional satisfaction.

What is time management?

Time management is one of the main pillars of productivity in business. It is a managerial skill consisting of the proper distribution of this resource to develop tasks and projects. Optimizing and using your time well is essential because time is limited: 24 hours a day and a life with days numbered.

You can't buy time, and even if we can outsource some activities, we will never have time to do everything. In the end, there is nothing more important for the self-employed person than to manage their hours well. Here, we offer you a series of productivity tips, methods and rules that will help you better manage your time:

Prioritize three projects and define objectives

Steps to take and applicable rules to manage time in your business:

1. Prioritize three projects, define objectives and tasks

If what you want is to be productive and not waste time, you should try to prioritize three projects, which will be reflected in specific objectives for each month and each week and will help you define the tasks of each day.

"Don't start a day, a week, a month without planning them."

We must put limits on our personal and professional projects since we cannot do everything at the same time. This is one of the basic premises if we want to develop our managerial skills.

For example, you can make a list of everything you would like to do, all the projects you have (example: start a business, participate in a marathon...) without setting limits and then classify these activities by priority, taking into account some criteria. Your criteria may be: the most important thing for the future, to create your company, your family, your health, etc.

After this activity, which requires a very personal reflection, you will have to choose the three priority projects and break them down into objectives and tasks. Eliminate for the moment other projects, the secondary projects, since the risk of having too many projects is that they lengthen. In the end, they never end, in addition to creating stress and demotivation. So, only three projects.

These projects must have a limited duration, at most one year. If they are long-term projects, you have to break them down into small projects. The writing of these projects and the description in objectives and tasks is a very good exercise to confirm the credibility of the project and the desire you have to achieve it.

And every month, every week, try to define the goals you have for these projects.

By having fewer projects, you will focus your energy on these projects and only on these.

Having accessible and gradual objectives, every week and every month, we will measure the progress—the situation of each project.

2. Steps to take and rules for time management in your business

Focus on what's important and prioritize. Try to apply the Pareto law in everything, without limitation, which says that 80% of the consequences come from 20 % of the causes, 80% of the results depend on 20% of the work, and 80% of the benefits of a company are generated by 20% of its products and customers. Try to delete everything that is not essential for your business. (Is it necessary, yes or no? If I don't do it, what happens?) Outsource secondary tasks to focus on the tasks that have the most impact on your future.

Classify the tasks to be carried out between urgent and important action, urgent and not important action, non-urgent and important action and non-urgent and not important action.

Organize your day before you start the day, not to let others organize your time. Define and write the three most important tasks of the day (TMI) that are normally a disaggregation of your projects. Try to start the day working on these tasks.

Limit the time of each task and set some deadlines. Parkinson's Law: A task uses all the defined tempo, or all work is delayed to occupy the available time. Don't say I need three weeks to do a job, but I need 4 hours.

Concentrate 100% on each activity: if I write an eBook, I write it, if I play with friends, I play. Seize the moment 100%.

Limit interruptions. Law of homogeneous sequences: without interruption, people need less time for their tasks because a few minutes are necessary to concentrate on each task. Tip: Isolate yourself and reserve a few moments for yourself, putting your phone in meeting mode and closing the Email. Note: email can be an important element of non-productivity. Two fundamental rules for emails: do not open the email at the beginning of the day and open your email inbox at certain times (at 10:00 and 16:00, for example).

Do right away, everything that can be done in less than 3 minutes (so you can get rid of small distracting actions).

Do the most unpleasant tasks during the first hours of the day (maybe they will be a TMI). The risk is that you will postpone this type of work every day until you reach a limit where you will have to work urgently.

Do not adjust your schedule too much; leave a little time for unforeseen events or delays. Tip: Over evaluate the time needed for a job (multiply the times with a coefficient) and reserve a few minutes between each meeting. Being optimistic in life? Yes, but not with time: Set realistic deadlines.

Change tasks and differentiate activities during the day. Not all activities require the same concentration, and we must be aware of the times when we are most effective in scheduling jobs at the right time.

Learn how to say "NO" to all the requests you have and that do not contribute to your projects achieving or that are not of clear interest to you.

Remember to take a few breaks to regain strength and inspiration.

Order your office or your space. Nature does not like emptiness: the more space we have, the more space we use. Consequently, we accumulate documents and then waste time searching for them, and we may even lose them.

Tip: on the computer, in the Email mailbox, and in the closet, try to have folders correctly identified (the fewest number of folders possible), rename the files to find them easily, immediately delete the useless documents and classify the others.

Changing habits and routines requires perseverance and determination, it is not as simple as it seems, and that is why, in many cases, the support of a mentor is very helpful.

We do not doubt, much less question our chores. In the end, we know how time can run, especially for those who own their own business.

The problem is when this becomes routine, and you run out of time to do everything you need every day.

However, it is good to know that, even with so many tasks, be they personal or professional, it is possible to organize better to increase productivity and do everything you planned.

To help you better optimize your time, we offer you ten tips that can make your 24 hours a day sufficient to complete your activities.

1. Create a goal

To improve your time management, you need to have an achievable goal.

Regardless of thinking about optimizing your time and increasing your productivity in personal or professional tasks, you must know that having a goal will help you better organize everything you need to do.

This happens because when you have a goal, you can think of ways to plan your time and actions further to reach that goal.

Therefore, you can establish short, medium, and long-term goals. Thus, you will be able to mount strategies to achieve those objectives, having as a focus a predetermined period for the completion of each task.

But be careful!

It is very common to set practically impossible goals. When you do this, in addition to not reaching them, it is very likely that you will get very tired and not be able to increase your productivity at any time of the day.

2. Make a list of your daily tasks

After defining your goal, you can begin to think about the actions you need to take to achieve that goal.

For example:

If you have an online business and want to attract a larger audience for your sales page, you can think of actions such as:

- Optimize your website;
- Create a blog;
- Write relevant content for your audience;
- Post more on your social networks;
- Create videos for your YouTube channel, among other strategies.

After thinking of everything, you can do to reach your goal, put these actions on paper.

It is very important to have a document with a list of everything you need to do to reach your goal. This will help you not forget about anything you have to do.

3. Prioritize what is urgent

With your to-do list in hand, it's time to tell what is urgent from what can be extended.

Think about the actions that are most important to reach your goals and put them into execution before the other tasks.

Now, do you understand the importance of the list that

we talked about in the previous point?

When you have written everything you need to do, it is easier to understand what is most important and cannot be left until later.

However, you should be careful not to over-extend the other activities. If you leave everything for later and do not establish order and a schedule with a start and end date for all your activities, you will end up doing nothing.

So even if you can complete a task later, don't forget to also implement it at some point in your day, which is what we will talk about next.

4. Have a calendar

Having a calendar with start and end dates for each planned activity is something that helps a lot with time management. Every time you set deadlines, you send intuitive commands to your brain that will know that something needs to be completed by that deadline.

With this, even if you have prioritized the most urgent and important tasks, you will never forget the other activities that you need to do later.

We advise you to use your Monday mornings to plan your weekly calendar. Thus, you will think about planning only a nearer future, which can help you better manage your time.

It is clear that some tasks take time, and may probably only be able to be carried out in 1 or 2 months. But if you already know of their existence, put them on your calendar so that when the delivery date of those activities is approaching, you remember that you need to complete them.

5. Do one thing at a time

It is useless to organize your tasks in order of importance, schedule your calendar with start and end dates if you do everything at the same time.

As we said at the beginning of this section, we know that it is very likely that you will have many things to do throughout the day. However, if you try to do everything at once, you will not be able to finish any activity, everything will be in the middle, and that can tire even more.

That is why you need to focus on a task to get to use your full potential in it. In this way, you will realize that you will manage to finish everything in the time that you previously programmed, and you will still do your tasks in the complete way possible.

Over time, you will find that organizing and focusing on one activity at a time will help in your time management, which will be better managed.

6. Avoid procrastinating

Even if you have to do more than one activity at a time, you mustn't put off what you can do now.

A very common mistake made by people who cannot carry out good time management is to postpone. Extending your deadlines too far makes you lose focus on the tasks that need to be done.

That is why all the tips we show here should be thought of as a whole. When you set deadlines to deliver certain tasks, even if it is a distant date, do not lose sight of it, thinking that you do not have to do anything now to accomplish that activity.

If you have time today to start something that needs to be delivered in two weeks, why not start and then have more time for other activities or unforeseen events that may arise?

7. Organize your work environment

Having a well-organized work environment helps a lot with time management. This is because, with an organized place, you will not waste time looking for something you need.

So even if you are your own boss, always have a separate space to carry out the tasks related to your business.

In this environment, put everything you need throughout the day near you, such as a computer, a phone, notebooks, pens and, if possible, even a good cup of coffee and a bottle of water.

8. Take breaks

Even with so many activities to do, it is very important to understand that you also need time to rest.

We know that many people, especially when they are very busy, think that it is necessary to work non-stop all the time. However, this is a great indication that you are not carrying out good time management.

Also, this is not productive either, since a person with a tired mind and body does not have good productivity.

That is why you need to take breaks during your tasks, and you should not forget to sleep well every day.

A technique widely used by various professionals to assist in time management during a break is the Pomodoro Technique. To carry out activities using this technique, you only need a stopwatch, which can even be the one on your mobile phone.

What you will do is:

- Use the list you made of all the tasks you need to do during the day;
- Divide your time into 25 minutes periods (called "Pomodoro") and set your stopwatch with those minutes;
- Choose one of the tasks that need to be done on that day and work on it without intervals;
- Pause for 5 minutes after the end of the first 25 minutes;
- Resume work after the break and work without interruption for another 25 minutes and repeat this action four times (4 periods of 25 minutes each, interspersed with three breaks of 5 minutes);
- After four pomodoros, pause for 30 minutes until you return to work.
- This can be a way to organize your time better and increase your productivity. Always remember to mark the tasks that you have

completed and, once again, think of the tips as a whole and do not start more than one activity at a time. Wait to complete one before starting another.

9. Avoid distractions

This tip is very important, mainly for those who work at home.

It is easy to confuse work hours with routine household chores.

There are also distractions like television, children, relatives, friends, and even pets that can distract you and make you stop doing the tasks you planned for a certain day.

The internet is also an environment in which these distractions constantly appear, whether in the form of social media, YouTube videos, and even interesting articles and sites.

Therefore, avoid leaving your social networks open while working and, when you are at home, remember to notify everyone who lives with you that you are working. That way, no one will interrupt you during an important activity.

10. Learn to say no

It is very important to know how to say no to some activities that you consider unnecessary.

For example:

Suppose you work with other people, and someone

wants to schedule a meeting to chat about a certain topic that could be solved with just an email. If so, suggest to your colleague to send the information and that instead of the meeting, the email would suffice to resolve the situation.

You will realize that the day will pay off much more when you start saying no to certain activities that are not mandatory at the time.

If you are the owner of your own business and have people who work with you, learn to delegate tasks. You don't need to do everything related to your company. You can find good professionals to work with you.

Make the most of your time

Knowing how to manage your tasks is the best way to be more productive and achieve good time management.

As we said from the beginning of this section, we understand that the exhausting routine and the number of daily tasks make many people lose focus. However, if you have come this far, you surely realize that it is possible to complete everything you need throughout the day without having to increase the number of hours per day.

Basic habits of successful people

For people, habit development usually comes about spontaneously, like when children learn to brush their teeth before going to sleep. However, there are others that we consciously need to build, since they are fundamental for growth, for example, learning to use a technological tool.

"To get different results, you need to have and develop the right skills." Some researchers mention that there are fundamental habits for people to be successful since each of them is a pillar to achieve the goals that each human being sets.

These are the ten habits listed by an expert:

1. Be proactive

We must take control of our decisions, since, although there are external factors that may affect the main objective, we must take responsibility for our actions.

2. Set goals and targets

It is the most important factor in achieving dreams. Having precise goals clarifies the progress that is made and determines the path that must be followed to get where we want. It is better to fragment a large goal into small achievable steps.

3. Face

Successful people have what in English is called accountability; that is, they face obstacles and mistakes head-on.

4. Identify areas of opportunity

Personal growth depends on one's ability to identify and work on the aspects that need to be developed.

5. Manage time

One of the great dangers that people face today, especially entrepreneurs, is spending the day doing what is urgent and not attending to what is necessary. Planning and acting based on priorities is an indispensable habit of successful people.

6. Empathy

It is the ability to put yourself in the place of other people, identifying feelings and thoughts that they might have. It is a crucial point to develop better communication with others.

7. Listen (not just hear)

This is about paying attention to what other people communicate and becoming aware of why, how, and in what way they act.

8. Assertiveness

That is, what you want to express frankly, directly and openly WITHOUT affecting others.

9. Find balance

Truly successful people set goals in all areas of their lives—physical, mental, social, emotional, and work—and manage to keep these facets in balance.

10. Generate commitments

It is not only to fulfill what is promised to others but to oneself as well. It involves constantly seeking to improve, learn, grow, and take on challenges.

CHAPTER 2

WHAT IS AMAZON FBA?

Amazon FBA is the acronym for Fulfilment by Amazon. It is a program of the North American multinational that allows any user in the world to sell their products through its platform in a very simple way.

It is precisely in this simplicity that one of its main advantages lies since you only have to create a professional seller account on Amazon and list your products on its central seller platform.

Once this is done, you only have to make sure that your products are well packaged to be transported safely to future buyers and send them all to the warehouses of the multinational founded by Jeff Bezos.

Once there, it is the professionals who make up the Amazon staff who are responsible for preparing and sending the orders placed by users.

A comfortable and simple method to sell online, don't you think?

In this regard, it is important to emphasize that Amazon FBA is not Amazon's affiliate program.

Through this program, what you will be selling are your products to the client through the multinational, being their supplier.

On the contrary, through the affiliate program, you do

not sell your products, but you sell those of the company, and you obtain as benefit a percentage of each transaction.

Advantages of Amazon FBA

Selling through Amazon FBA offers important advantages for those entrepreneurs who dare to embark on this adventure.

Here are some of them:

- Increased sales.
- You can do it without a virtual store.
- International expansion.
- Few barriers to entry.
- Amazon is in charge of the management.
- You can enhance your brand.
- Prime products.

Let's look into them.

1. Increase in sales

Amazon has a base of more than 300 million accounts that actively buy on its platform and hundreds of millions of monthly visits to the web made by users with a clear intention to buy.

With this in mind, it is not surprising that Amazon is at the forefront of online sales.

Also, selling products through Amazon FBA automatically gives the seller credibility and the trust of users, since the North American company is generally perceived as a company that offers excellence and high-quality service.

Otherwise, the seller would have to sell their products outside the framework and influence of Amazon, so that consumers would have greater reluctance to buy a product in a store that is unknown to them.

2. You can do without a virtual store

To develop your virtual store, you need technical knowledge, time and the budget necessary to be able to hire a developer to build it.

Also, once you have your e-commerce site, you will have to work on its SEO to give it visibility.

Amazon FBA offers you the possibility of not worrying about these details because we are talking about the largest marketplace in the world.

It is already developed, well developed, and with a level of visibility and brand image to which a virtual store could never aspire.

3. International expansion

Amazon reaches virtually every corner of the globe, so a seller can use this to their advantage to expand their market.

A retailer can create a product list at any local Amazon to try to reach a certain market segment, saving thanks to Amazon FBA, the inconveniences of local payment systems, as well as those related to logistics and operations.

4. Few barriers to entry

Starting to sell on Amazon is very simple.

Anyone can take the necessary steps to do so, and the cost is not high, so you can practically make sales from the first minute.

5. Amazon is in charge of the management

As stated before, one of the main advantages of Amazon FBA lies in how comfortable the sales process is for a seller.

The multinational will not only perform storage functions but will also take care of the administration and distribution of the product to buyers.

6. You can enhance your brand

Through Amazon FBA, you can sell products of your brand.

In this way, not only will you be obtaining benefits from your products, but you will also be working to gain visibility for your brand, promoting its branding, and, in short, you will be working for your project.

7. Prime products

Simply by selling through the Amazon FBA program, your products will be classified as 'prime.'

What does this mean?

This means that the user who purchases your product will not have to pay shipping costs, and, also, they will be able to receive the product even the next day, which will make your products more attractive.

Also, with Amazon FBA, your products will have greater options to win the Buy Box.

Don't you know what this is?

Winning the Buy Box means that, on product pages, every time a user clicks on the "Add to cart" button, it will be your product that is selected and not that of any of your competitors.

Getting the Buy Box is not an easy task because Amazon assiduously changes the variables by which it decides which seller should have a preference, but some factors can help you win it, such as:

- Having good ratings from your buyers.
- Quickly answering user questions.
- Having a competitive price.

Drawbacks of Amazon FBA

Unfortunately, despite all the advantages that Amazon FBA offers a seller, there is nothing entirely perfect, and this program is not perfect either.

It is true that in the balance, in my opinion, the pros weigh considerably more than the cons, but you should still know them if you plan to embark on this adventure.

Some of the drawbacks are:

- Fierce competition.
- Commissions.

- It requires a great organization.
- Intermediaries for payment.

Let's look at them more in-depth.

1. Fierce competition

It is to be expected, don't you think?

Selling on Amazon can be very, very profitable if your product is good and you do it correctly. So, logically, the same idea of selling products on this marketplace has been had by thousands of sellers before you.

Therefore, to compete in that market and make your place, you need to have a long-term strategy.

You must plan well the steps you are going to take, where you want to take them and that you do not leave anything to chance.

In this way, you will achieve better results.

2. There are commissions

Amazon FBA offers many advantages to sellers, and we just saw it a few lines above, but, unfortunately, all these benefits are not free.

Amazon has a bad habit of being a company and wanting to make a profit from its business.

What things though?

For each product you sell through Amazon, the company will take a predetermined percentage.

This percentage varies depending on the category to which the product in question belongs and can range from 7% corresponding to computer and electronic products to 45% of accessories for Amazon devices.

Also, as already mentioned above, to sell through this platform, you need to create an account beforehand.

For this, you have two options: the Professional Sales Plan and the Individual Sales Plan.

The first type of account, the Professional Sales Plan, has a monthly cost of € 39.

By paying this flat rate, you can sell products without limit, without having to pay the closing fee, which we will see below.

The other option is, a priori, cheaper.

The Individual Sales Plan has no cost, but you will have to pay a fee of € 0.99 for each sale you make.

Therefore, even though this type of account is ideal for testing Amazon FBA, if you anticipate that you will be able to close more than 39 transactions, it would no longer be profitable.

3. It requires a lot of order

For sellers who have full control over all phases of the sales process, this should not be a problem, but it is clear that not all people are cut from the same cloth or have the same organizational skills.

Selling through a marketplace like this requires significant management work so that none of your products are ever missing in the multinational's warehouses, with the loss of sales that this would entail.

4. Intermediaries for payment

When a user purchases one of your products, you do not receive payment immediately, but it is Amazon who receives that money.

Later, if everything went well during the transaction, the money will go to the seller of the product.

However, if the buyers put down the quality of the product purchased, the shipping process of the same or put negative reviews and low scores, the arrival of the payment could take several days, weeks, or even end up being canceled.

How to sell on Amazon FBA step by step?

Becoming a seller through the Amazon FBA program has a process that you must follow step by step.

Let's see what these phases are:

- Make a preliminary study.
- Create your account.
- Listing of products.
- Prepare your products
- Send the products to Amazon.
- Make sure there is always stock.

1. Make a previous study

This step should always be the cornerstone on which to build any type of project.

Carrying out a market study before launching into the adventure will allow you to have a better perspective of the current situation, which in turn will facilitate you to make better decisions.

Some of the questions you should answer are:

- What am I going to sell?
- Is there a demand for this product?
- Is there a lot of competition on Amazon to sell this product?
- Do competing products have many reviews? Are they positive?
- Are my prices competitive?

What profit margin will I have?

Depending on the answers obtained, you may have to discard a product and find new business opportunities, or you may have to lower or raise your prices, among other possible decisions. So you must carry out a good preliminary study to start your project in Amazon FBA on the right foot.

2. Create your account

Once you have the answers to your questions and have corrected the roadmap to optimize the results, it is your turn to register in the Amazon Sales center.

At this point, you will have to choose between the free account with fees and the payment account without fees mentioned earlier.

3. Listing of products

Once you have registered your seller account, be it the Professional Sales Plan or the Individual Sales Plan, it is time to add your products to it.

To do this, go to the "Inventory" section and click "Add a Product."

Next, Amazon will ask you to tell them what product you want to add to your list by searching among those that are already sold through the product's barcode or directly by name.

The database that the North American giant has is vast, so unless you want to sell a product that you have made yourself, you can surely find it in its catalog.

Once the desired product is located, several options will appear from other competitors who are already selling this product.

You will simply have to choose one of them and fill in the missing information on the page you will have reached after clicking on your choice.

In addition to this data (title, brand, color, weight, etc.), you will have to complete your product file by uploading images that represent it and setting a competitive price.

This step is essential, so you should take your time to get the best result; it may determine whether you get or lose tens, hundreds, or even thousands of buyers.

4. Prepare your products

It's time for you to make sure your products are prepared so that they can be safely transported to the buyer's hands.

Good packaging can be the difference between a satisfied customer and a negative review of your product that will frighten other potential buyers.

5. Send the products to Amazon

This step is key to benefit from one of the main advantages of Amazon FBA.

So that the American company can manage the preparation and distribution of your products and you can dedicate yourself to other tasks, you must have your products.

6. Make sure there is always stock

This is the last step in the process, although it is perhaps one of the most important.

Once you have completed all the previous steps and are unconcerned knowing that the management of shipments and returns of your products are in good hands, you continue to have a minimum of obligations to your project.

You must make sure that Amazon does not run out of stock of your products since, if this happens, it cannot make the shipments to your buyers, which would immediately hurt your sales volume.

Logistics by Amazon FBA or Fulfillment By Amazon allows any company or person to sell their products through the Amazon market, giving them the main tasks of online logistics (storage, preparation, and shipment of orders). For reference, in 2017, half of the products sold on Amazon were not owned by Amazon, but by third-party sellers in its Marketplace program.

However, despite Amazon's excellence in logistics and

the benefits that the FBA offers, there are certain considerations to make to understand whether or not the Amazon FBA program is the best option for your business.

1. How does the Amazon FBA program work?

If you have a product that you want to sell online, with this program, you can outsource all the tasks involved in the logistics process to Amazon in exchange for a cost for the service.

As a seller, you first need to prepare your products following Amazon's reception conditions. Once your product is ready, you send it to an Amazon FBA logistics center, and it is from this moment that Amazon will take control of the logistics process.

The services they offer are:

- Receipt and storage of the product in its logistics centers
- Product registration in the store so that you can search and buy on Amazon.es
- If a customer buys your product, Amazon handles and prepares the product for shipping
- Shipping the product to the end customer using Amazon transport accounts
- Amazon customer service for the buyer

2. What are the Amazon FBA costs?

In April 2018, Amazon updated its rate structure for the logistics services it offers.

FBA costs depend on the size of the product or the time

of year and are divided into two types: logistics management fees and storage fees.

The logistics management fee covers packing, handling and packaging, shipping, customer service, and product returns. It is charged per unit, and the cost may vary depending on the type, dimensions, and weight of the product. Today in Europe there are no differences in the logistics management fee during the year, but in the United States there is a difference between low season (January to September) and high season (October to December), so it is to be expected that Future Amazon.es will apply this difference.

The storage fee is charged monthly and is calculated based on cubic meters used per product with a difference in price between low season and high season. Since April 2018, the cost of this service is € 26.00/m3/month between January and September or € 36.00/m3/month between October and December.

Apart from these fees, Amazon also offers a series of optional services depending on the conditions and preparation needs of the product. These services include labeling, bagging, bubble wrapping, or an opaque bag and sealing.

3. What are the pros and cons of Amazon FBA?

Different factors must be taken into account when evaluating whether FBA is the best option for your business. Here are the pros and cons:

Pros

Access to Prime clients

Most customers who use Amazon FBA say that access to Prime customers is the main reason to use the program. When a product enters Amazon FBA, it automatically becomes eligible for the Amazon Prime loyalty program with free shipping. In addition to the credibility that comes with being a Prime product, Amazon Prime customers spend almost three times more than a regular Amazon buyer, so it is not a significant advantage.

The Amazon Prime seal practically eliminates the main reason for abandoning the shopping cart: the additional shipping costs. When you go to buy on Amazon, if there are two almost identical products online and with similar prices, but one of them is eligible for Prime with free shipping, you will surely choose the Prime product.

It is important to note that the seller will be charged the same shipping fee regardless of whether the customer chose to ship through Prime or not. That is, the rates for sellers do not change; what changes is access to Prime customers.

Greater visibility in the Buy Box

Amazon has become one of the leading shopping search engines, and many buyers only search for their products on Amazon. A seller who uses Amazon FBA receives greater prominence than another who does not use FBA in Amazon's Buy Box feature. When you consider that 82% of Amazon sales are generated directly by the Buy Box, any help to win the Buy Box is crucial.

Customer service and return management

Amazon's customer service is revered for its quality, and by using Amazon FBA, your sales will offer this service. Also, when you have an online store, you know that managing a return is a cumbersome process, so giving this process to Amazon is a great advantage. However, you should know that there is a return management fee depending on the size and type of the product.

Cons

Strict reception rules

For your product to be received, processed, and sold in Amazon FBA, you must prepare your product in compliance with certain rules before shipping to the Amazon logistics centers. Amazon's reception standards are highly strict about making the process as fast and standardized as possible. The product must be properly labeled and packaged to enter the stock, and there is no flexibility in this process. If you do not comply with the reception rules, you risk paying fines or rejecting the product and, if you repeat the infractions, your account as a seller will be deactivated.

Extended storage fees

Amazon Logistics Centers are designed to handle a large volume of orders with high turnover. For this reason, units that are in stock with Amazon FBA for more than six months are subject to an extended storage fee of € 500.00/m3. If you consider that this fee is almost 20 times more than your regular storage fee, you must manage and replenish your stock to avoid spending six months in an Amazon logistics center.

Additional cost per sale on other channels

Amazon FBA logistics is not strictly limited to Amazon customers, and they also offer the logistics service for sale in other channels. Amazon prefers to boost sales volume on its platform and therefore offers more attractive rates for sales on its channel. In Spain, logistics rates for sales in other channels are 50% more expensive on average than sales through Amazon and also include a flat rate of € 1.80/unit received at your warehouse.

Building your brand and customer loyalty

If you decide to sell through Amazon, your sales will surely increase. However, you have to understand with each sale made through Amazon, you stop building your brand and your customer base, transferring these benefits to Amazon. The content, photos, and text conditions that accompany some products are quite strict and greatly limit your ability to differentiate yourself from other sellers who sell similar products on Amazon. After all, when you sell through Amazon, the buyer of your products will most likely not even know your company or brand after receiving your product.

Loss of growth opportunities

The buyers of your products are likely to have been delighted with the product. However, since the end customer is not yours but Amazon's, you may miss growth opportunities for your store. By not having access to the buyer's data, you stop promoting offers or new launches to customers who are interested in your products.

Management and payment of taxes at the European level

When you enter Amazon FBA, they offer you the service from a logistics center in Spain or enter its Pan EU program(pan-European) distributing your stock in multiple logistics centers in Europe. The idea is that your product is closer to the users of the different Amazon platforms in France, Italy, Germany, etc. to reduce your delivery times and increase your sales. This is a double-edged sword, as each EU state has different tax laws, and there is no clarity on what a vendor's registration point should be to comply with their taxes. Amazon does not offer tax advice in this case, so if you are interested in entering its Pan EU program, we recommend having a tax advisor who can help you avoid future problems.

4. What alternatives are there to Amazon FBA?

If you are still not sure that Amazon FBA is the right service for your online sales, keep in mind that you have different alternatives.

Use a logistics operator

The closest alternative to Amazon FBA would be to use a logistics operator to help you with the comprehensive logistics management of your orders. The ideal is a logistics operator that works as a private label and allows you to send orders with your brand and packaging. In this way, you outsource the tasks of the logistics process while maintaining the construction of your brand and your customer base. It is not easy to identify a good logistics operator for e-commerce, so our main recommendation is that it be a logistics operator specialized in e-commerce since traditional logistics operators will not always have the technology and reaction speed you need.

Perform your logistics

There are different situations for which it is better not to outsource the logistics of your e-commerce. Having your logistics can give you a lot of flexibility and total control over all your sales, although it can mean an increase in your fixed costs. It is important to be clear when your online store should take care of your logistics or use a logistics operator.

Use a professional pre-FBA product preparation service

If you know that you want to use the Amazon FBA program for your logistics, you can significantly reduce your costs by going through a professional pre-FBA product preparation service.

This service consists of delegating the preparation of

the product before shipment to an Amazon logistics center to avoid pinching your fingers with fines for non-compliance with Amazon's strict reception conditions. In the United States, this service is known as prep-FBA, and the main tasks it offers are:

- Product reception and verification
- Preparation of packs, bundles or kitting
- Transparent or dark bagging
- Product labeling according to the Amazon standard

CHAPTER 3

WHY AMAZON FBA?

Selling products on Amazon vs. Selling products on your online store

One hundred and seventy million users monthly prefer to shop on Amazon over any other store. In 2015, they spent more than 100,000 billion dollars. Due to these impressive numbers, it is evident that all sellers should consider selling their products on Amazon.

However, the results that a seller will get depend on several factors, and what works for one seller will not necessarily work for another.

The Benefits of Selling on Amazon

How Amazon has successfully managed to blow our brains and establish itself as the number one spot for many buyers has been the focus of many marketing case studies. What we want to see is how a seller can benefit if he decides to sell his products with this industry giant.

More sales

You don't have to think about it. There are millions of active buyers every month visiting Amazon to buy products.

The numbers don't lie: With a base of more than 300 million active buyer accounts and more than 170 million monthly site visits, resulting in earnings of more than $ 100 billion, Amazon is the number 1 place for most buyers.

By offering their products on Amazon, each seller automatically gains credibility and trust. This is because many users prefer to buy a product from Amazon than from a store they have never heard anything about. Amazon's promise of excellence and high-quality service encourages many users to purchase the products on this website.

In countries where online shopping has not yet gained much popularity, most shoppers prefer Amazon over any other online store.

International expansion

Since Amazon is one of the biggest and most secure global shipping and buying platforms, it's very easy to start selling in various countries.

Magento has a Multiple Store view, but most "shopping cart" systems require you to create a new purchase for each different language; this is a lot of work without even knowing how the product will perform in this market.

With Amazon, any retailer can quickly test whether their products appeal to the general public by creating a product list on a local Amazon. It will not have the hassle of local payment systems, logistics, and operations.

Low Marketing Costs

Amazon already attracts millions of customers daily, and you have access to them.

Depending on your sector, and how active the market is, you can start selling from day one without making any effort.

Of course, the competition is tough, and you will need to stand out. Having a significant presence will help you stand out in the Amazon customer database.

You don't need an inventory

With more than 100 storage centers worldwide, you can ship all of your products to Amazon, and they will keep your inventory, list it, and distribute it to buyers.

The Amazon FBA (Fulfillment By Amazon) is your warehouse, administrator, and distributor for a very low price compared to the price you would have to pay in any other way. Aside from getting rid of the hassle of shipping, your products will automatically qualify for Amazon Prime Shipping and Buy Box Priority, which will significantly affect your overall sales.

The Disadvantages of Selling on Amazon

Even if no one can match the advantages of selling on Amazon, not everything is perfect, and there are many factors to consider before taking the big leap. Factors like high competition, high sales rates, and inventory management will have a big impact on your strategy and the price of your products, and for this, you must be very careful.

High competition

You probably already expected this, and yes, the competition is tough. You will need to have a long-term strategy, as otherwise you will lose to the competition and go to the last place in terms of price.

If you are selling the same product as other merchants, then you will be competing with them for the Amazon Buy Box. Unlike Google Shopping, which organizes product pages by vendors, Amazon's product pages are organized by product.

But Amazon must determine which vendor is best because many vendors offer the same thing for sale. When a customer clicks the "Add to Shopping Cart" button, the best seller's items will be added to their "shopping cart."

Other sellers will also appear in the "more purchase options" option, but as always, the winner takes it all. With the increase in mobile sales, winning the "Buy Box" is especially important.

Getting the Buy Box code right is almost impossible since Amazon constantly changes the variables considered when determining the winner of the Buy Box. Some things are under your control, and you should focus on mastering them: very good feedback, on-time distribution, quick response to customer questions, FBA, competitive pricing, and up-to-date inventory.

Commissions

All of these benefits mentioned above are not free. Amazon charges retailers substantial commissions for each product sold through its platform.

While in PPC channels, you pay for each click, regardless of whether that click is successful or not, in marketplaces like Amazon, you pay a percentage for each sale. Because of this, you need to make sure that your profit margins are high enough to be successful.

Depending on the category, Amazon CPA Commissions range from 8% to 15%.

If you are selling goods in low margin categories, you probably need to go to other categories because the numbers will not suffice.

Inventory management

If you are selling your products on multiple marketplaces, synchronizing orders is the first thing you need to consider. You need to ensure that Amazon orders are directly coordinated with your system for constant updating of the central order management system.

Fortunately, there are many tools on the market to help you ensure that the number of items available in your "shopping cart" is always up to date.

This ensures that retailers never promote out-of-stock products or spend money on clicks that don't end up on purchases.

In summary, for some merchants, Amazon Marketplace

might be beneficial to their sales strategy, but for others, it won't work from the start. Regardless of whether or not you sell on Amazon, the point is that you need to diversify your means of profit and never bet on keeping all your eggs in the same basket.

The ten advantages of selling on the Internet

More and more people start selling on the Internet before setting up a physical store. This is due to the minimal risk and investment that electronic commerce supposes and its massive reach, together with social networks. In this way, we can start by making ourselves known and getting to know the client before assuming the costs of real space at the street level. Next, we list the ten main advantages of e-commerce:

CREATE YOUR BRAND: You can create your brand with minimum investment and advertise it massively without spending anything through blogs and social networks.

BUSINESS OPEN 24Hrs: Customers can access your products and make purchases at any time.

NO GEOGRAPHICAL LIMITATIONS!: In addition to any time, they can also buy from anywhere in the world.

REDUCTION OF EXPENSES: The expenses of maintenance of e-commerce are reduced to the annual payment of the domain, accommodation, and certificates of secure purchase. Only with your Internet connection, you will be able to keep your business updated without worrying about rents, fees, and other invoices derived from the acquisition of premises. With your online store, you can test the market and, when you are sure that it is profitable, invest in a physical space.

KNOW THE CUSTOMER BETTER: Through the statistical tools associated with eCommerce websites and social networks, you will be able to study the behavior of customers in a faster and more reliable way: what time they buy the most, what products they prefer, at what times Promotions are more profitable, what suggestions or questions do you usually make regarding your products or services, etc. Also, customer service is faster and more effective through the Internet. All the time, people use social networks more to ask and comment on products, in addition to other tools such as blogs or chats owned by stores.

YOU DO NOT NEED TO HAVE STOCK: If you do not want to take risks or you do not know if the product is going to sell well, you can always work on request directly with the wholesaler. So you do not have to invest or store merchandise that, in case it does not Sell, will result in losses.

SPEED ON ORDERS: If you work directly with the wholesaler, he makes the shipment identifying the package as if it were from your company. Thus, you save time, and if you do it yourself, you have many options with different carriers for fast shipments that satisfy the client.

GROWTH SUPERIOR TO PHYSICAL STORE: You can expand quicker and attract more customers than with a physical store by having less money, and becoming a global platform. When you already have the shop, then you have already taken the most difficult step. Now you can multiply your benefits for the minimum cost.

MARKET ON THE RISE: Although the figures for online sales are growing at breakneck speed in Spain (more than 9 million Internet users who buy), 88% of businesses have no Internet presence. More and more people trust e-commerce and the opinions of Internet users when buying, distrusting companies that do not appear online.

PROFITABILITY: If you pick your niche well, and listen to your target market, you will earn a lot with little investment. And if for whatever reason, you don't do well, the losses will be minimal. If you already have a business to start from and want to give your products or services a presence on the Internet, you already have half the job done, so you don't lose anything and can earn a lot. What are you waiting for?

Where to launch your company with Amazon FBA

Are you aware that Amazon is today's largest marketplace? Due to its customer support, its delivery speed, and the fact that it offers all sorts of items at a very affordable price, a lot of customers go straight to Amazon when shopping for a product.

Yet what you do not know is that almost half of the goods Amazon offers are not their own, but are from third-party companies or business people. This is your case.

Therefore, every day more customers want to take the

risk to register as a retailer to boost their company profits taking advantage of Amazon's exposure.

And if you have an online shop and want to maximize revenue with another outlet, read this guide carefully because here you will learn how to sell step by step on Amazon. Read further because also included are 5 SEO tips and tricks to conquer your contest.

Benefits of selling on Amazon

If you've never tried marketing your goods on Amazon before, you do not know what benefits it would offer. And I want you to know the biggest benefits before I tell you how to sell on Amazon.

Multiply the popularity of your goods

The Amazon website is one of the world's most visited. If you're beginning, very few people know your company, or you want to greatly boost the revenue of your online store, with Amazon, you will meet a vast amount of potential buyers in a very short time due to the great exposure of this marketplace.

Present your goods to those interested in purchasing them

It's clear that by having them on sale at Amazon, your goods achieve exposure. The people who visit this website have a strong aim to buy. Therefore, at an early point in the buying process, you are exposed to customers who are more likely to buy from you than if they were discovered by other means.

The need to put up your online shop on Amazon can be

a good option if you don't have web development skills to create online shops, and you don't have a decent budget for anyone to design it for you.

All you need to do is build an account as will be discussed a bit later and start uploading your items with their respective images and apps. It is really basic and doesn't require you to have any sort of technological knowledge.

Internationalization of the brand

Due to the presence of Amazon in other countries, you will be able to make customers from many parts of the world purchase your goods and increase your profits accordingly. For example, you can sell on the 5 European platforms (Amazon.co.uk, Amazon.de, Amazon.fr, Amazon.it and Amazon.es) if you build an account in Spain, and therefore meet even more customers.

You create trust in your prospective buyers; Amazon is the world's most known internet shopping site. We all go to this site to buy almost any type of commodity, and we know it's a marketplace that operates like a charm. In addition, if we have some sort of question, or want to apply for a refund, we can do so without anyone asking why.

The inconvenience of marketing on Amazon

Advertising on Amazon has disadvantages. All that glitters isn't gold so it is also critical that you know what drawbacks there will be when you agree to add your goods on this platform.

Receipt of sales from an intermediary

Payment is directly provided by Amazon anytime a buyer orders one of the items you have for sale. Then if all goes well, you will transfer the money you have picked from the bank account.

However, if consumers argue about the price of their goods, their delivery or send you negative reviews and scores, payment can be postponed or even canceled for weeks.

You'll earn less than selling them yourself

As we'll see later, selling on Amazon isn't free of charge. They put this fantastic platform at your fingertips, and you can meet a lot of customers, so you'll have to pay the price in exchange.

Therefore, you have to deduct what you miss by listing your goods on Amazon from the normal profit margin on any transaction.

Selling on Amazon is also a strong platform for other companies and business people. This is why there are already thousands of vendors on this site, which turns into tremendous competition in many markets. This can lead other retailers to offer the same goods you have at a lower price, or Amazon, which is also a retailer, to choose their items before yours in searches.

Fees you have to pay if you want to sell on Amazon

According to the amount and quality of goods you wish to sell on Amazon, you need to build a quality of seller profile to apply for one fee or another. Thus, before telling you how to sell on Amazon, it is vital that you know all the prices of styles of accounts that exist to sell on this platform and see which one is most appropriate for you.

Fees for sale on Amazon

You'll have to pay certain discounts based on the sort of account you want.

Link rate: is the amount paid to you by Amazon on each order that is based on the product's gross selling price plus delivery costs. The figure will range from 5% to roughly 45% based on the group to which the company belongs.

Closing fee: on each commodity, it is a closed charge of € 0.99 and is deducted from the benefits. It doesn't matter what kind of commodity it is, or what it costs.

The sale price for items: this is the amount that Amazon charges you for every order you make through the marketplace. The most popular ones vary from € 0.81 to € 1.01 and refer only to books, songs, DVDs, apps, and video games.

Set monthly membership price: the price that Amazon pays to qualified vendors regularly for offering goods for sale in its market place. It has a fixed price of 39 euros a month.

Types of seller accounts

You will know when you register as a seller that there are two categories of accounts: the customer and the specialist. Everyone has their characteristics and circumstances, and we'll see through each of them in-depth.

Single seller account

This program is targeted at customers who sell fewer than 40 items a month and who just want to pay Amazon when they make a profit. And if you want to start selling little by little on Amazon to prove it works, this is a perfect choice.

Skilled vendor account

These types of accounts are best if you actively sell online (more than 40 items a month) and wish to leverage some of the benefits that profiles of these types have.

When you apply for this account, unlike individual accounts, you will be able to sell in all Amazon categories, build new items that are not on Amazon's list at the moment, receive more comprehensive information on your sales, upload your inventory instantly and, most importantly, you will be able to buy your goods with a swipe.

How to get started on Amazon sales?

Now that you know the prices, it's time to get down to business on Amazon and start shipping. There's a very easy method to do it.

Decide what to sell on Amazon. If you already have a store, or whether you want to start a new business and start selling on Amazon to make extra money, you must do a little research just to see the things that would be useful before you agree.

Were the items you'd like to sell on Amazon competitive enough?

The fastest way to see that a product is doing well on Amazon is to head to the product form page and see the best sellers list. It is a positive sign if the company you intend to market is in the first place. However, we do not know the exact demand that the commodity has in this way, and it will take a long time to do our research.

To solve this problem, we can use devices like Jungle Scout, which has a Google Chrome extension that will let you know how many sales each product has.

Picture, for example, finding an online appliance store and wanting to sell your robot vacuum cleaners. You have so many different models, though, that you don't want to start selling them all from scratch. You just want to sell the ones with the most interest.

See a column called "Business." In that result list, you will see the sales produced by each product, so we can get an understanding of the model which sells the most.

Furthermore, in the column "Revenue," we can also see the approximate profits produced by each purchase.

Are the items you want to sell dominated by a handful of retailers on Amazon?

So that you know whether a commodity is in high or low demand, it's time to see whether a handful of vendors control the market or not.

If one or more vendors were putting together almost all profits, I consider trying to sell another commodity on Amazon, as it will mean these sellers have a strong commitment to their buyers, and have very good opinions. It will be impossible to surpass them in the results lists.

To learn these details, we should go to the Jungle Scout extension again, to see whether or not the selling figures are being spread among many vendors.

If we see, by searching for "kitchen knives," that the markets are very scattered, and there is no definite dominator, the price is not going to be very high in general.

Will your goods get a lot of feedback from your competitors? Are they good?

An aspect that Amazon takes into account when putting a product in search results is the number of ratings a company has. So if the rival has a lot of reviews about the items you want to market, it can give you an idea that it's going to be difficult to overcome.

But, if a few items have a lot of reviews, and are also distributed across several different sellers, it will mean that there is not a lot of competition.

You can join the items and show their scores and ratings one by one, or use the Jungle Scout extension again so that you can look not just at the number of ratings, but also at their price. If you see that the items in the first positions have average or even poor scores, then it's a perfect sign to start selling yours.

If you are in that situation, I recommend reading the reviews that have 2 and 3 stars and see if your company can address the shortcomings that your rivals' similar products are blamed for. In this way, you can put a better product on sale on Amazon, which will get positive reviews and higher ratings.

Which margin of income will you be getting?

Finally, before you start making the account and placing the goods on Amazon for sale, you must measure the value you will receive from each product being sold.

It doesn't matter if you have your prices already fixed because you are only selling them in your shop at that number. The price may not be affordable on Amazon, and no one will buy from you. Therefore, one of the first items you need to look at is the pricing of the competitors and how you can place a comparable price on it.

If you can't bring the goods at a comparable price, I suggest not selling them on Amazon because all items are equivalent, customers are going to prefer the cheapest.

Build an account and sign with Seller Central

If you already know what items to sell on Amazon, the next thing you'll have to do is register at the Amazon sales center, supplying your nation, form of business, a credit card, a phone number, your personal information, and your bank details.

You may also choose between the two types of accounts. Notice there are two: the seller personally and the seller expert.

Most sellers opt for specialist accounts, but you can continue to try the personal account and go to the pro later.

To select the first product, go to the "Inventory" section and click on the "Select a package" tab.

Now Amazon will ask you to look at those already sold for your offer. You can scan either by barcode or EAN code, or the name of the drug.

You don't need to build a new product when you are selling an item you've created yourself.

After you've checked for your product, you'll certainly see some choices that other rivals are already selling on Amazon. Simply pick one, and you'll be taken to a page to finish filling in missed info. The nice thing about doing something like this is that the result will easily come out of the correct category and subcategories, as someone before you has already done this job.

If there is no company like yours coming out, you need to build a new page. In other words, to bring something on sale there, you can search for the categories and subcategories that have the most to do with your company.

So you should start filling in the product information fields such as names, model, weight, color, etc. Later on in this chapter, you'll find a set of tips and tricks to complete this information, so the company ranks among the Amazon search engine's first results.

In addition to the apps, in this phase, you have to upload the images of the product and build the versions if you have them. You must do it correctly because the first thing the customer will note is the graphics segment.

I suggest that you spend as much time as possible on this process because it will maximize exposure and reduce returns on your goods. Why? For instance, what if the colors of your product's picture do not conform to reality? The consumer will not be happy, will demand a refund and will definitely give you a critical rating.

Put a fair price on your goods

You will need to set a price on each of your goods after you have completed all of the fields. That is something you need to think very hard about because it can determine significantly the amount of profit you make and the return on investment.

Therefore, I recommend that you bear in mind the following points when deciding a price at random: measure the costs and benefits; leave aside the costs you face in producing or purchasing the product, and the costs of handling it. Then, set a minimum price at which to achieve a profit margin, that you will need to market the commodity chosen.

Analyze your competition: see the price your competition markets the same goods, or very close ones. Bear in mind that if a consumer sees your product cheaper from a different retailer, they can go for them and not you.

Look at other retailers' prices: what you need to worry about is that you're not just competing on Amazon with other sellers. You are also competing with local retailers who have their online shops.

Based on all of this, you'll already know what price you're going to pay and whether it's competitive for you to sell the commodity through Amazon.

When an individual has purchased one of your items, Amazon will contact you by email and with a message in your Central Seller screen.

You should have all the buyer's information when you go to the order page, and you can deliver the package within the agreed time. But, if you don't want to take care of handling the delivery and future order refunds, you should contact the Amazon Logistics company, also known as FBA (Amazon Fulfillment).

So what is logistics at Amazon?

It's a service that helps you not to think about anything relevant to delivering and storing your goods, which will offer you other benefits.

You will also send the goods to Amazon warehouses before you recruit them, meaning that anytime someone places an order in each of the 5 European marketplaces, Amazon can handle it without you needing to do something to deliver it to the customer easily.

In case you want to use FBA for the logistics of your business, you must pick them and click on "Transfer or restore inventory" after uploading your items to inventory.

Before that, you will put each product's units in order and build its labels. These marks should be stored as pdf before you give them to Amazon, and you can print and paste them on the packets.

You will then have to fill in the delivery details, choose the postal service where you want the box to be picked up, measure the prices, and print the delivery mark that you will use to add on the packaging that you are going to use. When Amazon receives your items, they'll immediately continue to be available on the website.

Receive your profits

Like what happens on your online store where you have your payment portal directly connected to your branch when you sell on Amazon, consumers can use the American giant's payment methods and gateways. Because of this, Amazon collects and handles the sales as a whole.

All this has its benefits and drawbacks.

The good news is you don't need to set up a POS, you just need to think about bringing your bank account in.

The unfortunate thing is you won't earn the profits from a transaction immediately, but Amazon will pay you after 15 days have elapsed.

What you need to take into account, of course, is that consumers have the right to refund their goods if they are not satisfied after they have received it. Amazon will then keep the value of the transaction for the time taken before the dispute is settled because the buyer is, for them, the first priority.

5 Tips and tricks added to Amazon to increase sales

Like I said at the start of the chapter, selling on Amazon has certain pitfalls, including strong competition. Many businesses and people are already selling their goods, so you'll deal with a lot of other vendors unless you've got a creative company.

But don't panic, because I'm going to tell you three good practices and two tricks that you can use now to increase the popularity of your products.

Rank your products on Amazon using appropriate and common keywords.

If your product can be named in many ways and have multiple ends, you must do a good search for keywords to maximize the title and content of your product file.

When we're talking about Google, finding resources that help us to find good keywords is very easy. It's not that easy on Amazon, though, because there are not as many options and some that don't have monthly search volumes. This is so because Amazon is not currently supplying this info.

However, there are some resources that allow one to know each keyword's prominence, depending on certain parameters. For example, Egrow.io.

This tool searches the top 10 items with the keyword entered from Amazon's search results and then analyzes the ranking of the retailer, number of stars, and monthly sales for each of them. Cross the data even with the Google search volume to learn its success in this other search engine to show you a ranking of success.

Another easier approach is to use recommendations from the search engine owned by Amazon.

If we have an iPhone case shop, for example, and we want to learn what kind of cases are most wanted, the reviews are a nice free tool that Amazon itself gives us.

Such tips are important long-tail keywords that are strongly sought by people who visit Amazon, and we can draw other ideas.

If we want a longer list of more keywords that we can export and add together, we can use the Amazon tab that has the keyword resource.

Simply select the country, language, and enter the main keyword, and the tool will show the Amazon keywords in the same order they were extracted from the autocomplete function. Amazon would usually place the most important keywords above the least.

If you've got the list of useful keywords, you'll know which items to start offering, how to name them, and what keywords to use in the Amazon label sheets.

Build an integrated SEO product sheet

Now that you've picked successful keywords, you'd have to do the company file's SEO On-Page to location for the specified keyword in the first tests. Not only that, but it would also be necessary for you to seek to place certain keywords and long tails relevant to it.

Title

The title is the most important area when it comes to placing the product, and, after a search on Amazon, it is the text which appears in the results lists.

It is, therefore, very important that you include the main keyword and others linked in this section to give Amazon priority as early as possible. You will not only have to use keywords, but adding other elements that we will see later is also necessary.

Attributes

Attributes or enumerations are the factors that separate the commodity and make it stand out.

Considering that this is potentially the second thing people would read after the title, a balance between inserting relevant keywords and sales pitches needs to be struck.

Definition

The definition is the next section we need to optimize. It's a section in which we have to define our company using the keyword and its derivatives. You can, however, stop placing a single block of text and instead use lists, highlight any words, make short sentences, etc.

Amazon Meta Keywords

Yes, you read it correctly. We all know that for years meta keywords have had little impact on the organic ranking of Google. Nonetheless, this does not extend to Amazon, which for now considers them for placement, as long as they are not used abusively by constantly inserting the same keyword.

In this context, I suggest you add the product's long-tail keywords, synonyms, and apps.

Other factors

In addition to the factors listed above, several other variables impact Amazon's placement of your goods, such as average ranking; a good score on your products directly influences better positioning.

Amount of feedback: It is important to try to get a lot of reviews on your products because they are taken into account by Amazon as you put up your products.

Comments Quality: When consumers view the comments of other customers favorably, Amazon will accept them.

Amount of sales: Once the company is selling well,

that means customers want it, and Amazon can take care of it by higher placement.

Creating appropriate titles and adapting them for Amazon's internal SEO

Like Google, Amazon always assigns tremendous significance to the title we allocate to our product, and we'll need to customize it according to its best practice indicators.

The length is as follows, based on where it appears:

- Names in the code search results: Between 230 and 250 characters.
- App search results for titles: Between 65 and 80 characters.
- Titles of the relevant article: Between 65 and 80 characters.

We would then have all or almost all of the items that Amazon implies but in an order that supports us.

Whether it's a common product that consumers are searching for without the name being used or it's imported, it's better to place the most appropriate and searched keyword first, and then the product logo and the other qualities that separate it and make it stand out. In the end, whether it is necessary or if multiple units are included in the same box, we can add the size and units in.

Nonetheless, there will be occasions when the term most looked for by consumers is the brand name and product name, and that's what we'll put at the top of our names.

Raise the CTR of your reviews by posting the product's URL

Have you started searching the Amazon products' URLs? Based on how they are accessed, the same link will have different URLs, e.g., certain parameters that are not in the original product URL are inserted when you click on a product from the search page.

And as happens with Facebook, a strong CTR is one of the criteria that Amazon takes into account when putting an article higher. Therefore, whenever we send traffic to that page, for example, posting it on social networks, Amazon would assume that users click on our page from the results list, resulting in a rise in the CTR and a boost of its placement.

Get ratings and feedback even if the brands don't have much exposure. Customers will always have an opinion about the goods they are purchasing. They seldom leave it written as a review, though, particularly when it's a good opinion.

So here are a couple of tricks to get them that few people know:

Give discounts in return for feedback

One way for vendors to counter the lack of comments and opinions on their goods is to submit items free of charge or at a substantial discount to customers who are eager to do an unbiased review of the product once they have sampled it.

Easy service. The seller publishes the ad focused on

receiving feedback in Facebook communities. The reviewer then pays for the drug, checks it, then grades it and makes a comment about it. Ultimately, the retailer returns to the Amazon network, either the maximum value or the equivalent of the discount negotiated publicly.

Request reviews from your customers from Amazon

Are you aware that you can ask for reviews from people who have already ordered from you from your Amazon Seller Central account?

Within your Amazon Seller Central account, you've got an order management tab in the Orders section, where you can see all the orders you sent.

The date, period, name, and other details relevant to each purchase order can be seen there. When you click on the name of the buyer, a text box will open, which will allow you to send a message to the buyer asking them to check your purchase.

Of course, it is very important that you choose the "Appraisal Request" option in the "Topic" area, and that you adhere to Amazon's policies in the message you send. This is, it will be a brief and formal text in which you thank the customer for their order and in which you politely and sincerely encourage them to judge your product truthfully.

Price to sell on Amazon?

Amazon is, as you've noticed, a very open platform for

all sorts of vendors, from startups looking to start a company and small firms trying to explore new outlets, to larger corporations selling hundreds of goods every day.

Selling your products on Amazon, though, has its benefits and drawbacks, and before starting it, I suggest that you measure the cost of placing your goods for sale on Amazon (in time and money) well, and the profit you will get from selling your items at a good price.

Another factor that you should keep in mind is that if you depend solely on this marketplace, and you have a very low-profit margin, I do not recommend selling on Amazon. Why? Just as you were able to add your goods on Amazon, by reducing the costs and pressuring you to do so, so will anyone.

And Amazon itself, once it notices that a company is selling a lot, will arrange better deals with the manufacturer or the likes, by offering the goods at a lower price.

CHAPTER 4

HOW AMAZON FBA WORKS

The sales process

At Amazon, there are several forms of sales, but if you are looking to automate your business to the maximum to travel or have more free time, FBA is the best option.

This abbreviation, which stands for Fulfilment By Amazon, refers to a logistics system in which Amazon is in charge of managing all your customers' orders, along with all returns.

This way, you can forget about having to make or order shipments when sales occur. And trust me, when you run a business internationally, this is an incredible help.

First, there is you and your brand. Your products will be made by a manufacturer who, in turn, will be in charge of sending the entire stock to Amazon warehouses under your coordination.

This means that you do not have to touch the product at any time, except for the sample that you can ask your manufacturer for to check the quality of the item in question.

It is a great way to automate the process since you can organize everything from anywhere in the world.

Then, once Amazon receives your stock, it stores it in

its warehouses and distributes it to your customers when sales are made, also taking care of returns, if any.

Finally, you will receive your money on time in your checking account every 15 days, once the storage and logistics commissions have been discarded, which are usually around 30% of the final sale price, as we will see below.

The commissions

It is very important that, before launching your product, you check whether or not it will be profitable once the costs for the fees are removed in FBA.

To be honest, not everything is worth selling on Amazon.

If you want to build a solid business with a future within any of the e-commerce giant's markets, the first thing you should do is calculate the costs well.

Here are some hints.

Fixed costs: Investment, reference, and logistics

First of all, you have to think about how much the product is going to cost you and try to buy directly from the factory to avoid intermediaries.

It is best to choose products that will at least double your investment. In other words, if you buy at €5, you must sell at least €15 so that your profit margin allows you to act smoothly.

On the other hand, you must take into account the reference rate, which ranges between 8% and 15% of the final sale price. This figure depends on the category in which you list your product, but the vast majority revolves around 15%.

Also, there are the logistics costs. As we have seen, with FBA, it's Amazon that stores and manages sales, and the final price will be charged from your earnings per package shipped. This amount will depend on the weight and size of your product.

You can check these rates based on these variables, although to give you an idea, the standard package is around € 3 if you sell.

Other costs: Storage and advertising

Finally, you should take into account the storage costs, which revolve around € 20 or € 25 per cubic meter depending on the time of year, along with the investment in advertising.

On Amazon, you must learn to campaign within the platform since this will allow you to gain visibility and start positioning yourself as a brand.

The investment in advertising does not have to be taken out of your pocket, but the number of your biweekly earnings will be subtracted.

I know positively that talking about finances is often unattractive to most entrepreneurs. But since it is an essential part of any project, here are ten tips to optimize your profitability and know what happens in your business.

What kind of products to sell on Amazon

By now, you have enough arguments to know that not just any product is valid to sell on Amazon.

If you want to do this professionally, the best thing to do is to secure your launch well before you start working on your brand.

We recommend that you choose a product that:

- Won't be fragile
- Weighs little
- Won't be too big
- You can customize

Not being fragile will save you a lot of headaches when your manufacturer has to prepare the shipment and when each order is placed.

Not being heavy or bulky will save you a lot at the level of logistics and storage commissions.

And being a product that you can customize will help you differentiate your brand from the competition.

Also, you must do a preliminary market study and analyze some variables, such as the density of the most searched keywords or the behavior of the competition.

To study this, we recommend using some professional software, such as Merchant Words or Jungle Scout.

How to build your brand

If, at this point, you are still excited about the idea of creating your brand and growing it on Amazon, but you don't know where to start, this section may help you to have a clearer picture of your roadmap.

To turn your brand into a business with thousands of hits a month and transform it into a passive income generator is possible, but only with know-how.

Concrete tips for selling on Amazon and not die trying

Don't jump without a parachute and train. You've already seen it, and Amazon takes a significant percentage of your profits in commissions. If you don't want to end up wasting your time and money, learn from the people who are today where you want to arrive tomorrow.

Manage your time well, and organize your goals. Take a look at these productivity tips. Surely they can help you:

Make sure your product is suitable for sale on Amazon. Do a good market study and calculate the costs very well. Analyze the behavior of the competition over time and find how to differentiate yourself as a brand.

Find a good manufacturer. Compare prices and qualities and, above all, make sure it is a serious company that will respond well to meet delivery deadlines.

Make a good listing on Amazon. Study the density of keywords and the most popular search terms. Take care of copywriting both in the title and in the bullets and the description. And above all, take good pictures, with a pure white background and highlighting all the qualities of your product.

Learn how to make advertising on Amazon an investment and not an expense. This will allow you to position your product faster on the first pages and lay the foundations to start making more and more organic sales.

It is true that if you decide to sell on Amazon doing FBA, you have to assume that approximately 30% of your profits will go to cover the costs of logistics, reference, and storage.

But have you thought about what it would cost you to have to keep renting a place to keep your stock? Or what would it take to hire a team of people to handle all shipments and returns?

For us, this type of sale has many more advantages than disadvantages, especially considering that you can take advantage of the reputation and professionalism of an e-commerce company that no other shadows globally.

Of course, this is a serious business and it is important not to jump without a parachute.

The best thing you can do if you do not want to end up crying in the forums is to train and learn from other sellers who are having results.

I hope this section has helped you to get a little clearer about how e-commerce works on Amazon and how it can benefit your digital business.

Essential first steps to start selling

Here begins the configuration of your Sell on Amazon account. You can familiarize yourself with selling on Amazon, the functions of Seller Central, and the policies that apply to sellers, as well as the products and services that can help you grow your business.

Quick start:

This is a short presentation from Seller Central. It also explains how to configure your account information, add your payment method, put your account in "vacation" mode, set your shipping rates, and manage your orders.

Sales plans, rates, and payments:

Explore each person's available sales plans and rates, discover how to track your payments and other transactions, and how Amazon disburses the funds derived from your sales to your seller account.

Add products:

Here you'll find information on how to publish products with the Add a Product feature, manage your inventory, and create product detail and variant pages.

Create your brand:

Learn about Amazon Brand Registration and Rich Content for your brand products. Find out how to create detail pages that help improve your brand recognition, visibility, and ultimately sales.

Sponsored Products:

Learn how to advertise your listings with Amazon Sponsored Products and create sponsored product campaigns.

Detail Pages and Buy Box:

Find out how to create a product detail page to help you increase the number of visits and sales. You can also get information about the Buy Box and how you can choose to win it.

Publication restrictions:

Find out which categories are subject to prior authorization by Amazon and how you can request approval to sell those products. You'll also find answers to frequently asked questions about other publishing restrictions or products that can't be sold on Amazon.

Shipping options:

It shows you an overview of the vendor-managed Prime program, as well as details on how you can sign up for the trial period of that program.

Amazon logistics:

Understand the basics of Amazon Logistics and how to change the products you currently manage to Amazon-managed. You'll also get information about Amazon's Small & Light Logistics Products program, how it works, and how you can start using it.

Creation of promotions:

Here you will find information on how to create and manage Flash Offers. We will also talk about the Amazon Logistics Amazon Giveaway program.

Performance as a seller:

Find out how to ensure that you publish your products correctly to ensure the best shopping experience for customers.

Amazon Sales Tutor:

Learn about the Amazon Sales Tutor and how to configure personalized recommendations to adapt them to the needs of your business.

Unified account for North America:

Learn how to create and manage product offers, customize your listings, and manage your prices and inventory in the United States, Canada, and Mexico from a single interface.

International sales with Amazon:

Get an idea of what you need to sell internationally on Amazon. You will also discover the importance of translation and localization when selling on Amazon websites in other countries.

Automate prices:

Here is an overview of the Automate Pricing feature. Learn how it works, how to create or modify a pricing configuration, and how to update the prices of your SKUs accordingly.

Amazon Business:

Learn about the features available in the Amazon Business Intercompany program and how to get started. You will also be able to see the Sell in Amazon Business rate table and the reduced rates available for some business transactions.

Benefits and Advantages of using Amazon tools Optimization Software

Main benefits and advantages of using sales optimization tools or software on Amazon:

- **Time-saving:** Whether you want to find keywords for your products or send internal emails to each of your thousands of buyers, these Amazon tools will save you hours and hours of work that you can spend on whatever you want.
- **Adaptability:** Internet sales vary more and more quickly. With these tools, you can make massive changes to your listing, your strategies, or monitor your competition or your data to be able to adapt more quickly to the changes.
- **Convenience:** They are not only time-saving but these tools are also easy to use. With a few clicks, you change prices, modify a strategy, etc.
- **Optimization:** Optimizing everything related to your Amazon sales business is vital to avoid headaches, problems you don't see coming, etc. Can you imagine having your stock

management well optimized? What a relief it would be!

- **Profitability:** It is true that these Amazon marketing tools have their cost, and sometimes high. But it is an investment that will make your business profitable... ALWAYS make the most of the tool. As a business owner, you have to know its potential and organize that it is managed correctly. If you have them and don't use them well, you will throw the money in the trash.

Tools to know what products to sell on Amazon

In all work, some tools help us with our tasks or make our work easier and more effective. And to increase sales on Amazon as well.

There is an infinity of platforms and tools for very useful purposes, from the simplest such as the Amazon Tools that are used to investigate which are the best products to sell or other more advanced ones such as the Amazon Tools Spy or those that do A/B testing.

Also, there are tools to generate accounting and tax calculations produced by the business relationship with Amazon, such as the Amazon FBA Calculator, to calculate the benefits of your products.

Therefore, you must know all the different types of Tools to sell on Amazon that there are to determine which ones you need the most.

Types of Amazon FBA Sellers Research Tools

To do keyword studies and improve the SEO of your products.

To monitor your listing and control the rankings of positioning.

To optimize Amazon ADS campaigns and control your profit.

To do email marketing on Amazon.

To control the price of your products and automate strategies and offers.

Amazon Tools Analytics: These are tools that monitor all the data in your account: Sales by units, by marketplaces, expenses, rates, etc.

Amazon Power Tools Sales: Tools to specifically control how you are selling, daily, monthly sales, the variation of daily sales, etc.

Amazon testing tools: These tools allow you to test to see how things work before using them.

So as you can see, there are many options you have to optimize your business on Amazon and make the most of sales.

Which will translate into higher income for you? Don't wait any longer, keep reading, so you know the great variety of tools that promise to take your business to the next level.

9 product research tools on Amazon

The first step to being able to generate good sales is to have an attractive product. Not only in quality but in price and positioning. One that allows you to know, before making any investment, that you will be able to recover your money and generate considerable profits; in the shortest possible time and also that the public is sure to be interested in.

But don't be scared. You won't have to do complex calculations or graduate from pure math to find out which articles are best for your online business. Today there are many Amazon product research tools, which are responsible for doing all the heavy lifting for you. You only have to take care of acquiring the tool of your preference.

Also, you will have to follow some very simple and routine steps to be able to carry out the searches and that, as if by magic, the tool allows you to know data that not everyone knows, about the article you are interested in; classified information. It will help you make the right decision since it will help you to know how sought after that product is.

Jungle Scout is an amazing product research tool, whose operation is only effective on Amazon platforms, regardless of its country of origin. With it, you will be able to access a host of extremely useful data about the product you are interested in selling; to know if it is truly profitable or not.

Jungle Scout is a tool that is responsible for conducting

a market study; to be able to show you with numbers, what are the items you should, without a doubt, include in your sales catalog. There is a lot of data that it throws at you for such a purpose, such as the name, brand, and price of the product, as well as the category to which it belongs and the rank it occupies.

The latter refers to the position in which the article is at the time of searching on Amazon, about its competing products. Still, not everything is there since Jungle Scout also offers data regarding income, sales movements, number of opinions, rating obtained, daily sales, and type of seller of the items.

By vendor type, Jungle Scout refers to the nature of the vendor-Amazon relationship, that is, whether it is an FBA or Fulfillment By Amazon, the same Amazon or a third party. All the mentioned data can be found through a simple search on Amazon of the product that interests us and clicking on the Google Chrome extension so that Jungle Scout can proceed.

But the Jungle Scout extension for Google Chrome is not the only presentation in which the tool will be available on the internet. Since it also comes in web application mode; it has a different cost than the Chrome extension and that can be complemented; interacting wonderfully with each other, since with the application you can get other options.

Strong Points or Advantages of Jungle Scout

Get profitable products that generate considerable profits for your company.

Analyze the products and the public's interest in it before even making any type of economic investment.

Feed your inventory with items that are fast selling.

Obtain an automated market study in seconds, without the need for you to carefully examine each product for it.

Presence of an application to deepen and further improve the experience.

Egrow is a wonderful application for all those people who work as sellers at the most popular mall in the world, Amazon. Without importing under any circumstances, Egrow is in charge of analyzing thousands and thousands of products daily to its large customer portfolio.

The same that has been given to the task of acquiring the Google Chrome extension; the Amazon article explorer tool, Egrow, can provide you with information about the best items on the market; those that are truly profitable and very interesting to the public to ensure that your sales are effective and significant in volume.

With Egrow, you can choose the most attractive item for your market segment, so that you cannot resist the incredible options that your product catalog brings; which guarantees that you will have a large number of sales and that, also, you will recover the investment in the blink of an eye, allowing you and your business to grow by leaps and bounds, thanks to the right decisions.

Strong Points or Advantages of Egrow:

Possibility of tracking the same product for up to 90 days, thus being able to know the differences existing in that item in the stipulated period.

Egrow takes into account the comments and suggestions of its customers, so it constantly makes changes to improve the experience of its users and to satisfy their needs.

Accurate calculations, which guarantee Egrow customers and users that the data thrown by the tool is 100% reliable and true.

Zonguru is a very useful tool when deciding to dedicate yourself to selling items on Amazon; since this gives you the possibility to choose the best product; so you can feed the physical and digital inventory of your company, in the best possible way; with high-quality products, attractive sales numbers and very good positioning in the Amazon search ranking.

With Amazon Tools Zonguru the decision is totally in your hands; since the tool gives you precise data about the prices of the products, the ranges of the best sellers, customer reviews, ratings obtained by the items and, also, the estimated sales; a tool that undoubtedly represents a great help for any trader, be it, beginner or expert.

It is presented to you as a compatible extension and intended to be used only with Google Chrome; being able to acquire it with a monthly or annual investment plan, depending on your preference. But, the most incredible thing is that you can have a free trial for seven days, without a contract and pay the plan of your choice when you decide to continue using Zonguru.

Also, another function that will leave you captivated with Zonguru is the baptized "business board"; with which the tool analyzes your company, this time, thus allowing you to know what your earnings are, how much you have spent or invested. It also generates sales comparison charts, so you can evaluate how your company is doing.

Strong Points or Advantages of ZonGuru:

Presentation of accurate and reliable data to analyze the steps that you must follow with your business.

Possibility to experience a free trial of the Google Chrome extension for seven days and without a contract.

Monthly and annual payment plans, so you can decide on the one that best suits you and your finances.

Function "business dashboard," which allows you to analyze all aspects related to the purchases, sales, investments, and interaction of your company; so you can evaluate their performance and get better every time.

Unicorn Smasher is another of Amazon's product explorer tools. With this incredible extension that you can use in Google Chrome, you will be able to access very important data when choosing which product you will invest in to offer your clients; so that your company is even more prosperous and fruitful than you have always been dreaming of.

In addition to its incredible design, which is highly attractive to its users, Unicorn Smasher is also in charge of attracting the attention of its clients for having the goodness of being a completely free extension. Yes! This means that you can download this tool and use it to grow your business without having to pay a single euro! Simply incredible.

Unicorn Smasher was designed by the creators of Amazon Tracker, a very popular product positioning tool on Amazon platforms; which means that Unicorn Smasher is an extension created by experts; which, without a doubt, means that you can trust the tool with your eyes closed, giving you reliable and accurate data.

You can enjoy it immediately, as it is an Amazon product explorer tool, totally free.

Expert hands created it in all aspects related to Amazon, such as those of the designers of Amazon Tracker.

100% reliable, accurate, and safe data.

You and I know that when looking for a product on the internet, and even more on a platform as big as Amazon, we will find the same item, offered by various sellers at very different prices; even though because it is the same product, it retains the same characteristics in all offers. That is why you, as a seller, must go one step further and go to AmazeOWL.

With this tool, you can have the guarantee that AmazeOWL will be in charge of analyzing the market you are trying to enter for you. Being able to do so with prior knowledge generates a great advantage that, surely, will be reflected in the sales numbers of your company, making it more prosperous and profitable, which can only result in endless benefits.

With AmazeOWL, you will be able to find the answers to important questions when choosing a product for your catalog, such as, "What is selling the most?" "Which item is not too expensive to send?" "Which product has low competition on Amazon?" This desktop application promises to be very useful when searching for items to feed your sales catalog.

Strong Points or Advantages of AmazeOWL:

Chooses the most suitable product for sale, thanks to its incredible search engines, which give you accurate and reliable calculations.

It is a detailed and easy to use desktop application, you can manipulate and understand it as soon as you start using it.

You will not need spreadsheets or other documents to store your search data, AmazeOWL allows you to save listings directly from Amazon; making the experience easier and simpler.

It is not an extension, but an application, which means that you are not required to have the Google Chrome browser to be able to use AmazeOWL.

AMZ Hook is another of the Amazon product analyzer tools that you can find on the web. AMZ Hook gives you a wide, comfortable, and complete experience, so that you meet your goals and, without delay or effort, you can find the ideal product to grow your Amazon sales catalog.

With AMZ Hook, you can put many filters to your search that will help you find what truly interests you. These filters can be by category, the ranking occupied by the article, the price; by the valuation received by the product, the critics, the weight or the amount of competition in the market.

As if that were not enough, AMZ Hook also allows you to add an extra keyword to filter the search to your liking; or, exclude some other; which means that with AMZ Hook you can carry out a 100% personalized search in seconds, saving you time, money and effort. Because the faster you find the ideal product, the faster you can buy it.

But, without a doubt, the best thing about AMZ Hook is that it is a tool that you can use without paying a single euro since it is 100% free.

Strong Points or Advantages of AMZ Hook:

Perfect for carrying out 100% personalized searches, being able to filter them with the included keywords, or add and remove others according to your taste and need.

Easy to use and understand tools for any type of audience dedicated to selling on Amazon.

It promises to help you find the best product so you can sell on Amazon FBA and make your business evolve.

You will not have to pay for it, and it is 100% free.

Evaluating the market you are entering or thinking of entering has never been so easy and simple, and with AMZ Scout, it is a simple task that you can do in the blink of an eye. It only takes a few clicks to search for the product you plan to invest in, and AMZ Scout is in charge of analyzing all the data related to it, for you.

You will be able to find new data and evaluate your niche, all from one place and from the same source, your AMZ Scout. You can also closely monitor the activity of your main competencies so that you can have data on their inventory, sales level, income, and prices and thus improve the offers and services you offer your clients so that they prefer you and Your business.

You can also track the sales history of a product; to see if there are significant variations in the demand for any product due to variables such as the time of year or the current fashion. In this way, you will make sure that you invest in an article that is profitable in a constant way; to assure you of continuous and frequent sales.

Strong Points or Advantages of AMZ Scout:

Find the ideal product so you can grow your business. One that generates profitability and high levels of profit due to the great interest it arouses in your niche.

345

Evaluate the activity of your competition so that you always go one step further and nothing takes you by surprise.

The free trial period when choosing a plan; which allows you to assess whether the tool meets the benefits it promises and thus acquires it definitively.

User Reviews:

AMZ Scout has very good reviews regarding the effectiveness of the benefits offered by the tool.

As suggested by the testimonies that we can find on the AMZ Scout web portal; such as Jeremy Scott, Ann Robins, and Om Shah, it has been agreed that the AMZ Scout extension is very useful for their businesses and has represented great advances that have given way to their evolution and growth.

If you want to find the perfect, correct, and successful products to sell on Amazon and make your business grow by leaps and bounds, you can use Asinhunt. With Asinhunt, you will be able to track those products that you want to incorporate into your sales catalog, before making a final investment in them; to evaluate if these are as profitable as you consider them.

In this way, you avoid having a disappointment when offering your products on Amazon that do not instill enough interest in your niche; causing you to have both money invested and stagnant inventory. This means that you will not be able to invest again until you manage to leave the purchased merchandise. That is why Asinhunt has come to make your business easier.

With it, you can estimate the daily sales volume of a certain product and know if they are truly profitable for you and your business. Furthermore, its use is very simple; you just have to make a list of the items that interest you, and Asinhunt will take care of giving you the price, the units in stock, the name of the merchant, the number of reviews and the ratings obtained.

Strong Points or Advantages of Asinhunt:

You can choose a plan and start with a free trial to assess if the tool is what you and your business need.

Ease to use the tool, and a simple interface.

Obtaining data in seconds, optimizing your time and, thanks to the precision of the information, also the money of your company.

A/B Testing tools for Amazon.

Just as there are tools that help you explore what those "star" products are, which only promise to increase the sales levels of your business and return the capital invested in the blink of an eye, there are also other tools, just as important for other aspects; such as A/B testing for Amazon.

These are nothing more than tools that allow us to make comparisons between two web pages on the same platform. That is, two similar versions are made to a portal but still different from each other; to evaluate which one captures the user's attention in the greatest quantity and, in this case, that the purchase is made, since, as we know, the design must join the psychology for it.

The versions of the web page, baptized by its designers as "A" and "B," appear randomly to users of it; to evaluate which of them generates a better experience for the client and, therefore, for business.

Once conclusive results have been obtained that dictate which version of the website obtained the best and most favorable interaction with users, we proceed to opt for this option definitively and abandon, definitively, the other proposal of the portal that did not generate such good numbers.

From the same creators of Jungle Scout comes Splitly, an Amazon A/B testing tool for products on Amazon; Which promises to improve the volume of your sales, get more web traffic and significantly increase your profits. All this through algorithmic division tests or "A," "B" versions of the same digital platform, to assess which has the highest profitability.

Using artificial intelligence and the testing method, you can scientifically test each item that makes up your sales catalog; and thus achieve better results and a higher volume of sales. With Splitly, you can also evaluate the rank of your keywords; and thus monitor them over time, for which Splitly provides detailed reports.

Strong Points or Advantages of Splitly:

So far, a total of $ 125,005,000 has been generated from additional sales, thanks to the A/B tests performed.

Time optimization, with functions such as testing keyword lists, helps you eliminate manual labor and direct your attention to other important issues.

You can start your experience with a free trial.

User Reviews:

Those who have had the opportunity to have Splitly as allies of their business on Amazon report that they do not regret it. It has been one of the best decisions they have made about their sales with the help that Splitly offers in terms of positioning and A/B testing. Furthermore, it has made their sales and web traffic levels grow in incredible ways.

Such is the case of Scott Voelker, owner of "The Incredible Seller"; who relates that he was struck by a simple test such as the change of the main image. Both affected the number of sales of his business; receiving a total of $ 4,000 more now than it was before trying the A/B testing that Splitly offered.

If I start by telling you that this next tool is free, surely I already have your attention, and you will be interested in knowing what it is about; but its null sale price is not the only benefit that this incredible tool has. Listing Dojo is a wonderful helping hand when it comes to performing A/B testing or website version testing to evaluate its profitability and acceptance.

And it is not just about comparing. By testing, you can achieve big changes in the company's finances annually, however small the additional income may seem at first. Listing Dojo lets you test up to 7 variations of each listing price, title, images, and description. And it is here the magic begins to happen.

Listing Dojo lets you know how each variation you make to the page affects the user experience; that is, which changes generate more clicks than before and which ones generate fewer; so that you can keep those that attract the customer the most and are more likely to take them to make a purchase.

Strong Points or Advantages of Listing Dojo:

It is a free Amazon Tool, making it easy to reach even if you are starting your business.

You may make up to a total of 7 changes or variations perversion; so you can evaluate the effectiveness of each one, measured by the clicks of the platform-client interaction.

Accounting and tax tools for Amazon

As a merchant, you should know that whatever activity you carry out, you have to be very attentive to paying taxes. But it is not a secret for anyone that performing these types of calculations is usually tedious and even complicated. That is why today, the web is full of resources that promise to ease the burden of all matters related to accounting and taxes of Amazon.

With these tools, you can, without any problem, focus on other important aspects of your business; such as making customers fully satisfied so that your business is on the rise, since the accounting and tax resources for Amazon take care of all the calculations for you, and tell you how much you should charge and how much you should pay to cover the taxes.

Among the tools or resources aimed at taking care of the accounting and taxes of your business, are the following:

Taxify is a more than ideal option for any type of merchant, be it small, medium or large, since it promises to help you place the costs of the products, so that, in this way, you can cover the taxes generated by the sale of the item and have no surprises when it comes to counting your earnings. With Taxify, you will not lose a single euro again due to errors in the calculations made.

Besides, Taxify helps with other accounting aspects, such as reconciliations; information about the taxes that may be being generated in the place where Amazon stores your inventory if you are a merchant of the FBA program. And last but not least, the tool is also responsible for declaring taxes on your behalf, to remove the heavy load.

Strong Points or Advantages:

- Valuable assistance is a really important matter for your company; especially those related to the accounting area of the same.
- Customer service through the free phone number and Taxify email support.
- Possibility of evaluating the experience with a free trial before finally purchasing the tool.

User Reviews:

Taxify has been of great help to the accounting area of many businesses, such as those of the owner of Forrest and Harold, who explains that owning two businesses and taking care of both, caused him to neglect the accounting aspect of them and fell behind in their declaration and payment.

But after he decided to trust Taxify, everything changed, and he was able to focus on other aspects that required his immediate attention, without the need to leave the accounting of the business to abandon.

Fetcher is an accounting aid tool that was designed and created for ordinary human beings, specifically for those who do not have a very good relationship with mathematics and calculations, or who simply do not have the time to account and manage as they wish carefully. But this is no longer a problem, thanks to Fetcher.

Plus, Fetcher promises to bring you accurate, sync data on Amazon every five minutes; which guarantees that the margin of error is practically nil and you can trust the tool with your eyes closed. The fact that it is a sister resource to Jungle Scout and Splitly confirms this.

Strong Points or Advantages:

- It is a tool that was created and designed by subject matter experts such as Amazon sellers, software engineers, and data fanatics.
- You can start the experience with a completely

free trial of one month.
- Low prices and different plans according to the level of your business.
- Synchronization with Amazon every five minutes.

TaxJar is another incredible tool that promises to help you extensively with accounting for your online business. This tool is capable of providing you with automated reports and sales tax files if you are a multi-channel seller.

Also, you can, through the application, directly connect shopping carts to the online site or market where you only sell them once, in which case the tool will be responsible for downloading the data and preparing them to file sales tax returns; quickly and easily.

Strong Points or Advantages:

- Ease in all accounting aspects of your online business.
- Plans at very solidary prices.
- Possibility of starting your experience with a 30-day free trial.
- Automatic preparation of reports, presentation, and tax declaration of your online business.

Avalara is the solution you were looking for to automate the calculation, presentation, and declaration of all sales taxes generated by your Amazon items. You will simply have to synchronize your data, and the tool will take care of giving you the amount, date, and value of each period of payment of the taxes, in such a way that you eliminate all the manual and tedious work of the calculation.

Strong Points or Advantages:

- Automation of sales tax reports of your products offered on Amazon.
- Start your experience with a free 30-day trial, for which you will not need to present any credit card.
- Customer service through the telephone line; Avalara promises to help you and accompany you at all times.

User Reviews:

Adrienne Kosewicz, the owner of "Play It Safe World Toys," states that she has been a user of Avalara's services for more than a year to date; and that, in all this time; has rigorously and promptly complied with sales taxes; thanks to the Avalara team who are dedicated to doing Adrienne's job so much easier.

Advertising platforms

We know that nowadays, everything is managed through the internet, that is why it is full of how much information and data we provide to the network; e-commerce platforms are no exception.

In order not to remain on the last pages of results, it is necessary to apply certain advertising and web positioning strategies.

These help us, precisely, to go climbing positions time by time, so that, combining the correct strategies and fulfilling the appropriate steps, we may appear on the first page of the results, or as close to it as possible; which, without a doubt, translates into greater exposure to the public and potential sales.

CPC Strategy is a tool that promises to accelerate your Amazon sales; it does the implementation of market strategies based on a design that ensures the long life of Amazon's businesses.

All this is done from the optimization of the listing; that is, CPC Strategy is in charge of capturing those keywords that go with your article, and they can generate greater searches and interaction with customers thanks to their use. Besides, it constantly campaigns and offers, inside and outside Amazon, to increase web traffic.

Strong Points or Advantages:

-   CPC Strategy provides you with weekly reporting from the executive panel; so you can evaluate the progress of the implemented strategies.
-   Constant supervision of the main account of the seller, in addition to optimizing it with strategies that promise to improve sales performance.

To start experiencing the changes that CPC Strategy brings to you, you must first fill out a form to evaluate your strategy as an Amazon seller. To do this, enter the web platform.

Kenshoo is another tool that you want to be part of

your online business. It is an excellent idea to advertise your Amazon items and optimize their sales. Kenshoo connects, thanks to its machine learning intelligence, with other platforms, as is the case with Amazon, to boost the performance of your business.

It uses the customer's intention signals and links them to the knowledge of the article to be able to offer them in an optimized way, providing a better and greater sales result to your business.

Strong Points or Advantages:

- There are more than 3 billion keywords managed through Kenshoo.
- They currently have over 1 million active campaigns for advertisers around the world.
- Request a "demo" or a free demo, and then, if you like it, purchase it definitively.

To do this, you only have to enter the web platform of the tool.

Seller Labs is an incredible Amazon Tool of great advertising help for your business on Amazon, with which you can dominate and control the advertising of the platform, automate your comments and those of your buyers, discover useful keywords for your articles, as well as profitable products, and also simplify your business's inventory and financial reports.

Strong Points or Advantages:

- Customer service whenever you need it, thanks

to the extensive service hours that run from Monday to Friday.

-   Wide range of experts at your disposal to solve your concerns.
-   Great help in all advertising and extra functions in the PRO version of the tool.

User Reviews:

The results obtained once you adopt Seller Labs as part of the business are impressive and evident. Such is the case of Chris C., who testifies that his online business went from having 184 comments on Amazon, to more than 600 in just four months.

Sellics is an advertising support platform aimed at Amazon sellers, whether they belong to the Amazon Seller or Amazon Vendor program or Amazon suppliers. With Sellics, you will be able to increase the organic web traffic of your business, automate advertising campaigns and, as if that were not enough, track your earnings.

But that is just a small sample of all the benefits that Sellics will bring to your online business.

Strong Points or Advantages:

-   Possibility of using a personalized plan for your type of business, being able to choose between the Amazon Seller or Amazon Vendor options.
-   Start with a 14-day free trial, then take it upon yourself to purchase the tool.

User Reviews:

Good opinions about this incredible tool abound. So much so that it currently has the approval and satisfaction of 93% of its customers. Generating up to 42% of an increase in the income of users who have joined the Sellics experience. The multiple testimonies that you can find on the platform of the tool show it.

PPC Scope is one of the tools or Amazon Tools that are leaders in terms of advertising support; With it, you can increase the number and volume of your sales, without the need to increase your budget.

With PPC Scope, you will be able to identify the keywords and those that have worse performance easily, so you can focus on making the performance of your online business as high as possible. You will be able to see those terms used by clients when searching, and also, have a global and up-to-date view of the results of your advertising campaigns.

Strong Points or Advantages:

- Free trial of up to 21 days, in which you can find out if the tool is truly useful for your business.
- Higher profits for less effort, PPC Scope takes care of making the task easy, so you won't have to spend hours preparing your business advertising.
- You do not need a credit card to use the free trial.

If you want to be part of the great book of happy and satisfied users of PPC Scope, you only have to access its website and acquire the tool that will change the sales volume of your business right now.

CHAPTER 5

PREPARATION OF THE PRODUCT FOR SALE

Once you have read the Amazon Seller Agreement and associated policies and guidelines, the next thing you need is key information to sell on Amazon successfully.

New Amazon sellers often have experience with other selling services and sometimes assume that they all work the same way. They think that it is not necessary to pay too much attention to the details of the seller agreement or the policies and guidelines of the program. So sometimes there are people saying, "I didn't know I had to..."

So that you do not find yourself in that situation, here are some of the aspects that new sellers tend to overlook.

Things you need to know

- You create a special seller account for your company by registering as a salesperson on Amazon.
- Important: Managing and maintaining multiple seller accounts is prohibited.
- You can build customer trust by offering clear and detailed information about your sales policies.
- Please note that your return policy should be at least as advantageous to customers as Amazon's.

Things you have to do

- Type the name you want to show up on Amazon to remind consumers of you or your company.
- Make sure that your contact information or that of your company is up-to-date (email address and telephone number, if you have one) so that you can be contacted if necessary.
- Keep your credit card information and bank details updated to make payments and disbursements.
- Publish your shipping and return conditions to build customer confidence.
- Describe the message and gift wrapping services you offer.
- Upload your store logo to your seller account - the logo image must be exactly 120 x 30 pixels.
- Enter only specific company information about how you manage your business on Amazon.
- Set the delivery prices, and consumers are familiar with the shipping costs that relate to your goods.

Things you have to avoid

- Registering multiple seller accounts.
- Including the URL of your website or third-party websites in product files, in your company name, or other company information.

PUBLISH PRODUCTS

Things you need to know

- Publishing products in the right categories and with the right information is essential to keep customers happy and for stronger seller results.
- All your listings must comply with the standards described in the publication guidelines of the corresponding product category.
- Amazon customers expect their products to be properly packaged and to arrive on time.
- The product information sites are not part of a single retailer.
- Set your shipping rates, sales prices, and promotions in Seller Central; do not include this information in the product details.
- Your deal with Amazon sellers specifies that the price at which you post a product on Amazon, as well as the other terms of the bid, be the same or greater than that you provide on other e-commerce platforms for the same product.

Things you have to do

Product Titles

- It provides information only about the specific product.
- Be brief, but include the key information.
- Titles cannot exceed 100 characters.

- The title should begin with the brand of the product (if applicable), not the name of the seller.
- Include model number, if available.
- Use only plain text (do not use HTML format).
- Pay attention to capital letters and use them correctly.
- Use figures ("2" instead of "two").

Images

- You must show only the product that is for sale, without accessories. In other words, the image must show what the client is going to receive.
- Use a pure white background (RGB values 255,255,255).
- Provide images with a minimum of 1,000 x 500 pixels.
- The product must occupy at least 85% of the image area.
- The format of the images must be JPEG (.jpg), TIFF (.tif) or PNG (.png). JPEG format is preferred.
- Use professional photos.

Things you have to avoid

Product Titles

- Promotional information or any other information that does not describe the product itself (e.g., "x% discount," advertising messages, URL of your website, name of the seller in the title).

- Classifying your product in a category that does not correspond to it according to Amazon's navigation structure.
- Including HTML code.
- WRITING ALL IN CAPITAL LETTERS.
- Including symbols (! * $?).

Images

- Showing accessories or decorations that are not sold with the product.
- Photographs for the main image showing scenes from everyday life, for example, with people using the product.
- A single image showing multiple colors or views of the product.
- Color backgrounds.
- Graphics, illustrations and animated images are not allowed.
- They should not have borders, watermarks, text, URLs, or include the seller's name or logo.
- Nudes.
- Mannequins.
- Drawings or artistic representations instead of photographs.

CUSTOMER ORDERS

Things you need to know

When you set up your seller account, you will be informed about the shipping expectations that you will have to integrate into your order management and shipping process. You will also be asked to confirm the shipment of each order to Amazon so that they can charge the customer and keep them informed of the status of their order.

To get the invoice, you must confirm to Amazon that you have already shipped the order. When doing so, they will also send the shipping confirmation email to the customer, informing them of the expected delivery date.

Book, Music, Video, and DVD orders must be shipped within two business days. The rest of the products must be sent on the date you have specified.

Things you have to do

- Review your default shipping settings and customize it to suit your logistics management model.
- Check your seller account at least once a day to see if you have new orders.
- Use the order reports to track your orders and all the information about them.

Things you have to avoid

- Including advertising material in the product packaging.
- Trusting only notification emails—emails can be lost or deleted.

CUSTOMER SERVICE

Things you need to know

Amazon's return policy allows for the return of new

and unopened products within 30 days of delivery, with the right to a full refund. It is mandatory to accept returns and issue a refund to the customer by Amazon's return policy.

Amazon will send all order and shipping confirmation emails to customers; you do not need to send any. This is to avoid conflicting messages that may confuse the customer. Note that shopping on Amazon needs less consumer contact than other providers because Amazon handles a large portion of the correspondence.

You are not permitted to present customers with direct mail, or to divert them in any way from the Amazon buying and selling process, including through permitted communications, such as responses to their questions about your products or their orders.

Things you have to do

- Manage all orders within the promised preparation and shipping time, and ship exactly the published products for sale.
- Clarify the procedures and processes for delivering, returns, and refunding and all other related details.
- Do not send customers more messages than necessary to manage their orders and provide the corresponding customer service.
- Quickly respond to customer questions about the status of their orders.
- Don't forget that customers expect the same quality from Amazon that sells when it comes

to customer service. You may have to negotiate with unsatisfied consumers if you don't follow the standard.

- Be courteous and be polite with clients as they request documents, returns, or refunds.

Things you have to avoid

- Bribing customers to send positive feedback.
- Using customer communications for commercial purposes or directing customers to your website or third-party websites in your emails.

Branding On Amazon

One platform, dozens of marketing possibilities. Since its launch in 2000, the Amazon marketplace has been driving meters. In 2016, Amazon represented more than two million sellers worldwide, 10,000 in France, and tens of millions of potential buyers. In France, out of 90 billion euros spent on the Internet in 2018, 6.6 billion were spent on Amazon compared to 5.6 billion in 2017 (Kantar). The "marketplace" represents 49% of purchases on Amazon.fr and contributed to 80% of its growth last year, reminded Frederic Valette, director of fashion & retail insights from Kantar departments. However, while Amazon is already the leader in France, far ahead of its main competitor Cdiscount, the share of e-commerce in France is still limited (it should reach 10% this year).

Initially, it's a simple way to make extra money on the marketplace—buy a generic product and sell it under your brand. But what is the catch? Even an easy idea has its drawbacks when it is not executed correctly. Let's look at the common pitfalls.

1. Not conducting in-depth product research

Product research is the first trap that online sellers make when trying to become a private label on Amazon. Either by choosing the product themselves or by deciding whether it will make a profit or not.

First, by choosing the wrong product category, sellers can make a big mistake. This is where online sellers get into trouble and fall into common product categories like clothes, children's toys, food... It doesn't mean that you will fail if you choose one of these categories. But they are particularly challenging to promote compared to the competition.

Once you have carefully studied the product category chosen, you should purchase the product.

Here are the fees that new sellers sometimes forget to consider:

- Original packaging cost and product weight.
- Shipping to Amazon Shipping Center.
- Marketing costs like promotional gifts or PPC (pay-per-click) which make final margins much smaller than expected.

In the end, if you are looking for product data and information, combined with your business understanding, you will be able to make an informed decision on the best products to choose from as private labels.

2. A weak product listing and no customer reviews

We all know that it is easy to be skeptical of a product when the product page is not up to par. If you're a regular Amazon buyer, you're probably well aware of imperfect product lists, with incredible images, unsuitable titles, or misleading descriptions. This can be exacerbated by a lack of product advice, which challenges reliability to your customers. While many online sellers can undervalue this, Shopify data shows how nine out of ten consumers read about ten reviews before they form an opinion about a business.

Here's how to improve your product page performance:

The listing: think about what your potential customers can look for to find the type of product you are selling. With that in mind, design a long list of keywords to target to get more views on your product page. Make sure your title, image, and description present your product in the best possible way.

Opinion: Positive opinions are essential when it comes to trusting your brand, especially if it is a private label. The beginning will always be the most difficult moment. Still, once you have implemented an effective strategy with more and more opinions from your customers, new customers will be able to trust you more.

3. Choosing the Shipping Type and Inventory Problems

It's easy to research mediocre products that can

capsize your private label in the first place. This leads to terrible long-term decisions, such as believing that Fulfillment by Merchant (FBM) is a cheaper and easier option compared to FBA (shipped by Amazon). As an online seller, you save a lot of time bypassing this responsibility on to Amazon. You can ship your inventory to any of the FBA warehouses, and Amazon will store, choose, package, and ship all of the orders you receive to consumers. Whether you choose FBM or FBA, be sure to buy enough inventory for each lot. If your online business can afford it, plan to buy 500 to 1000 units first.

4. Not collecting sales taxes

When you sell on Amazon, you are working on your account. This means that you must fill in your tax information in the "tax settings" in your central Seller, in the same way as if you are an online seller using the FBA service. Often, new sellers forget that even if they ship part of their inventory to an Amazon shipping center, if Amazon ships to a different country, the taxes will be higher. Online sellers who ignore this point are left with tax surprises at the end of the year.

Can private labels be successful on Amazon?

To be successful on Amazon with private labels, you have to think outside the box and be persistent, even if you don't see the profits right away. Whether you've already experienced one of the above points or are new to the matter, beware of these traps and get ready from the start!

Advertising on Amazon

Who has never visited the Amazon site? An essential electronic commerce platform is, however, often neglected in favor of better-known advertising interfaces such as Google Ads and Facebook Ads. However, Amazon Advertising is destined to become an increasingly important player, deserving of being included in the web marketing strategies of companies wishing to increase their notoriety and especially their sales. Little documentation exists, which helps to make advertisements on Amazon, so here are five tips to start your campaigns on the advertising platform of the giant e-commerce.

1. Understand How Ads On Amazon Work

Advertising on Amazon is similar to the way Google Ads works: you set a budget for your campaigns and only pay when someone clicks on your advertisements. These are distinguished from the non-advertising content of Amazon pages by the mention "sponsored."

THE "SPONSORED PRODUCTS"

The first type of ad is called "sponsored products." These ads work by keywords. They appear on product sites and in search results (at the top and while scrolling on the page). A click on this advertising content leads to the product page highlighted.

"Sponsored Brands"

The second type of advertisement corresponds to "sponsored brands." This is content appearing mainly in search results, which, when clicked, can lead to different destinations, such as a product page or a store. It functions for keywords and is recommended for approaches on exposure.

A quest for "critical oil diffuser," for example, can show several advertisements for marks.

" Product Display Ads "

The second type of ad is called "display product advertising." These are banners displayed on the entire Amazon network, whether on the pages of its site, those of partner sites, or the devices in their product range.

" Video Ads "

The last type of ad applies to video content. Amazon recommends using them in addition to campaigns on the Display network, to ensure an even stronger presence and thus improve the notoriety of a brand name.

2. Use Your Account To Make Amazon Advertisements

Now that formats have no secrets for you, it's time to find out how to advertise on Amazon. And for that, go for Amazon Advertising. It is at this stage that things start to get complicated. The Canada website, on the one hand, is only available in English and, on the other hand, the choices differ based on the sort of advertising you choose to make.

Create Sponsored Ads

Supported advertisements include two of the four above ad types: supported goods and sponsored signs. You will either have an account (Seller Central, Vendor Central, or Vendor Agent) to move to the next level or build one.

If you haven't set anything up yet, Amazon has two options for getting a Seller Central account. If your product catalog is less than 20 items, the "Individual sales program" formula will only incur costs on your sales ($1.49 per sale + additional costs). If it is cheaper, you will need to apply to a premium account at $29.99 a month, and each transaction will also entail additional costs.

Display Or Video Ads

For advertisements on these types of placements on Amazon, it is important to go via Amazon DSP (formerly called the Amazon Advertising Platform), a portal built primarily to connect marketers to pages belonging to Amazon, for its allies.

But these campaigns can't be launched without the help of an Amazon advertisement contractor. In this scenario, the first move is to have a direct touch with them.

3. Build Your Amazon Advertising Campaign Well

It's time to bring your Online marketing campaign to life until you are linked to the site. But before going headlong, it is always good to remember some good practices by (re)discovering how to create a PPC campaign, because, in order not to waste time and money, you have to build your account in a structured way.

Prepare The Structure Of Your Amazon Advertising Account

If you've ever run Google Ads campaigns, this will help you understand how to do Amazon ads. If you have never done it but are interested, you can count on our expertise on the subject. The best is to have a clear idea of your product categories and create a campaign for each one. Next, think about the product families that make up these categories, as this will give you the ad groups, which will themselves be composed of your keywords.

For example, imagine that you are selling wellness products and want to highlight several of your categories. You will create a campaign whose ad groups would be: "diffuser," "essential oil," "aromatherapy," etc.

Choose Keywords And Make Them Even More Relevant

The list of keywords is very important since it is your choices that will determine when your ads will be displayed and thus direct your expenses since you will pay for each click on one of them.

We advise you to stay concise in your lists (up to 30 keywords). If you're teeming with ideas when advertising on Amazon, chances are you can still split your ad group into several groups. Consider this action, but don't waste it!

Also, it can be interesting to choose keywords corresponding to the names of your competitors and their products. The cost per click is still fairly low, which helps you to gain exposure from Web consumers who know less about your brand than your rivals do.

Finally, to ensure that you don't excessively spend too much time at the start, choose those keyword matches (exact and speech in this case) and try to avoid words that are frequently associated with your goods but not applicable to you. This move is very critical, sometimes ignored, to get more eligible clicks and thus optimize your return on investment.

4- Work On The Content And Monitor Performance

Once your advertising account is well structured, it's time to tackle the content so that you can finally publish your campaigns.

Make Amazon Ads With Engaging Content

The style of Amazon ads is distinct from that of Google Advertising, so it is helpful to learn how to create a successful text or video ad on it. You can follow the same precepts by modifying them, from the title of the offer to the quality of the landing page, which must be reasonably persuasive and informative to contribute to the order.

The object of your advertising is, of course, to draw

attention and get clicks. For the same, there is something on Amazon. How many times did you visit a web page when you clicked on a link without even knowing if it suited what you were searching for? To avoid this, it is necessary to put as much information as possible in the titles.

Let's take the example cited earlier with your wellness shop. Suppose you have bottle commercials for natural oils. A customer would want to know from the title what kind of essential oil it is, whether the commodity is priced by unit or by the ton, the power, etc. That refers to all the sheets of your company, whether you sponsor them or not.

Follow The Results Of Advertising Actions

Monitoring the success of your campaigns from the outset is important for understanding how the consumer responds and being able to change the situation. Do not hesitate to test several things, because this is how you will find out what works best. When you advertise on Amazon, the interface also recommends doing five campaigns in the first weeks of launch, but that, of course, depends on your product catalog and your budget.

As previously recommended, continue to exclude irrelevant keywords that you find in the search terms of Internet users. You can download reports to check them to have a maximum of qualified clicks and reduce your unnecessary expenses.

Also, if you haven't already done so, be sure to check

out what the competition is doing. Change your bids, track your costs per button, review your outcomes, in short, control your campaigns, and, most importantly, don't abandon them. At least two or three days a week, you can review your account and make sure everything's perfect.

5. Do Not Forget To Make Amazon Advertisements Specific To Seasonality

One of the great strengths of Amazon is its popularity during holiday periods or for the highlights of the year, which are synonymous with discounts. Neglecting these dates is possibly drawing a line under the largest share of your turnover.

Prepare your projects long in advance (the site allows you to prepare up to 4 months in advance) so that it's all set for both early buyers and last-minute buyers. The ideal is, of course, to have different advertising content, which adapts to purchasing behavior and the conversion funnel.

Initiating a sense of urgency is a common practice, as it is generally successful. Do not hesitate to put forward discounts or limited-time offers when you advertise on Amazon, especially since the site is specially dedicated to direct purchases.

At the same time, while some of your products may sell very well throughout the year, perhaps for other products, it would be wise to campaign for a limited number of weeks.

To summarize, to start your campaigns well, you must

first understand the possibilities that Amazon Advertising offers to be able to create a well-organized account and obtain qualified clicks to maximize your performance through regular management and capitalization on the highlights of the year.

5 Biggest Mistakes When Selling On Amazon

You take a chance when you choose to become a vendor on the Amazon website. The slightest mistake could cost you precious time and money, or even worse. A mistake could endanger your business before it starts. The world of Amazon can be confusing, but by arming yourself with lots of information, you can maximize your chances of success. So if you're a new Amazon FBA seller, you're in luck. Here's a list of the top 5 mistakes to avoid.

1. Sell a product at too low a price.

When you start selling on Amazon, it is normal to start low. For you, this is a new activity, and inexperience may cause you to lose money. But you should avoid selling products whose price is less than 10 €. Even if you think you can make a small margin. There are two reasons for this:

Fixed costs will absorb your margin. By fixed costs is meant your monthly subscription to Amazon, the fees of your accountant, etc.

On the other hand, if you are an FBA seller and if your product has a sale price below 25 €, it will not be eligible for free delivery by Amazon under the Prime subscription. This could put off many potential buyers.

You are going to have to preferably search for a product with a sale price between 20 and 50 euros. So why the price between 20 and 50 euros?

Below that, it will be difficult for you to make a margin.

Above that, your initial investment may be too large for a first experience. Also, for a purchase of more than 50 euros, customers will prefer to think it over, talk about it with their spouse and will be less inclined to make an impulse purchase.

2. Make a profit margin

Many sellers are losing money on Amazon. Over 90% of Amazon sellers fail in their first year. You should not forget that selling on Amazon is not as simple as buying products in China and reselling them on Amazon.

There are also costs to be expected. Whatever product you sell, you need to make sure you can sell it on Amazon for a profit.

This means that your income per item must be higher than the total cost, such as samples, product cost, shipping costs, storage, packaging, Amazon fees, PPC ads. This is called the margin. You will need to consider these many costs before you get started. You have to think about your margin when negotiating with your supplier. You also need to think about your margin before setting your selling price.

When you sell your products on Amazon, keep in mind that all the basic fees and costs of the products must be covered. Ideally, the product you have chosen should allow you to benefit from a margin rate of at least 30 to 35%. This margin rate is not fixed: it is a starting margin rate, which you can improve over time. When selling on Amazon, your profit margins are an essential variable to your success. Without margins, your business will not survive, and there is no point in engaging in a fight lost in advance. Just because you have products to sell doesn't mean you have to sell them at a loss to compete with your competitors. Otherwise, you will go straight to disaster. Profit is paramount in business. Remember to integrate the manufacturing costs, shipping, storage, and sales. Closely monitor your profit margins to achieve success finally.

3. Choose a saturated niche

The most common mistake of an Amazon seller is not to do a thorough study of the product before getting started. You may be tempted to choose a product that sells a lot without trying to analyze the market. You must know the number of competitors. Competition is a good thing. This usually means there is demand, and there is money to be made. But when you start from scratch, it will be difficult for you to compete with other sellers who already have several years of experience, with a large number of comments and a low BSR. Some product niches on Amazon are saturated with competition, and it will be very difficult for a new seller to tell the difference. There are many opportunities on Amazon to launch products that have high demand, without there being hundreds of competitors already. So if you have to choose between 2 different products to sell on Amazon and one has 10,000 competitors, and the other has only 50, you will have to choose the one with only 50 competitors, even if the demand is slightly lower. You should always choose a product that sells a lot but with little competition. For example, you can use the tool called CEREBRO supplied by HELIUM 10. You enter the ASIN number of the product of one of your competitors. And the application displays a note, "the CEREBRO IQ Score," based on the HELIUM 10 algorithm, which analyzes the level of competition. The higher the score, the easier the competition will be.

4. A non-optimized product listing

The customer who will consult your listing will buy the product based on the information you will provide. The person who will be viewing your listing may never have seen your item in-store. Photos, descriptions, and comments are elements that will allow him to take action. A badly worked page will not convert. And a page that does not convert will be sanctioned by Amazon, which will attribute a bad BSR to it. In other words, a botched listing will rank poorly in an Amazon customer's search results. Amazon, in its algorithm, will take the number of comments. Unfortunately, when you launch your product, you will leave with 0 comments. But Amazon, fortunately, takes other factors into account when determining its ranking. The algorithm will analyze the quality of your listing, which must be as attractive as possible. Here are the most common mistakes you should avoid to improve your ranking:

- A title that does not describe the product
- Having poor quality pixelated images
- Limited, poor quality description
- Few optimized keywords in the Frontend and Backend
- Not mentioning the benefits that the product will bring to the customer in bullet points

In practice, you can rely on a tool called SCRIBBLES of HELIUM 10. With the help of this powerful SEO tool, you will never forget to include a precious keyword in your listings. You should love the simplicity of making enticing advertising in the front and key sections of the product page. Even without comments at the launch of your product, you can improve your BSR ranking.

5. Not paying attention to customer comments and questions

Today, each customer takes note of the opinions of other buyers before making a purchase decision. If your product has no reviews or negative reviews, it is unlikely to be added to the shopping cart. In case of negative comments on the product, take the time to analyze the problem, and thank the customer for the help he gives you with his review. Try to find an amicable solution so that he revises his comment and corrects his rating upwards. Optionally, proceed to a refund of the product. Because it is estimated that it takes about 12 positive opinions to compensate for a single negative opinion. When you receive a request for information on a product, try to answer it within 24 hours. If customers do not receive a response, they may not be looking for your product. On the other hand, if you still haven't received feedback for your product, you can request it from your customers in a very professional manner. This process can be automated with the Amzcockpit auto-responder. It is a web application specially dedicated to Amazon sellers. You will be able to automatically send an email to your customers to ask their opinion. The Amzcockpit Web App is connected to your Amazon seller account. You do not need to know the email address of your customers, and emails always leave after the delivery of your product. Positive comments always reassure visitors and make them want to trust you. Please note, gifts or discounts in exchange for positive feedback are forbidden by Amazon.

HELIUM 10

The HELIUM 10 software suite currently contains a suite of 18 tools. Today it is one of the best performing applications. But HELIUM 10 is also the complete application on the market. HELIUM 10 tools are designed to save time, search for profitable products, discover profitable keywords, delete unused keywords, spy on your competitors, identify FBA refunds for damaged or lost inventory, and optimize your product list.

HELIUM 10 is quick and easy to use, whether you are a

beginner or an experienced user.

We highly recommend this app. You can make your own opinion by testing it for free.

It offers a 50% reduction coupon on the first monthly payment.

It also offers a coupon of 10% reduction for life on your subscription.

SEO Strategies To Improve Your Rankings On Amazon

Amazon has become a game-changer for e-commerce businesses. More and more customers are starting to benefit from the rising network of Amazon. Using Amazon services as one of your main platforms can give your business several benefits. However, this requires strategic planning and execution to leverage your competitors.

Amazon continues to grow rapidly

With more than 2.5 million active vendors and 310 million registered users, Amazon is currently one of the leading e-sites. Amazon hosts, on average, more than 197 million people worldwide per month, more than Russia's entire population. Furthermore, a new survey reveals that 89 percent of customers chose to shop from Amazon ahead of other e-outlets.

Convenience, reliability, and great customer service are among the reasons why Amazon is today, the most preferred online shopping location. Innovation also plays a significant part in Amazon's growth. They continue to improve and add new features useful for Amazon sellers and buyers. One of the main features to watch out for is the Amazon Best Seller (BSR) ranking, which allows customers to see the most popular items on the market. Many sellers also take advantage of Amazon BSR to promote their products and services.

Amazon's competitive market

With Amazon's growing network, it is quite surprising that only a few companies have managed to use this platform. This is due to the level of competition, as the number of sellers continues to increase as well. Also, most Amazon sellers have no idea how the algorithm works. They generally think that integrating your business with Amazon will immediately generate sales.

With an overall 8% increase in competition from last year, it's imperative to find more ways to boost your Amazon product lists and brand pages. It's true that using Amazon services will help boost sales for your company. However, that doesn't mean it'll give you immediate results. As for every other site, you need innovative marketing strategies from Amazon to outperform the competition.

Act on the marketing plans you have. To achieve trust with the target audience, consider the Amazon BSR metrics. Try other useful approaches, such as introducing SEO strategies on Amazon and improving the product list.

What is BSR for Amazon, and how to win it?

Amazon assigns each product using different catalogs

called Best Seller Rankings, formerly known as Amazon Sales Rank. Amazon BSR shows the location of your products and brands. To gain exposure, the product must generate more sales. Products with more sales will be featured at the top of Amazon's page.

Amazon also takes into account historical sales data for a specific product. It is updated every hour and classifies each element in each of their categories and subcategories.

Keep in mind that a product's BSR rate can work differently from other Amazon markets. For example, you can appear in the top 5 of a subcategory page on Amazon.com, but the lower ranking on Amazon.

The overall BSR rate on Amazon should indicate its level of sale compared to other product lists. But according to Amazon, that doesn't always show which items are selling more than similar products. That's why they created the bestseller list of categories and subcategories, which makes it more convenient for both sellers and consumers.

You can find the Amazon BSR score for the product in the Details section of the list. By default, Amazon offers some of the most popular subcategories for higher ranking items associated with other products in this subcategory.

Other popular ways to make your product pages more available on Amazon:

As noted, Amazon calculates the best seller ranking based on recent sales and historical sales data. Note that Amazon's algorithm for the top seller list does not include product reviews, seller reviews, prices, and keywords when calculating the BSR. However, these factors can give your products and brand pages more credibility with consumers and generate more leads.

Although the Amazon BSR weighs heavily on sales, optimizing your Amazon product lists remains an ideal option. The most successful companies use this platform, the strategies of Amazon SEO and the campaigns of Amazon PPC to promote their brand and increase their sales.

Here are some of the most powerful ways to customize the Amazon Product Lists and send you more ideas:

Understand the use of relevant keywords

Amazon's search algorithms are not that different from popular search engines, such as Google, Yahoo, or Bing. Performing thorough keyword research is essential for determining the primary and secondary keywords to use for your Amazon marketing campaigns. Just like optimizing a website through SEO practices, relevance, and search volumes are key factors to consider.

Following the same principles, you have to be careful with keyword stuffing. Focus on readability and content optimized for conversion. Always check Amazon's keyword guidelines and search terms to make sure your optimization strategies are well defined.

Optimizing the title and description of the product

This is one of the reasons why many Amazon sellers find it difficult to compete with their competitors. According to research, 90% of product lists do not meet Amazon requirements. Many companies overlook the importance of optimizing product titles and descriptions.

Like Google, Amazon performs regular updates with its algorithms. Simple details, such as using character limits for titles and product descriptions, can have a significant impact on Amazon's search results.

Here are some things to consider when creating product titles:

- **Make descriptive titles**

Amazon users prefer this platform because it is fast and convenient. If they can't understand your products at first glance, you are losing valuable leads. Be creative with your product titles. Use the 200 character limit from Amazon. Provide concise titles to provide an understanding of the product to your audience without clicking on the page.

- **Incorporate keywords**

Please use important keywords in the Brand names. Try to use the keywords at the beginning of your title. This makes sure that your product page is indexed for particular keywords. Again, avoid keyword stuffing for better search results.

- **Focus on user intent**

This applies to titles and product descriptions. Consider your audience when creating the content. Put yourself in their shoes. Do you find the information useful? Will the title give you an indication of the goods you are selling? Simple details like this can help improve your product lists.

- **Follow best practices**

Always follow best practices or the recommended format when creating Amazon product titles. Here are a few:

- Capitalize the first letter of the main words.
- Provide the exact details (size, volume, color, measurements, etc.).
- Use numbers for numbers.
- Avoid using an ampersand.

For product descriptions, use bullets to separate and highlight the main features of the products. Avoid lint when providing details and try to incorporate some of the keywords.

Optimizing product images

The images on your product list speak volumes about your business. This is one of the most important factors that Amazon users take into account when shopping online. Use bright, clear, high-quality photos to optimize the zoom function. Take photos using different angles synchronized with Amazon's A9 algorithms. The recommended image must be at least

1280 pixels side. If possible, provide ultra-HD 2560 pixel images on the longest side.

Get customer feedback

Customer reviews are essential to your Amazon business. In general, sellers get reviews based on product quality and customer service. There are other ways to increase the number of reviews. The use of package inserts, for example, may encourage customers to give feedback on your products and services.

Be proactive in maintaining a high product evaluation score. Respond to comments, even negative comments. Be professional and find ways to solve their problems. This reflects good customer service and could persuade the customer to make changes or remove bad reviews.

Conclusions

In general, the best way to improve your Amazon BSR is to increase your sales. This should not, however, limit your strategies and goals. Focus on other actionable elements, such as improving the visibility of your brand pages and product listings in Amazon search results. Take the time to understand Amazon's metrics. Improve your product list with ethical optimization guidelines. Explore different Amazon SEO approaches. Do your research and contact Amazon marketing professionals for expert help.

CHAPTER 6

THE BEST STRATEGIES TO MAXIMIZE YOUR PROFIT
ON AMAZON IN 2021

Method To Analyze The Market

To investigate a market is to carry out a process of analysis of the environment of the company to obtain the necessary information for the establishment of the corresponding commercial strategies.

The reasons why market research may be carried out is to find business opportunities, learn about the viability of a product or service, and solve problems, among other aspects.

Below are the steps to follow to know how to analyze a market:

One of the first steps to develop is knowing why market research is being carried out, and what it is intended to achieve. The needs and objectives of the organization must be analyzed.

Another important issue is to identify the information you want to collect, where it should be based on a research objective.

The determination of the sources of information will be determined once it is known what the information to be collected will be. It may come from the target audience, from the company's customers, from research carried out, from past data, or from publications, among other sources.

Define and propose how the collection techniques will be. This process will be completed with the determination of what the information will be and where the sources will come from. The techniques, methods, or ways of collecting the information can be:

Observation techniques:

It is the observation of people, facts, objects, actions, situations, among other elements, by visiting the places consumers frequent, where their behavior will be observed.

Experimentation:

It is about knowing the response of consumers to a certain product, service, or idea directly.

Focus Group:

It consists of gathering a group of people to interview them and generate a debate about a product or service, to know their opinion about it.

The survey:

It is a simple and economic methodology where oral, simple, and objective questions are asked to obtain the same type of answers.

Then will come the process of collecting the information, where who will be in charge of carrying it out will be determined, as well as when it will start and what its duration will be.

The next step is the analysis of the information, where

they will try to interpret and draw their conclusions in this regard.

Decision making and strategy design will be the endpoint after knowing how to analyze a market.

How To Know The Needs Of Your Clients Better Than Them

Sometimes consumers trust their emotions, others listen to the facts, and then a mix of both. They read honest and false reviews. First, they want this, then they want that, while what is useful to them may be something different.

Making sense of all this and identifying the customer's true needs and expectations is a difficult task.

Needs ≠ Desires ≠ Expectations

Two people walk into your corner store, and you hear one say to the other, "I'm hungry! I'm going to buy Mars." It is clear that this client needs to fill the void in his stomach, but also that he has a conflicting yearning: his cravings for a chocolate bar.

You know that the sugary bar is not the best option against hunger. What you need rather is a wholemeal sandwich. But it would be haughty, and perhaps even conceited, to tell him that his solution is not a good one. Who says that Mars does not give you more satisfaction?

Desires and needs are not the same things. This can be quite confusing for companies about best practices in such situations. These are two different motivations for the client, and differentiating them is essential.

A definition of need suggested by Jorge Baba from Game-Changer is "something that solves a real or imaginary problem."

A wish is simply something we would like to have for whatever reason, be it rational or irrational.

The expectations are anticipated circumstances of a purchase. They involve all the consumer process phases, all the client experiences, as well as the purchasing and experience impact, the realistic advantages, and the emotions. Customers value a company's performance for their ability to meet their expectations.

The client often wants a more powerful motivator than they need. This manifests itself when you listen to your customer after asking why they want what they want. Usually, he has a burning desire to get what he wants, and he just wants you to show him how to achieve it.

Jorge Baba, Game-Changer

Needs, wants and expectations are key motivations that drive your customers, and ultimately, anyone.

1. Get conversation info

Conversations in customer service serve as research on customer needs and expectations.

Your customer service and support department are the points of entry for consumers who find it difficult to identify the product they want, don't know what product they need or want or don't want to search for it.

Listen, ask, make a difference. To discover customer motivations, your first step is to listen carefully. This boils down to differentiating and asking the right questions.

This is critical since many clients themselves do not know the difference. Another might say, "I need a new laptop," and one would say, "I want a new laptop." For you, this difference could suggest a different strategy or approach to better help each of them. For them, it may just turn out to be a semantic issue. With the help of the following questions, you will be able to understand what they refer to.

Many clients know what they want or need, but have trouble expressing it on their own. It may be that they don't have the vocabulary to articulate their feelings, or because they're confused in the goods or services jargon. In the above case, consider eliminating obstacles by the introduction of a more compassionate vocabulary in both regions.

An unidentified killer of positive customer experience? Speak specialized jargon to your clients instead of using simple and direct language.

Micah Solomon, Forbes

Not all clients, either for themselves or for service personnel, are specific about what they want and need.

"What would you like to get from the product?"

An attitude that reflects on the actual value the consumer is looking for. It is designed to pick the product offerings that have the features that give said value. When the consumer does not need a product but wants one (remember the difference), the product's profit is more theoretical and not concrete—such as its recent nature, its style, or its pattern.

"What is the matter you want to resolve?"

A similar question, but through an indirect approach, the focus is initially on the problem that the client has. It works particularly well when customers only have a vague idea of what they need but are aware that something is wrong. The ability to fix the problem is the benefit of the product, and this is what the customer is looking for.

"How much are you willing to pay?"

Money is an important factor for almost all customers, but it can be difficult for them to recognize a good or bad price for value in a given product area. For example, prices may vary for software offered through subscription, and the value of its features is difficult to list. Get ready to follow up with comparison pages and itemized price breakdown.

Tony Allesandra has posted a list of 23 questions on HubSpot to ask consumers to help them, and you learn what they want and what they need. Both work in direct contact with the client and with feedback surveys designed in a B2B context.

2. Categorize feedback

It's worth making an effort and reaching out to your

customers for suggestions and feedback. This will help you identify patterns and make assumptions about the probability that they will behave in a certain way or contact you in a specific way.

Although this is a continuous process, also think of it as a step before communicating with the client, as it will give you an idea of how to start direct contact with your "average" client.

Gregory Ciotti from Help Scout made a list of 7 categories to organize your clients' suggestions and comments:

- Email and contact formats for clients
- Customer satisfaction surveys
- Usability testing
- Exploratory customer interviews (this coincides with the previous point of direct customer contact)
- Social listening (with voting on social networks)
- Field activities
- Space for comments

These feedback channels will likely be used by your clients orally or in writing. The evaluation of said information is subject to subjective biases, and to obtain reliable conclusions, it is necessary to collect and categorize the contributions.

Ciotti suggests using apps like Campfire and Trello to make organizing such feedback a project for the entire team. Putting data from various sources into collective tools will tell the story of your customers and give the opinions of your base customers. Eventually, it will also show their needs and expectations.

3. Obtain information from customer statistics

You know you did something right when you kept a customer active and brought him back for a certain period. Therefore, the metrics that describe retention, loyalty, and satisfaction also inform you if you have satisfied the needs and expectations of your customers.

It is easier to get more of this type of metric, and unlike the qualitative information provided by customers, you will get numbers that speak for themselves. You can track the trends found through them and be sure that strong figures back them. These are the ones that will immediately provide you with digits:

- Customer Satisfaction Index (CSAT)
- Net Promoter Score (NPS) recommendation index
- Customer Effort Index (CES)
- Things Gone Wrong (TGW) failure rate
- Social media monitoring with tracking tools

4. Gain an understanding of the community

One of the best things about social media is the freedom of expression; it makes people feel. They may dramatize and glorify unique experiences with a company to be heard by a wider audience, or out of sheer emotionality. Their motivation leads them to talk about what moves them. This means that if they do, it is relevant to them, and also to you.

Obviously, Facebook and Twitter are platforms that must be tracked, but it is also worth looking at Quora, Yelp, TripAdvisor, and Reddit, among others, this depends on your industry.

Here are some useful tools to monitor and evaluate which ones are interesting for you and your social networks:

- **Google Alerts.** This alert service from Google notifies you when your brand appears in an important position.
- **Mention.** A powerful freemium tool that alerts you when your brand is mentioned on the net. It is very practical to track social media, something that Google Alerts does not do.
- **Social mention.** A free tool that analyzes the social mentions of your brand on the internet. Among others, it shows the probabilities that your brand will be discussed online, the proportion of positive and negative mentions, the probability that people repeatedly mention your brand and the range of influence.

Also, consider a feature request page where users can vote on issues and requests. It will give you specific opinions and wishes of people acting in their interest, but they often know your product quite well.

Request management systems like Receptive will help you draw the right conclusions.

If I had asked people what they needed, they would have told me a faster horse.

Henry Ford

The Ford quote says a lot about innovation but also customer needs and expectations. Sometimes the client does not have the necessary information or the right mindset to request the best possible product, and even, in this case, the desire to be respected and considered is still present.

Ford took the bold path by replacing horses with horsepower, but he also paid tribute to his clients' desire for approval and consent. He understood that they need to be assured that what they want is the right choice. And in the end, the first carriages had a great similarity to horse carriages.

With a mix of flexibility, respect, experience, and the right information, you will understand how to make your customers happy in the long term, or at least during a fleeting encounter.

How To Recognize A Profitable Niche On Amazon

There are tons of niches you can attack within Amazon, but not all of them suit you. Here is a method you can use to find profitable niches. Simple and actionable for everyone. Let's dig in!

Niche Ideas

The first step is to look for ideas for niches to analyze their profitability and feasibility later.

For niches, Amazon is very simple, go to their website and browse the categories. Write down all the ideas that you are getting in a notepad, and keep in mind the following parameters.

- The categories where the commission is a minimum of 5%.
- The products that have enough and good opinions.
- The prices that are not very low.

Analysis of profitability and viability of niches

Now, do you have a notebook full of ideas for niches? Then it's time to analyze the competition in the SERPs one by one to assess whether it will be profitable to get into it or not.

Potential organic traffic

The first thing you have to look at is that the niche has the potential to capture enough traffic to generate a good income. To do this, simply Google "best #product_name," take the first three URLs, go through Ahrefs and look at the "Organic Traffic" metric.

Organic Traffic is a metric of Ahrefs trying to calculate the monthly organic traffic from the domain. It is usually far from reality, but it is usually enough for us to estimate an approximate amount of organic traffic that a domain can generate.

One very important thing to keep in mind: if the domain to be analyzed is a generic website that, apart from this niche, attacks others, only pass the URL with which it is ranking the niche that we want to investigate. If it is a website focused on that niche, use the entire domain. Why? For two reasons:

If you analyze the organic traffic of the entire domain

of the generic web, you will get a very high figure and not at all representative of the potential of the niche to be analyzed, since being a generic website, you will be analyzing many niches at the same time.

If it is a website focused on the niche, if you decide to get into it, you will probably create something quite similar, so by analyzing the domain completely, you will have an approximate idea of the total traffic you can generate.

Another thing you have to consider in combination with organic traffic is the price of the product. The smaller this is, the more traffic you will need. Unless the price of the product is very high, if the Organic Traffic of the competition is less than 2K, I would not get involved.

Resources needed by the competition

You already have a niche where the competition is attracting a good amount of organic traffic, and also, the product has a good price, perfect.

But now you have the most important step, estimating how many resources the websites above have needed to get there to determine if it is worth getting into. It depends on what type of website you are going to analyze; the way to proceed is different.

Specialized websites

Your direct competition and the mirror you have to look at. The first thing you should do is check the amount of content they have published, it does not need to be exact, but you can determine if it is a lot or a little. I do it by checking the indexed URLs with the site: URL command and taking a look at the number of words in the main articles.

The second thing you have to look at is the number of incoming domains the domain has and the quality of them, again using Ahrefs.

Based on these data, you can already get an idea of what it will cost you to attain the position. And based on your available resources, you will have to decide whether it can be profitable or not.

The less content, incoming domains, and more Organic Traffic, the better it looks to get into a niche.

Generic websites

There are hundreds of generic websites created by SEOs that attack all the Amazon nodes literally, without scruples. To analyze the resources that you are going to need to overcome this type of website, look at the quality of the content in question, the trend of the domain, and the incoming domains it has with the URL that is ranking above.

These websites usually have a lot of authority and content. But they are not your direct competition.

If you find SERPs plagued by these websites (very common) but no specialized website, it is a good sign. Generics usually have a disadvantage compared to a specialized website for their keywords in question.

Niche Analysis Example

So far this has been the theory (which I hope has not been boring), now here's how to analyze two possible live niches, to consolidate the acquired knowledge.

Niche example 1: Express pots

The first thing to do is google "best express pots" and take a look at the SERPs and find the following:

Position 1

- Analysis URL: https://10mejores.top/olla-rapida/
- Traffic Organic: 2.3K
- Incoming domains: 0
- Content: 5000 words. Well laid out and focused on search intent

Position 2: YouTube videos

Position 3

- Analysis URL: ollaexpress.net
- Traffic Organic: 4.8K
- Incoming domains: 88
- Content: 341 indexed URLs

Taking these data into account, I can determine that the niche does not interest me at all since:

The article of 10mejores.top is, without a doubt, a tough nut to crack. It is dominating, with rich snippets included. It is a website in pure growth, and it does not look like the SEOs behind are going to stop.

That there are YouTube videos between the top1 and top2 is not good either, that takes away a lot of visibility from the top2; the poor must be receiving a few clicks. It is something that can always happen to us even after creating the niche, but if we see it first, it is certainly a negative point.

The specialized website has invested quite a few resources without very good results.

The Traffic Organic potency is too low for the price of the product in question.

Mind you, probably with a 100% vertical niche, we could sneak into top3 and even exceed 10best. But consider that there are better niches if you do a little research, hence it is not the best place to put your money.

Niche example 2: Bakers

Search for "best bakeries," and find the following:

Position 1

- Analysis URL: http://enmicasalomejor.com/mejores-panificadoras-domesticas/
- Traffic Organic: 439
- Incoming domains: 0
- Content: 2200 words

Position 2

- Analysis URL: https://mejorpanificadora.com
- Traffic Organic: 608

- Incoming domains: 14
- Content: 40 indexed URLs, long content and very focused on search intent

Position 3

- Analysis URL: http://pan
- Traffic Organic: 2.2k
- Incoming domains: 25
- Content: 24 indexed URLs, content that can be improved

I like this data much more, and I tell you why:

- Top1 is easy to beat with a specialized website; in fact, I do not think it will take time to go down to top2.
- The top2 is showing that with a good SEO job, you can dominate this niche. He has only been online for a couple of months, and with few invested resources, he has sneaked into top2. Of course, the contents are very elaborate and focused on the search intention.
- Top3 confirms that potential organic traffic is interesting. Also, unlike top2, your SEO on-page is not as elaborate, it has less content, and it has not needed many links to capture traffic. In the coming months, your organic traffic will probably drop to the benefit of the top2, which presents a better job.

Although it is not a bad niche, it is far from being top. It is simply a normal niche, which perhaps gives you € 50-100 per month investing few resources.

I think I would not get involved, as it is too small, and niches that can give you from € 300 are preferred. If you are starting out, it may not be a bad option at all, although you will stick with other SEOs.

This is a method you can use to analyze the profitability of a niche in a few minutes. You will have to analyze a lot of data until you find a good gold nugget, and something quick and actionable is what you need.

Extreme Importance of reviews

Do you know the importance of product reviews on Amazon?

If the answer is "no" or "I don't know," don't worry, in this section, we will discuss everything you need to know about how to use product reviews to improve your business within Amazon and boost your sales.

Do you know what benefits reviews provide for your business on Amazon?

Reviews are a fundamental piece for all Amazon users, both for those who sell their products on this Marketplace and for all consumers who make purchases there, since reviews play a crucial role in the decision making of users when the time to buy comes. So a good review could become that "little push" for an Amazon user to finally decide to make a purchase. However, that is not all; And if you are really smart, you can get the most out of reviews to improve your business within Amazon.

In this chapter, there are four important aspects that you could take into account to gain more reviews on your products and thus generate a positive impact for users when they are visiting your publications. Also, these tips will teach you not only how to generate good reviews for your account, but you can also use your competitor's reviews to innovate in your business.

Observe and Study your Competition

Reviewing your product reviews can help you develop good ideas for future improvements, but have you considered seeing what your biggest competitors are doing?

Applying a follow-up strategy to the reviews of your competition can help you boost the growth of your business since it will help you greatly to generate more ideas to improve the performance of your account. To consider the possibility of promoting new products now, idealize new ways to differentiate your listing from the competition.

Be in control of your ASIN

Reviews of your products are a valuable component of your overall reputation as a seller on Amazon, so it is important to monitor the reviews that you receive from all your customers periodically. It will allow you to learn what things to hold to give your clients the best shopping experience.

Tracking feedback of the product over time is a smart way to collect valuable details straight from customers. Are there any quality problems that could be solved in the manufacturing process? Do customers mention innovative uses for those products or request related products that could also be sold as a kit?

The truth is that this type of continuous improvement will differentiate your Amazon business from your competition. For this, it is important to stay in tune with the end-user experience with your product.

Determine which products you want to have in your catalog

Adding more products to your Amazon listing can help you to expand your reach within Amazon further, but it is very important to ensure that there is a real demand for the products you sell or are going to sell. Obsolete inventory costs you money and storage space, regardless of your compliance model, but it is very important if you are an FBA provider.

Between inventory performance index and monthly assessment of long-term storage rates, it's more important than ever to market your products regularly.

The more details you will find, the less bet you would have, before making a big order for a new product. Tracking the ASINs of the products you are considering stocking (or items similar to the one you are considering developing) can help you gain valuable market intelligence. Carrying out this type of research can help you better understand a new business niche before diving into a large order for a new product without knowing if it will sell as you expect.

Stay Afloat and Renew According to Trends

Constantly monitoring your product reviews will help you stay on top of market trends, possible improvements you can make to your product, and more. And it is also a very important aspect of your reputation as a seller.

Product reviews can provide essential data for the continued growth of your Amazon business. They can even provide data that can help you better manage your inventory if you are considering adding a new product to your catalog.

It is important that you take a look at your reviews from time to time, and study your competition, both the comments it receives on its products and its listing in general so that you can take action plans if you are looking to increase your sales and expand greatly, plus your reach within the huge Amazon marketplace. Renew your catalog if necessary, with the use of strategies that fit your line of business.

How To Get Tons Of Reviews

One of the most important factors that directly affect the user's purchase decision in a marketplace is product reviews and comments. In this section, you can find aspects to avoid and enhance to highlight your business against the competition.

The opinions that customers leave on an e-commerce site or a marketplace have unmatched value. And on Amazon, even more. If you have part of your business on this platform, you will have already gone through several steps: improve the position of your products in the ranking, increase their visibility and, as a consequence, increase the sales of your business.

If you are already at this level of the process, congratulations, you have achieved the most difficult. But there is still work: you have to promote an element that users take into account when choosing one product or another: valuations and opinions on Amazon.

Much of the success of this marketplace is related to the trust of its customers, both present and future, and to a large extent, they have achieved this due to their good number of opinions.

So now it's up to you: since comparators trust Amazon, if your products have good opinions, they will buy insurance. Therefore, you have to achieve optimal reviews and ratings of your products.

It is not an easy task, but neither is it impossible. You just have to follow a series of guidelines and, above all, do not stray from the main premise: your product must respond to a need and be of quality.

On many occasions, we become obsessed with the number of reviews we have on our page. You do not need to have hundreds of comments and reviews since your potential client will be worth the first 10 or 15 positive evaluations to trust your product.

Therefore, the first thing you have to do is assess whether your product is really good and meets a need. If so, reviews will come. Getting the first opinions indeed is the most difficult since there is none; the potential customer does not have any reference to help him buy.

But be patient, you will get it, and once it has started, it will have a snowball effect.

Step one: what you should never do

Before giving you a series of recommendations, let's better start with what you should not do in any case. By following this guideline, you will be closer to achieving your goal.

The first thing you should know is that it is possible to buy reviews or get false opinions. There are private Facebook groups and other series of platforms that carry out some fraudulent tactics to get users to comment on the products.

But be careful, if they are detected by Amazon (and it happens many times) your account and products will be affected, losing positioning or even being removed from your website.

In addition to avoiding the purchase of false opinions, we recommend that you follow these rules set by those responsible for the marketplace:

- You cannot offer compensation or discount for reviews.
- You cannot send review requests to anyone.
- You cannot ask anyone to modify or delete opinions.

Amazon uses an algorithm-based robotic program to

detect this type of behavior. For example, there is a maximum daily number of reviews, if any of them are not verified (that is, if it is verified that there has been no real previous purchase) or if they come from suspicious users or accounts, the platform will block your reviews, for several days nobody will be able to write opinions of your product.

And as we said previously, the next step can be the outright deletion of the account.

Tips for activating positive reviews on Amazon

Once you have seen and analyzed what you should never do, it is clear that the best option is to get true reviews that help you get the first positive reviews for your products, as well as improve and activate the current ones if you already have them.

Here is a list of the most useful recommendations you can follow:

» **Improve your services and your product as much as possible.** Review negative reviews, if any, and analyze them for improvement and to give no reason to any future customer to rewrite reviews of this type. Even if you still have time, Amazon has 60 days to modify or update a negative review if you have resolved the problem with the buyer.

» **Offer the best customer service.** This is key to get positive ratings when selling through Amazon. The marketplace itself gives a series of essential tips for you to carry out this task accurately:

- Don't just listen to your customers, you must also understand them.
- Covers each of their needs.
- Respect the current customer, do not focus only on potentials.
- Don't be afraid to apologize.

» Start with promotional products or at special prices. If you are starting out and your products are of good quality, and you do not have much margin to make big discounts, there is a tactic that usually achieves good results.

It is about creating your brand and making it known, introducing as a starting point some product of necessity and with a competitive price. If necessary, adjust it to the limit even if you do not earn any benefit. The goal is to achieve significant sales volume, and that will start to generate a lot of valuations. As soon as you have visibility, you can incorporate other products that leave you more margin.

» Use Amazon Vine. It is a service offered by Amazon through which samples of products are sent free of charge to certain users considered as top authors of reviews. They test them and write their opinion. The truth is that the marketplace does not guarantee 100% the creation of valuation, but it is a system that usually works very well, especially if the product is good.

» Request an assessment from the platform itself. You can contact the buyer directly through the Order Management page, using the option "valuation request." This is the official way to do it.

» Add a personalized note with your package. You cannot ask for a review or opinion, or offer any incentive for the buyer to leave a comment, but you can thank them for their purchase. With this gesture, the user may be more satisfied and want to help you by giving a positive evaluation.

Finding Something to boost your initial sales

Amazon is now the world's largest online marketplace and has given third-party advertisers an outstanding opportunity to make a living.

Not unexpectedly, its success among retailers continues to rise; Internet Retailer recently reported that four times more people make a million Amazon purchases relative to eBay. With $88,000 spent on the web globally every minute, here are some tips and tricks to help improve your sales, starting today.

1. Get Feedback

Customer reviews have enormous power; 88 percent of customers now claim they value both online reviews and personal recommendations.

Try thinking beyond the simple, look for media-including comments. Visual reviews or a critique of a picture of the product will do wonders. When you know people who have loved your company personally, go to them. Conduct study at a local university to find students to support you with the idea, this would cost only a small amount of money, or it could be completely free.

Around 90 percent of Amazon shoppers don't leave any feedback. Using software such as Five Comments will help raise the number of comments received and help you remove some unfavorable and derogatory comments. Amazon highlights the value of vendor success and ranks the products in the highest positions.

Should you not ask out-of-Amazon vendors to have feedback? The advantage of this is that if you receive derogatory or constructive comments from some consumers about your product, this can help you improve your company without withdrawing from your reviews. It is an especially effective tactic when you launch a new product.

2. Give it away for free

Stay with me here; though this is a bad move in the short term, this can have a large long-term effect. As described in the previous chapter, it is important to get feedback to show off your goods. So to bring them together, sell a 99 percent Discount Coupon Code to consumers (Amazon does not authorize you to give 100 percent) in return for a review. It will dramatically boost the Amazon search rating and potentially guarantee that the next time you choose an item to sell, more buyers will think of you.

One way to get rid of the obsolete inventory is to send the customers presents to create goodwill. That means they are more likely to return when they want to purchase an object in the future. Linking your Amazon Seller Central to other distribution platforms helps you find those products and handle your inventory better.

3. Improve SEO

Aside from the ranking and price of the retailer, Amazon also looks at the keywords in the product description to rate the listings. Amazon's keyword stuffing choice for a product title is very much reminiscent of the strategies that SEO companies used in the early 2000s to introduce and boost Google rankings.

You have a 500 character cap on the product description, of which you can use as many keywords as possible to guarantee that the name is noticeable. In this area, Amazon offers brand, definition, product range, type, color, size, and quantity.

I will also recommend using the Amazon Keyword App, which uses the AutoComplete feature of Amazon to identify common long-tail keywords with a score of 1-10. You can export to Google Keyword Planning Tool, where you can calculate the search volume of these keywords, those that are most appropriate for you and import them.

Amazon also offers you, divided by the product description, to insert the details in a keyword area. It's worth noting that the use of keywords you've already used in the product description is not successful, as Amazon will ignore it. Here you can insert five keywords, or keyword phrases, so use them wisely!

4. Keep competitive and win

Purchase Box: Many critics have the illusion that it's too hard to keep selling on Amazon. While 55% of its sellers record a profit margin of more than 20%.

Amazon notes that price is essential to win the buying box, along with quality, reliability, and customer service.

Repricing tools such as FeedVisor or Teikametrics tracks the costs of the rivals 24/7 to ensure that they are sustainable. Only entering because you want to be $0.01 less costly than someone else might be the deciding factor. It is a huge help as they work in real-time during the day. For example, if one of your rivals has no supply of a certain commodity, your replicator would immediately increase the price to achieve full benefit.

5. Get publicity

Whether you're just starting or looking at your company with as many eyes as possible, this makes the view of the goods under the results of the scan, in the right column, or on informative pages.

Amazon also confirmed that they are going to extend this feature and make the advertisements more noticeable early as well. Invariably they give free credit to get you going too, so it's a no-brainer!

6. Discount

Similar to #2, discounts are an effective means of attracting highly inspired consumers and creating lifelong relationships.

Daily offers and substantial discounts for your product category could carry you to #1. This also opens the door of being on the "Hot Sales" and "New & Interesting" lists on the Amazon homepage, which would produce immense traffic volumes.

This also offers relevant goods visibility and can be seen on the website. This helps buyers to show other deals at a glance and maybe entice them to buy one of the discounted products at full price.

7. Marketing outside of Amazon

While email messages and direct calls to action that alienate Amazon customers are banned, that doesn't mean you can't market customers to your Amazon shop. Post writing and blogging is a perfect way to do so because you can use WordPress to address your respective content niche for free.

Another successful way to create customer satisfaction is to add a coupon to the bottom of the packaging list. Flash sales, BOGOF, one-time deals, and free delivery are some of the reasons customers can be tempted to reorder.

Amazon coupons

Did you know that Amazon customers love promotions and discounts? Would you like to create your own promotional coupon campaign? Here's How to Create a Promotion on Amazon, everything step by step! It does not matter if you are developing the private label or arbitration model, this information will be very useful to you.

Step by step guide to create a coupon promotion for your products on Amazon:

1. The first step is to access our Seller Central account and position the cursor on the "Advertising" menu at the top of the page. From the drop-down menu, select "Promotions".

2. On the "Promotions" page, we will use the initial "Create a promotion" tab that offers five options (Free Shipping, Money Discount, Buy One and Get One, External Benefits and Give Away). For the purpose of this section, we are going to choose "Money Off".

Note: When creating a promotion, the Money Off page is divided into three sections - Conditions, Schedule and Additional Options. Let's start with the first section, Conditions.

Terms:

3. In the conditions section - "At least this quantity" indicates the quantity of products that a customer must buy in order to obtain the discount. If you simply want to offer a coupon code for a single product, choose option "1", if they are more, we must indicate the amount we have decided on.

4. Then select "Create a new product selection." This option is at the end of the line "Purchased Items." This will allow you to choose which products in your inventory you want to apply the coupon or

promotional code that you are going to create.

5. From the drop-down menu, I recommend selecting "SKU list" or "ASIN list" as they are easier to find. Now click on "Create Product Selection". At these times you can indicate to which products the discount can be applied.

6. On the "Create Product Selection" page, enter the name you want to give to the campaign product, then include an internal description and finally enter the SKU or ASIN number of the product to which the discount coupon can be applied. (Don't forget that you can find your SKU in the "Manage Inventory" section of your Seller Central account.) After you have chosen the SKU or ASIN, click "Submit."

7. Once the product selection has been created, you will be redirected to "Create a new product selection." Now, in the "Purchased Items" of the drop-down menu, you must choose the product that you have just chosen for the promotion.

8. In the line "Buyer gets", you can choose between offering a discount in money or in percentage. This value already depends on your profit margin. It is advisable to handle the discounts in Money.

Note: Amazon does not allow 100% discount on a product, but you can offer the full amount in money.

9. Now we go to the line "Applies to", select "Purchased Items" and voila.

Congratulations! You have finished the first section!

Let's move on to the second section, which is pretty easy...

Programming:

10. In this step it is important to ask yourself the following question: How long do you want this promotion to be available to customers? If you already know then choose the start and end dates and times of your promotion. Please note that Amazon requires 4 hours to process and enable your promotion code, so you must choose a start time of at least 4 additional hours to the time you are defining the promotion.

11. Now you must enter a promotion theme or reason in «Internal Description», which is entirely for your own reference and, on the other hand, you do not need to enter a tracking code, since Amazon offers one for you.

Well, we have already completed the second section! It was easy, now let's go to section three.

Additional options:

Be careful in this step, many sellers make big mistakes that quickly turn into loss of money. So pay close attention!

12. In the "Claim Code" section, we must check the "Single Use" option and then a sub-menu is displayed in this section, which we will select with a little "One redemption per customer" and "Exclusive".

13. Next in the section "Customize messaging", we uncheck the option "Detail page display text". If you

don't uncheck it, each customer will be able to see the details of their promotion and the coupon code in their profile and the idea is that you share the coupon to a specific community.

14. The rest we leave as we find it and we click on "Review", immediately a new page loads which is just a matter of checking the promotion and clicking on "Submit".

Remember: We must wait at least 4 hours for amazon to finish processing the codes and discounts can be applied. If you want to check the status, from your seller account, enter the Promotions section and there you will see if the promotion is in process or complete.

15. Finally, to obtain the promotional codes for our products, simply enter the "Promotions" page, and click on the second tab "Manage Your promotion". A list will appear where we must select the one we have just created.

16. Now we click on the button "Manage Claim Codes". Once inside, it will ask us to indicate to which group or niche we are going to give the Amazon coupons. Select the amount and click on the "create" button.

17. Once the codes have been generated, we see how a new item from the list of promotional coupons is created at the bottom, it is just a matter of clicking Download and voila!

Congratulations, you have finished creating the amazon coupon or promo code campaign for your customers or community! That's all, I hope this information has been useful to you.

Alternative Strategies With Social Media

To drive the most social traffic to your store, it is vital to understand the value and benefits each network brings to your marketing strategy. Let's take a look at the protagonists of the universe of social networks:

Facebook

With more than 1.3 billion users, Facebook is the most popular social network, and it is an excellent space to share visually rich content and attract new customers through affordable and effective advertising, directed at specific market segments.

When it comes to traffic and sales, Facebook is the king of e-commerce, with almost two-thirds of visits to Shopify stores and an average of 85% of purchase orders coming from this social network.

Besides, with the purchase button for Facebook, you can display your products directly on your Facebook page, from where you will have the option to redirect your buyers to your website to make the payment or finish the purchase process without your customers having to leave Facebook.

To get the most out of Facebook, be sure to share great resolution photos of your products, as Facebook photos have been shown to generate more than 50% more "likes" than average posts.

Pinterest

Although Facebook is unrivaled, Pinterest is another

excellent channel for you to promote your products. It accounts for 13% of all social media traffic to Shopify stores and is particularly useful if you sell products for a specific niche, such as antiques, collectibles, books, or magazines. Pinterest is a highly visual platform, so be sure to create a spectacular photo collection.

Twitter

Twitter is a platform where users exchange content with their followers, who then share it with their followers, and so on. It has more than 232 million users around the world, with special penetration in the United States. The format of this platform makes it particularly enjoyable to grow the social reach of a business. Visually rich content such as photos and videos is especially valuable, generating 35% more retweets compared to text-only content. We recommend using shortcut links to drive traffic to your website and track results.

LinkedIn

With more than 250 million members, LinkedIn is known for being a professional social network and is particularly popular with businesses that sell to other businesses. Like Facebook and Twitter, LinkedIn lets you post to reach audiences that aren't following you yet.

On LinkedIn, people are mostly interested in discovering information about their industry, especially content that helps them improve their jobs. On the other hand, it also allows them to show their networks their knowledge and expertise about their profession and area of knowledge. In this sense, you can share information about the industry of your business, make contacts, and learn about new trends that you can consider to buy the next products you want to sell. Avoid using LinkedIn to sell your products at all costs, as your readers will not well receive it.

Instagram

Instagram is a fast-growing social network, where more than 300 million users worldwide sharing photos and videos. Brands have leveraged Instagram's highly visual community to connect directly with their audience, making it a great platform for visual marketing campaigns. Although you cannot share links in their posts, you can use this platform to promote your brand and share the URL of your website on your Instagram profile.

The focus of this social network is the beautiful visuals. If your product is not especially visual, use the platform to make your company more personal, and people can identify with it. Use images to illustrate the personality of your business and how special it is. Also, capitalize on user-generated content and encourage your customers to share (with corresponding credits) images of other people with your products.

CHAPTER 7

SO WHY NOT ADVERTISE ON AMAZON TO SELL YOUR PRODUCTS?

If you are already investing in Facebook Ads and Google Shopping, it is time to take the leap and see how one of the most extensive online advertising platforms works.

To help you in the field of Amazon, this chapter will tell you everything you need to know about advertising on Amazon, its concepts, and how to make an announcement step by step.

What are Amazon ads, and how do they work?

In the same way that Google's search engines work, Amazon's sponsored products are keyword-based ads and product targeting.

They appear at the top and bottom of search results pages, within organic results, on individual product pages, and under the label of "sponsored products related to this item."

The word "sponsored" allows us to identify that this is an advertised product.

The advertising system is very similar to that of Google Ads, and it is the PPC system (pay per click).

This means that the advertiser will only have to pay for their ads, if users click on them and not for impressions, as it happens on other platforms such as

Facebook ads.

Advertisers who want to gain greater visibility of their products on the Amazon platform, pay to fill these positions.

Also, another reason to bet on advertising on Amazon, is that sales history is a key factor for the platform to position you at the top of the ranking in organic search.

Types of advertising on Amazon

There are three types of advertising campaigns on Amazon:

- Sponsored products
- Sponsored brands
- Stores

It is as if it were a free buffet; these are the solutions that Amazon offers as self-service, and as we said, there are three types of campaigns.

1. Sponsored products

Within search results and product description pages, certain types of advertisements are shown, leading Amazon customers straight to a particular product available on the website.

This type of ads helps you increase the sales of your products since it is related to search terms.

They are usually displayed above or below the search results page and also on other product detail pages.

Sponsored products are activated by keyword, and advertisers have the option to choose between different match types, set a daily budget, and the duration of the campaign.

2. Sponsored brands

These ads include your brand logo, title, and up to three products, allowing you to increase your brand recognition.

The main feature of this ad is that you can create a personalized page as if it were a mini landing page of your brand and products within Amazon.

Users will reach this personalized page when they click on the title or the logo.

If you click on one of the products on this carousel, it will take you to a product detail page.

3. Stores

Stores are pages created for your products and categories with predesigned templates or content blocks.

You don't have to advertise on Amazon to create one, but you do have to be the owner of a brand that sells products.

We could say that stores are a portfolio of your brand, being able to direct users through a unique URL that Amazon provides you.

Notice that in the URL, you will see the word store.

The benefits of advertising on Amazon

As with any advertising platform, advertising on Amazon has strengths and weaknesses, but we will focus only on the benefits that will allow us to boost sales.

If people go to Facebook, they do searches and compares, but when they go to Amazon, they have in mind a single product, and there is a desire to buy it.

Perhaps, for this reason, the average cost per purchase is € 75.

A good number, right?

Advertising on Amazon allows us to optimize the performance of our ads by being able to select the budget, the start, and end date, and adjust the keywords to the search terms.

According to Patrical Ecommerce, the average cost per click on Amazon rarely exceeds € 0.31, which makes its ads cheaper based on CPC compared to other platforms such as Google Ads.

Also, we must bear in mind that Amazon searches show a clear transactional intention.

Finally, the different types of ads, as we have seen previously, allow sellers to choose the most appropriate ones depending on their advertising strategy and the available budget.

If you are looking for brand recognition, bet on sponsored brands, while sponsored products will allow you to compete with other products with similar or related characteristics.

How to make an advertising ad on Amazon step by step

Once the steps to take are known, it is time to get into the Amazon advertising platform.

1. Register with Amazon Seller Central

First of all, it is necessary that you are registered on the platform as a professional seller and that your account is active.

To create your account, you have to go on Amazon Seller Central and follow the steps to register, and you will have to provide data such as your country, password, and contact telephone number.

In the next step, you will have to fill in the information regarding your business, bank details, and taxes; you accept and confirm.

If all the data entered and the verifications are correct, Amazon will redirect you to your main professional sales account panel.

2. Inventory management

One step that we should not forget is uploading our products before creating an ad.

To do this, in the upper navigation bar, we go to "inventory" and select inventory management.

We upload the image, the product characteristics, the details, and we accept.

3. Creating your campaign

Now you must go to the "advertising" tab, located in the Amazon sales tutor, and click on start (the yellow button).

4. Budget, duration, and segmentation of your campaign

Write the name of your campaign; remember to write a name that allows you to identify what products you are promoting quickly.

In the next step, select the daily budget (remember that the minimum is € 1 per day) and the start and end date.

Amazon makes two types of segmentation available to us:

- **Automatic targeting:** Amazon will automatically decide how to display your ads considering the search terms most used by users in products similar to yours.
- **Manual targeting:** In this case, it's up to you to decide by which keywords you want your ad to be shown.

5. Creation of your ad group

If you run Facebook Ads campaigns, the structure with advertising campaigns on Amazon is very similar.

A campaign is composed of one or more ad groups, which, in effect, include different items.

Pick the goods you want to include in this promotion

and the default price, which is the average amount you're able to spend for a click that users make on your ads.

To establish a real average, Amazon gives you the option to see the average of the winning bids by category, this way, and you will have an idea of what the maximum amount is and adapt your bid.

If, in the previous step, you have selected manual segmentation, you must choose the keywords.

Amazon puts at your disposal a list that they consider interesting for you, but you can also set yours.

6. Your campaign is ready

If you have followed all the steps correctly, a message will appear that your campaign has been created correctly, and you will be able to view it in the Amazon campaign manager.

Please note that sponsored brands and stores will be subject to review within 72 hours before publication and commissioning.

You have created your first campaign on Amazon!

Also, as in any advertising platform, we must keep track of the statistics and data produced by our ads.

From the "reports" tab of the main bar, we can understand how our ads are working and conclude with the different KPIs that the platform shows us.

Welcome to Amazon!

Now your products and your brand will be reaching

the right people, and you will be building a consolidated relationship with users.

Take advantage of the full potential of the Bezos platform to have a presence from just one euro a day, combining the advertising strategy with other platforms.

CHAPTER 8

SHIPPING VIA FBA STEP BY STEP

The purpose of this chapter is to help you successfully send your first shipment of products to Amazon FBA. Since Amazon has fairly strict shipping guidelines, we will review its preparation, packaging, labeling, and delivery requirements to ensure that your first delivery and your first encounter with FBA go smoothly.

If you're new to selling on Amazon, you will first register on Amazon as a seller. To create a seller account on Amazon, simply follow the step-by-step instructions. Choose "Fulfillment by Amazon" (FBA) option when you're ready to list your orders. Amazon can stock, box, assemble, and ship the order to a retailer with this option, as well as handle customer support and returns. Your primary duty as a retailer is to keep track of the inventory and, if necessary, restock it.

An overview of the FBA process

In what follows, we will outline the process of selling your products on FBA. Follow these steps to make sure that your first shipment of FBAs to the Amazon distribution center goes smoothly:

1. Decide which products you want to sell on Amazon FBA (and contact a supplier).

2. Sign up for a retailer account with Amazon.

3. List the goods you want to sell on Amazon FBA and use your seller account to build a shipping schedule!

4. Choose a forwarder who can transport your manufacturer to the designated fulfillment center (the chosen forwarder will know and comply with Amazon's planning, packaging, marking, and shipping specifications for your products).

5. Your goods are shipped to the designated Amazon fulfillment center.

This chapter will focus on steps 3 through 5 and cover everything you need to know for your products to be successfully delivered to Amazon FBA.

Build your shipping plan on Amazon

Once everything is set up, and you are ready to send your products to Amazon FBA, you log into your Amazon Seller account and create a new shipping plan. First, you need to specify the products you want to send to Amazon. Then you have to specify whether you sell 'individual products' or 'packaged products.' Check the "Individual items" box when you send boxes containing one or more products of variable quantity and condition. Select Products packed in a box if all the products in your box have an SKU (unique product identifier) and a corresponding condition, i.e., each box containing the same product contains the same quantity and has been pre-packed by the manufacturer. Then,

- Define the quantity for each product
- Provide the preparation guide depending on the type of product you have
- Print labels
- Review and approve your shipment to FBA

The shipping method with details of the carrier: For this step, you also specify the number of boxes and print your shipping labels. (If your shipment is eligible for the Amazon Partnership Shipping Program, this is also where you plan and pay for your shipment.)

A summary of the shipment process, where you can review the contents of your shipments and track your shipment and its receipt status at the FBA warehouse.

For steps 2 and 3: If you prefer not to prepare and label your products yourself, Amazon FBA offers to solve this problem for an additional cost via its FBA label service and its FBA preparation service. You just need to select 'Amazon' from the 'who-prepares' drop-down menu and 'Amazon' from the 'who-labels' drop-down menu.

Finally, make sure your shipping plan is accurate and reflects the products you want to send to Amazon. When you are satisfied, continue to approve your shipment (s). Based on your shipping plan, i.e. what products you ship and from where you shop, Amazon assigns you an order processing center. In other words, you do not influence the warehouse to which you will ship.

When you are satisfied with your shipping plan, the

actual shipment of your products is as follows:

Sending your products to an Amazon distribution center

When you send your products to an Amazon distribution center, you have three options:

- Sending to Amazon FBA with a forwarder
- Ask your supplier to ship your products directly to Amazon
- Select to ship with Amazon partner partners via the Partner program (only for small package deliveries and to Amazon European markets)

Whichever option is chosen above, Amazon's preparation and labeling requirements must be met. Otherwise, you risk losing your shipment through Amazon, which would delay your time and money enormously.

Choose your supplier to manage preparation and shipping

If your supplier sends your products directly to Amazon, you will save time and money by eliminating the middleman. However, you should instead carefully tell your supplier the Amazon preparation and labeling guidelines, as well as the labels to follow that your supplier will place correctly on your products. Everything must be perfectly aligned so that delivery to Amazon is not mistaken. It is certainly possible, but we do not recommend this solution for small package shipments.

Another thing to consider is the fact that if your supplier ships your products directly to Amazon, you run a potential risk that once your supplier becomes familiar with the FBA requirements and process, nothing prevents your supplier from you cutting you off and selling its products directly to Amazon in the future.

Finally, if you choose this solution, make sure that your supplier ships your products with duty paid (incoterm DDP), because Amazon will not pay any shipping or customs fees for your account.

Sending to Amazon FBA via a forwarder

The logistics of getting your products to Amazon FBA can potentially take an enormous amount of time, energy, and money. Therefore, your freight forwarder must understand the process of transferring international goods to Amazon.

As soon as your shipment exceeds approximately 135 kg, it is no longer advantageous for you to use the well-known (express) courier services, such as DHL, UPS, FedEx, etc. Instead, you need to find a freight forwarder to process your shipment from your manufacturer to Amazon FBA.

A freight forwarder will first be able to coordinate each step of the shipping process for you, which can be very helpful if you are inexperienced in the shipping industry. Besides, if you go to an appropriate freight forwarder who is knowledgeable about FBA activities (which we highly recommend), they can even prepare your goods for smooth delivery to Amazon. This includes, but is not limited to, the following:

- Check your goods for damage
- Check that the size and weight of the box does not exceed Amazon's requirements
- Label your boxes for yourself according to FBA guidelines
- Pack your cartons on pallets, including stretch film and labels
- Schedule an appointment for delivery
- Transport products to the specified distribution center

The obvious advantage of these solutions is that you (i.e., your freight forwarder) control the quality of your products and make sure that Amazon's packaging and labeling standards are met, which reduces the risk of rejection of your shipment by Amazon FBA.

The downside to this solution is the extra cost you pay to an "intermediary" to prepare your products or the extra time you have to spend doing it yourself if the products are sent to your address instead of leaving a freight forwarder to do it. And finally, the cost of the additional handling between your supplier and the Amazon processing center. However, we know from experience that it is worth spending a little more because a lot in this process can go wrong. By trusting your products with an experienced Amazon FBA forwarder, you will greatly benefit from their expertise and resources, and you will have the guarantee that your products will arrive safely at the final destination.

Partner Program with Amazon

If you only carry small quantities, you may be able to benefit from the Amazon Partnered Carrier program—depending on the shipping location and the size of your shipment.

To be able to benefit from the Amazon Partnered Carrier program, the length of your box must not exceed 75 cm and the maximum weight to bear without other conditions is 15 kg. If your package weighs between 15 and 30 kg, it must be marked "Heavyweight/team lift," visible from above and from the sides of each heavy unit.

The partner operator program allows sellers on Amazon to take advantage of Amazon-negotiated messaging rates. This partnership transport program is only available for small packages in Europe. For shipments abroad or to overseas departments and territories -DOM-TOM-, you must organize the transport yourself.

Also, if your shipment is more than half a pallet, it must be palletized, and the Amazons partner program will not be available. Once the size of half a pallet is reached, you must find your forwarder, and a delivery appointment must be made between the order processing center and your transporter.

Now let's get to the basics of using the Amazon FBA service: Prepare your products according to Amazon requirements. Whether you do it yourself or have a third party manage it for you, you must do well to prevent Amazon from refusing your products on delivery.

FBA Delivery Guidelines: How to Prepare Your Products for Shipping and Delivery

At first glance, Amazon's shipping requirements for sending your products to an Amazon fulfillment center may seem complicated and overwhelming. For your shipment to go smoothly, you must prepare and label your products according to Amazon guidelines. Otherwise, Amazon may refuse to receive your shipment upon arrival at its distribution centers.

Preparation conditions

When you register your products with your Amazon Seller account, Amazon provides you with a detailed guide to products requiring special packaging and preparation directly online.

The list of special preparation categories includes:

- Brittle
- Liquids/gels
- Textiles
- Plush/Baby items
- Sharp Objects
- Small Objects
- Adult items

Whether you're selling baby products, liquids, or fragile items, Amazon has recommendations for everything.

Labeling and barcodes

All products sent to Amazon FBA must have a single, readable, and correct barcode so that fulfillment centers can identify and register them upon arrival. If Amazon cannot read your product's barcode, it may face problems, such as determining the content of your item, its membership, or its destination. The correct application of this label ensures that the correct unit is received and that your inventory is accounted for.

Amazon FBA distinguishes between products that you must label yourself and products that already contain a barcode from the eligible manufacturer. Therefore, these things they call "sticker-free and mixed inventory" are items you can send to Amazon distribution centers without even having to sign them. We'll explain the two barcodes submit choices to FBA in the following: using the current manufacturer's barcodes (only for qualifying products).

Print barcodes/labels from your Amazon Seller page.

Mixed inventory, without the sticker

Some products meet the requirements for using the manufacturer's barcode. If your preference is set, the manufacturer's barcode will be used to identify and track your inventory throughout the Amazon fulfillment process. Note that when you choose this option, your products will be mixed with items of the same products sold by other sellers.

For a fact, that ensures that if a buyer orders one of your goods, Amazon will distribute the available product nearest to the same buyer, even though it's not "your" goods, that is to say, you didn't submit that particular product to Fulfillment. This takes core. In such a scenario, Amazon will transfer an identical product from the warehouse to the vendor whose product has been used to satisfy the order of the buyer, and you will, of course, collect credit for the sale as usual.

Finally, when you use the manufacturer's barcode as a label option, it allows Amazon to provide fast shipping for that particular product while saving you time and money because you don't have to apply Amazon barcodes to your products yourself.

Eligible manufacturers' barcodes include UPC, EAN, and ISBN codes. To be able to use them, your product must respect the following elements:

- Your product(s) will have one scannable barcode in the Amazon Catalog that fits a standard ASIN (Amazon barcode).
- The expiration date of the product(s) must not be set.
- Your drug must not be either consumable or topical (for example, oil, shampoo, or cosmetics).

Label your products yourself

If your products are not eligible for mixed inventory without a sticker, you must label them yourself with FBA labels, and you must follow the label requirements of Amazon for your shipment to arrive at Amazon distribution centers quickly and accurately. Amazon barcodes include ASIN and FNSKU.

When creating your shipping plan, the third step will allow you to print your labels. These must be sent to your forwarder if you do not label the products yourself (and the boxes).

Each of your products requires a label that can be scanned—this applies to all products. In other words, if you have a large box containing ten headsets, each set should be labeled with a barcode. It is not enough to label the box containing your products. Besides, it is essential that the label is placed on a smooth surface and covers all existing barcodes. Do not put the mark around corners, curves, and tops, as this can jeopardize the probability of scanning them and slow down the receipt process, thus slowing your unit's availability.

For products requiring additional preparation, such as bagging or bubble wrap, you must make sure that the labels can be scanned without opening the packaging. This also applies to mixed inventory without a sticker. Also, the barcodes on the labels cannot be smeared, discolored, or torn, as this would also complicate their scanning. The same goes for labeling your shipping cartons: the labels should be placed on the carton (s), away from seams, edges, or corners, and if you are reusing cartons, be sure to cover the old labels.

Be aware of the requirements for pallets

If you're delivering pallets to an Amazon fulfillment center, it's important to know the following requirements:

- When delivering pallets to distribution centers in EU countries, the pallets must measure 80 x 120 cm (standard European pallet).
- When delivering stock to the UK, the pallets must measure 120 x 100 cm (British standard pallet). Other pallet sizes will be rejected.
- The maximum height for single stacked pallets is 1.7 m and 1.5 m for double-stacked pallets (including pallet height).
- Pallets must not exceed 500 kg gross weight, including the weight of the pallet.
- Pallets should be wrapped in a clear plastic.
- Pallets imported internationally must comply with standard ISPM15 (heat-treated pallets).
- The maximum weight for each carton on the pallet is 15 kg. If it exceeds the 15 kg limit, it must indicate "Heavy Weight" on the top and sides of the box.
- All shipments other than small package deliveries must be palletized.
- All pallets containing mixed but visually similar products must be labeled "mixed product" or "mixed SKUs."
- All the pallets must contain the following information in the upper right corner of one of the sides:
- Name of the supplier
- to and from addresses
- Order number (s)

- Number of boxes
- Number of pallets ("Pallet no. ___ sure ___.")

Requirements for scheduling deliveries to Amazon FBA

Scheduling appointments to deliver your products to Amazon must also follow certain guidelines.

You must complete the booking form and specify the requested information, such as the number of pallets and cartons, and the purchase order number, which is your Amazon reference ID. Once you have filled out the reservation form, you send it to your transporter, who must then contact the designated distribution center and make an appointment for delivery. In addition to the purchase order number, the carrier must also provide a PRO number and a bill of lading number (B/L).

For all incoming deliveries, the appointed courier will require a delivery date at least 24 hours in advance. Since Amazon demands that FBA orders be shipped at very precise hours—often late at night and in a very short timeframes—this will create delays in the actual delivery period we are delivering to you. As with any other airline. Finally, all palletized deliveries must be made on a truck weighing at least 7.5 tonnes. This ensures that the truck can reverse to the loading dock and allows an electric pallet truck to access the back of the truck. Private vehicles such as cars and vans will be refused.

Deliveries went wrong

No one has to talk about the orders and ships. Therefore, you must be aware of the most common issues that may cause delays or even rejection of your goods during the delivery period. Be mindful of the following mistakes to ensure your goods are shipped successfully:

- If your goods are not correctly packed for shipping.
- If goods are mistakenly labeled or have illegible labels.
- If your shipment includes unexpected items: e.g., several packages in the same package, no record made, or you delivered more than specified, etc.
- If products are "gone," for example, point of sale packets used as packages or when sets of several items are incorrectly labeled.
- If the state or explanation of the product does not suit what is stated in Amazon programs, for instance, an incorrect version, condition, or relation.
- When the pallet's height reaches the 1.7 m limit for a single stack, and 1.5 m for a double stack.
- When dangerous items present a risk to safety.
- Where various goods use the same barcodes.
- When liquid goods are not sealed properly and leaked.
- When you bring in the outer box, wrapped goods with a single name when attempting to

distribute several items.

- When you have many barcodes in your company, and have not hidden the old ones.
- When you place the barcode sticker on the outer bag, and it might have come off.
- If your boxes are too big, without an alarm mark (> 15 kg).

Taxes and duties

It is important to note that Amazon takes no responsibility for the taxes or duties to which your shipment may be subject. Then, make sure that the package is processed by inspection so that fines, fees, or other costs are charged in advance before being shipped to Amazon. Therefore, upon arrival at the Amazon factory, the order will be denied. Amazon does not serve as the official importer or final purchaser of imported products from you.

Risky products

Be mindful that Amazon FBA imposes limitations on particular goods that you are not permitted to sell through FBA. The list below does not cover all those fields, but offers some examples:

- HAZMAT products: compressed gases and flammable products. Sending lithium batteries requires additional product information
- Perishable products/expiry date: for example, food and pregnancy tests
- Heavy goods exceeding 30 kg
- Tobacco, firearms, prescription drugs, alcohol, liquid containers larger than 1L, knives

What happens next?

When your products have been purchased and scanned by Amazon, they stock them at the distribution center, and your goods will usually be available for sale on Amazon within three working days.

In your Amazon Seller account, you can review, monitor, and track (if applicable) your shipment simultaneously. Visit the "View Summary" page to track the progress of your shipment as FBA receives it. If there is a problem with your shipment, you will also be informed.

If, after 72 hours, your shipment has not been fully received, please contact Amazon Technical Support for assistance.

CHAPTER 9

WHAT IS PRIVATE LABEL ON AMAZON?

To start selling successfully, you will have to make a vital decision. What product will you sell? Making this decision is the number 1 obstacle that prevents new Amazon sellers from starting their business.

Choosing the wrong product to sell on Amazon can cause your business to fail before the event begins.

What is Amazon Private Label?

Selling and making money with Amazon is one of the goals that many merchants and brand owners have set for themselves during this last year, some have achieved great results, and others keep trying. Without a doubt, we know that starting an online business may seem simple, but everything behind it is what makes the business work as expected.

A private label product is manufactured by a licensed or third-party supplier and is marketed under a supermarket or retailer's brand name. Like the store, you specify everything about the product—made from, how it is packaged, what the label looks like—and you pay to have it produced and sent to your store. It compares with purchasing goods from other firms that have their name on them.

For example, Target sells a variety of snack brands from companies like General Mills and Frito-Lay, but it

also sells its cookies under the Archer Farms brand—
which is Target's private label brand.

Beauty salons often create their brands of shampoo,
conditioners, and styling products for their consumers
to purchase and take home. Restaurants often decide
to make a private label for their seasonings or blends
that have become popular with their consumers.
Grooming services can make a line of private label
household cleaners, and pet stores can make their line
of pet food and grooming tools.

Private Label Categories

Almost all consumer product categories have both
private label and brand offerings, including:

- Personal care
- Drinks
- Cosmetics
- Paper Products
- Household cleaners
- Condiments and salad dressings
- Daily use items
- Frozen food

While private label goods remain in the minority,
accounting for 15 percent of U.S. retail revenues,
according to the Harvard Business Review, certain
types of private labels remain to experience
tremendous success, according to a Nielsen survey.

Advantages

Stores interested in filling their shelves with products

with their brand name have a good reason. Some of the great advantages of private label are:

- **Production control:** The factories work under the direction of the store, offering complete control of the ingredients of the products and the quality.
- **Price control:** Stores can determine the cost of the product and a profitable price.
- **Adaptability:** Smaller stores can move quickly to obtain a private label for production in response to growing market demand for a new feature. At the same time, larger companies may not be interested in a niche.
- **Brand Control:** Private label products carry the brand name and packaging design that the store created.
- **Control of profitability:** Thanks to control of costs and prices, stores can control the level of profitability of supplying their products.

Disadvantages

The disadvantages of adding a private label are few, as long as you have the financial resources to invest in the development of such a product. The main disadvantages are:

Manufacturer dependency: The production of your product line is in the hands of a third party manufacturer, so it is important to get involved with well-established companies. Otherwise, you may lose opportunities if your manufacturer has problems.

Difficulty building loyalty: Well-established home brands include the margo frying pan, which can be sold at several retailers, sometimes. Your goods can only be available in your shops, thus limiting customer access. Of course, limited availability can also be seen as a perk, giving consumers a reason to come back and buy from you.

Even though private label products are sold at a lower price, some private label brands are positioning themselves as premium products, with a higher price to prove it.

The Private Label of a product means that you work with a manufacturer and buy a generic product that you can make your own by adding your own brand/logo to that product.

Amazon is a super competitive place to sell, and as more people jump on the Amazon FBA bandwagon, it naturally becomes more difficult to find low-competition products to sell.

What it consists of?

To start, the first thing you need to have is your private label, and if you already have it, you are likely thinking of launching your product on Amazon. We will look at five steps that will help you make sure you have done everything necessary before you start selling your private label on Amazon.

The most important business objective for more than 30% of sellers on Amazon during the past year 2019 has been the launch of new private brands to market within the Amazon marketplace.

While investing in a private label from idea to practical execution takes time and extensive research, an increasing number of Amazon sellers and brands are doing so because they have witnessed the success of others and are drawn to the lack of direct competition in private label ASINs.

Private Label Products

Private label products are mostly products made by a third party and sold under your brand. The manufacturer of those products does not have any right on the label or brand you decide to use, and you can decide on the design of the product and its packaging, your brand logo, labeling, and all other creative elements that you can use to identify the product with your brand.

Starting an Amazon private label business can be highly profitable if approached with detailed strategy, the right resources, and the necessary industry experience. In this section, we'll clarify how to get started on Amazon with a private label business model and offer realistic advice on how to ensure success.

Start with the Private Label in 5 Steps

Step 1: Research To Identify The Correct Product That Can Be Added To Your Catalog

When figuring out what products might make sense for a white label, you should look for a product that is endorsed and can realistically become a best seller.

Brainstorm about the activities, services, or product categories that interest you, and then make a list of the products associated with each of them. Start with a broader list that you can narrow down gradually to make sure you cover all of your bases.

Be sure to take into account existing or potential demand, including fluctuations in sales or seasonality. On the other hand, find out if you can create a recurring demand. It is recommended to search Amazon, including lists of best sellers and new releases, products that work well, and have little or no competition. You can also research social media to uncover any budding consumer trends.

Step 2: Partner With A Supplier And Manufacturer With Enough Experience

Your distributor plays an important role in the success of your private label products. While cost will be critical in determining the correct provider, it may not necessarily be the only factor. The cost of labor and material must be taken into account, as well as the estimation of the currency if it is a foreign supplier when evaluating the options.

It's best if you only consider vendors with expertise in products similar to the ones you want to create, to make sure they are credible and reliable. Try to establish a relationship over the phone and visit their production facilities to have a clear understanding of how and where your products will be manufactured.

Step 3: Conceptualization And Approval Of Your Brand Logo And The Design And Packaging Of Your Product

An advantage of selling private label products on Amazon is the lack of direct competition, which means that you can automatically win the Buy Box on the ASIN. While you may face indirect competition, no one is selling the same product.

In addition to the physical components of a product such as the product itself and packaging, you can also differentiate your brand from the competition with a compelling value proposition and brand story. These two most intangible elements of your brand can help promote brand awareness, consumer engagement, and social proof.

Aiming to attract potential buyers, bold and unique colors, fonts, and design elements can be infused into your logo and packaging, and consistency must be maintained across all additional products added to your private label line to demonstrate the consistency of the brand. When creating the brand concept and physical design, let's not forget the target customer and make sure that the decision we make is attractive to him.

Step 4: Request Product Samples To Do Quality Control

Once you've developed your product, ensure you ask your supplier for samples to be sure that quality and other specifications are exactly what you're looking for before hitting the market. By sharing the prototypes and packaging with various groups of people, including potential buyers, you will be able to get any feedback that needs to be addressed before placing the initial bulk order.

Step 5: Determine Your Amazon Compliance Strategy

Before you decide whether to fulfill your Amazon orders through a merchant fulfillment operation (Fulfillment by Merchant or Seller Fulfilled Prime) or through Fulfillment by Amazon, you will need to understand which products have proven successful with each method of compliance.

Do your products need special handling? Are your products more prone to damage from extreme temperature fluctuations? Do you want to have the Amazon Prime badge on every product you sell? Do you have the bandwidth to handle customer service and returns?

To determine which products are best suited to each compliance method, whichever route you finally choose, you must consider the size of your operation, your product categories, and your business goals for the year.

CHAPTER 10

CONCLUSION

It is always said that "if you are not on the first page of Google, you are nobody, you do not exist." Well, it's the same on Amazon. If you are not in the top 10 results on your keywords, your product sales will suffer the consequences. Discover in this final chapter how to be well-positioned on Amazon and thus generate more sales...

Introducing A9: Amazon's Algorithm

A9 is the name of the ranking algorithm made on Amazon. Since this is a guide to properly referencing your products on Amazon, let's start at the beginning.

A lot of the work is done before the customer even touches the keyboard. Once the customer presses the "Enter" key to perform a search, the A9 ranking algorithm provides the results through a two-step process:

It's a fairly simple process basically:

- First, they sort the relevant results from their extensive "catalog" of product lists;
- Then they sort these results in an order that is "most relevant" to the user.

Now, some of you SEOs might think, "Wait for a second... Providing relevant results is Google's domain. I thought Amazon only cared about conversions!"

The response is simple: Amazon's importance doesn't mean the same as Google's. Read the Amazon A9 quote carefully to see if you can tell the difference:

"We don't give the visitor what they are looking for, but what they would like to buy. We must anticipate. For this, our algorithm uses human judgments, programmable analyses, case studies, and of course, the results of concrete and analyzed conversions."

Understood?

Google says, "What are the most accurate results to meet the searcher's query?"

Amazon says, "What products are researchers most likely to buy?"

The difference between these two questions is the difference between how Amazon measures relevance to Google.

Ranking on Amazon is easier than ranking on Google because you essentially cut the work in half. A complete Amazon SEO plan uses only internal factors to determine the ranking of a product. Backlinks, social media, domain authority... These are all things you don't have to worry about on Amazon. Officially no... Unofficially... yes!

Cockpitlab tip: Send a ton of traffic to your Amazon listing, with super URLs and analyze the positioning of your product.

Keep these three rules in mind:

- Amazon's main goal in everything it does is

always to maximize revenue per customer (RPC);

- Amazon tracks every action a person takes on Amazon, to where their mouse is on the page;
- The A9 algorithm exists to link the data tracked in #2 to the goal stated in #1.

So far, so good?

What Influences The Amazon A9 Ranking Algorithm?

Conversion rates - These are ranking factors that Amazon says have a statistically relevant effect on conversion rates. Examples of conversion rate factors include customer feedback, meeting Amazon image requirements, and pricing.

Relevance - Remember the first step in the Amazon A9 ranking algorithm? They collect the results and then decide how to record them. Relevance factors tell A9 when to consider your product page for a given search term. Relevance factors include your title and description of your product.

Customer Satisfaction - How do you make most of a single customer's money? Make them so happy they want to come back here. Amazon understands that building consumer satisfaction is the key to optimizing an RPC. It is much more difficult to get someone to spend € 100 once than € 10 ten times. Ranking factors for customer retention include seller feedback and order defect rate.

AMZcockpit Note: Amazon uses both expected and

actual conversion rates for product classification. For example, because your product is priced over other equivalent items, Amazon would assume a lower sales rate for your ad and use that figure before it is checked by the actual results.

All correct! Now, we are about to continue learning about the Amazon rankings. What you'll see below are variables on the Amazon list, whether supported by Amazon itself or by individual advertisers.

The Most Important Amazon Ranking Factors

Amazon is not like Google, where they go to great lengths to hide the factors they use in their algorithm. In Amazon's Seller Central, they'll blatantly tell you many of their main ranking factors.

Ranking Factors For Conversion Rates

1- Sales classification

After just a little research on Amazon, it should be pretty obvious that the number of sales compared to other similar products—also known as "Sales Rank"—is one of the most important ranking factors.

Even now, in their search results, Amazon is testing a new feature where they instantly apply a #1 Bestseller banner to the top-selling items in the search genre.

It's very simple…

More sales mean better Amazon ranking, and higher Amazon ranking means more sales!

It sounds like a virtuous circle, but fortunately, there

are still many ways for new sellers to make room for themselves. If you have a problem with "Amazon hijackers" listing hackers, make sure you know how to protect yourself first!

2- Customer reviews.

It is probably not necessary to say that the number and positive nature of your comments is one of the most important ranking factors of the Amazon A9 algorithm. How you respond to your comments is also important!

3- Answers to questions

It's one of those metrics that Amazon doesn't specifically point to. But, this is the data they have access to, and the questions and answers are listed near the top of the product page, which usually means that this is important for conversions.

4- Image size and quality

Amazon continues to tighten its product listing logo size and Price Policies. Right now, some categories don't even show results that don't have at least an image of 1000 × 1000 pixels or more. These are called "deleted lists."

The image size of 1000 × 1000 pixels allows Amazon to offer its customers the Zoom feature, which has a dramatic effect on conversion rates.

Apart from the artistic side, when your cursor hovers over the image, Amazon automatically displays an enlarged version in the product information panel.

Note that it is not the number of images that is

important here. The yoga mat in the example cited earlier is the #1 product for the keyword "yoga mat," but it only has five images. Since the image is large enough and informative enough to give the customer all the information they need, that's all it takes to make Amazon happy.

You can be ranked higher if you have a single large, high-quality image than if you have multiple images of normal size. I don't mean that multiple images don't convert better than one, just that the benefits quickly fade after the first one.

5- Price

Remember earlier, when we talked about how the Amazon rating algorithm uses both predicted and real conversion levels to decide what items to include in its search results?

One of the most important ranking factors that Amazon uses to determine the expected conversion rate is the price—they know that customers tend to look for the best deals. More importantly, Amazon uses price as a major factor in choosing the product to display in the shopping box, which is the part of the page containing the Add to Cart button (we'll talk about that later).

Note, for example, that the product ranked best for the search term "juicer" has fewer customer reviews, a lower customer ranking, and a lower sales ranking than all other ads in the top 3. It is better ranked than competitors because it has a lower price while having a good rating and maybe its image is 1000 * 1000 compared to other products...

Note that comments are vital. And the price is not the only reason why the juicer ranks quite well.

6- Parent-child products

If you have a list of (parent) products and decide to offer a color or size variation, these are known as (children's list). They appear on the same list as the variations. It's best to use the built-in parent-child product functionality of Amazon Seller Central to direct all customers to a single product page.

This has several advantages:

- It maximizes feedback from your customers, as Amazon will combine your like products into one page of primary products;
- From the UX point of view, this is the only rational solution; having consumers on the same page increases the probability of purchasing the product; Amazon has demonstrated preferential rating of goods with several choices on their catalog.

7- Time on the page and bounce rate

Remember, Amazon can measure all of a customer's interactions with its website, so it's easy for them to track detail on-page time and bounce rate statistics.

Here's exactly what these similar but different measures mean on Amazon:

Time spent on the page:

Amazon estimates the time a customer spends on your product page is a good indicator of their interest in your product. A customer who reads the full description of your product, reviews, and investigates questions and answers is much more likely to buy than one who spends a few seconds browsing through the features.

Rebound rate:

A "bounce" occurs when a customer searches, visits your page, then returns to the search results or clicks on a related product offering. Bear in mind that Amazon has a much more reliable bounce rate metric than Google, mostly because all user interaction is occurring on their website.

8- Completeness of the product list

Finally, the last conversion measure to optimize is the completeness of the product list. The different sections of the product list mainly have to do with relevance, but the completeness of the amazon product sheet affects the conversion rate.

In general, the more complete your ad, the better. Do your best to fill in all fields on the product configuration page to maximize your chances of appearing at the top of product search results.

Relevance Ranking Factors

9- Title

On Google, you want a concise and engaging title with your keyword from the start.

On Amazon, all you care about are the keywords. You want to pile up as many keywords as possible in about 80 characters.

You can go beyond 80 characters if you want, and it's better to have too many keywords than too few. I saw products at the top of the list with titles that make no sense and that have more than 200 characters:

Note that Amazon is starting to crack down and normalize product titles - keep your eyes open for the future.

10- Characteristics/Bulleted list/Bullet Points

As with images, the features are so important that Amazon no longer allows products without chips to be presented in the shopping box, and not having them is a serious obstacle to ranking well on Amazon.

11- Product description

The description of your product is basically where you develop your features. It is also the part of the page over which you have the most control. If there is somewhere where there is a lot of effort to be made to get involved, it is in the description of the product.

That said, keep in mind that unlike Google, there is no benefit in having a keyword appear multiple times on the product page; if it appears at least once in your list of products, you will be able to position yourself on it.

12- Manufacturer's brand and part number

Something that each of the best products specifies is the brand and manufacturer number first in the product title. If you do the research yourself, it is not until the 20th result that Amazon shows us a list of products without the brand and manufacturer number included in the title.

You always, always want to include a brand in your title .because it allows your product to search filters AND allows you to capture customers looking for a specific brand. And if you find yourself in a niche where customers use the manufacturer's number to search for products, you want to include that keyword in your title.

However, this strategy works for well-known brands.

I place my keywords first and then my brand.

Nothing official, but either there is a weighting of the first words, or it will come from Amazon A9.

13- Technical characteristics

This is the section of the website on which you mention the product's technological and physical details.

It is the last tab on the creation or modification of a product on Amazon Seller Central fr.

This includes size, shipping weight, color, date of

publication (if you are making books), technical specifications, and more.

14- Category and sub-category

You may not have noticed this, because if a customer has reached a category, any other searches they perform on Amazon would be limited to that category by default.

When making your list of products, be sure to place your product in the most relevant and narrowest category possible.

15- Search terms

In addition to the categories, you can also specify the search terms you want to associate with your product.

Even if Amazon lists five different 50-character search term fields, you'd better think of it as a large 250-character text box where you can enter all the possible search terms you can think of for your product.

16- Source keyword

This is one of Amazon's most secret means of assessing the suitability of an ad for a particular product quest. It is also another example of how Amazon tracks every detail of a customer's activity on its website.

Therefore, if I were to buy the yoga mat, Amazon would know that this list is very relevant to the term "yoga mat." The next time a customer searches for this term, this list is more likely to be ranked at the top of the list simply because by searching for this keyword, there is a conversion, so the relevance is checked.

Here's a good little Amazon ranking hack that you can do to take advantage of this factor:

- Build a URL for your product list using the query [& keyword = your + keyword] (add the code in parentheses to your product URL);
- Use a link shortening service like bit.ly to create a shareable link to this URL;
- Direct traffic to the shortened link.

Now, every time you make a sale from one of these links, you are deceiving Amazon by telling it that the sale was made with a specific search word.

Customer Satisfaction Ranking Factors

17- Negative comment from the seller

Why do I list negative comments from sellers in particular, as opposed to comments from sellers in general?

It is interesting to note that Amazon claims not to follow positive feedback from sellers, at least not in the interest of their product classification algorithm.

Instead, they track sellers' negative feedback rates or frequency. No matter how bad the feedback is—any negative feedback is the same, and everything counts against you too in terms of ranking the search results.

To be clear—as a third party seller trying to win the shopping box, you want your seller feedback to be as high as possible. However, the negative feedback rate is the only measure that has a known effect on product search results.

18- Order processing speed

Amazon understands that quick and reliable delivery is one of the easiest ways to make consumers happy. Therefore, a supplier or seller who has demonstrated consistent and efficient order processing is more likely to rank higher than a supplier who has had complains of inaccurate or slow deliveries.

19- Stock

Customers hate when they want a product but can't get it. One of the most common reasons for this issue is when an item is out of stock, or when a seller does not keep proper inventory tracking.

Whether you are a first seller or a third party seller, it is essential to keep your inventory in stock to maintain a high ranking, both in the search results for A9 products and in the purchase box of your product.

Two of the main indicators of customer satisfaction are the percentage of orders refunded and the percentage of cancellation before execution. In both cases, Amazon has found that sellers with low inventory rates tend to have higher refunds and cancellations, which is bad for customer retention. This principle is especially for sellers Amazon FBM (Fulfillment by Merchant or Shipped by the seller) because with Amazon FBA, stocks are up to date.

20- Percentage of perfect order (POP)

POP is a measure of the number of orders that go perfectly from the moment the customer clicks on "Add to cart" until the product arrives at his home.

When you have a high percentage of perfect order, it means you have a high stock rate, accurate product lists, and fast delivery. This is exactly what Amazon wants for each of its customers, so they will naturally rank the most popular sellers before the less popular ones.

Don't forget customer satisfaction!

21- Order defect rate (ODR)

ODR is the opposite measure of POP.

Each time a customer makes a complaint with an

order, it is considered as an order defect. Here are some of the most common ways in which an order can be faulty:

- Negative feedback from buyers;
- Guarantee request from A to Z;
- Any type of shipping problem;
- Chargeback by credit card.

Each of these examples alone would count for your order defect rate, which is the number of order faults relative to the total number of orders executed over a given period. Amazon says all sellers should aim for an ODR of less than 1%.

Important! Negative comments withdrawn by the buyer do not count towards the calculation.

22- Exit rate

How much time does a consumer use and leaves Amazon on your ad? This is the threshold of exit.

When your page has a departure rate above normal, Amazon will take it as an indication that you have a low quality ad. Generally, a high exit rate is attributed to a low stock-in-stock rate on your offer, or because your commercial is not complete.

23- Packaging options

It's a measure I didn't think Amazon was using for ranking, but recently I've seen things like this in product search results:

It is clear that packaging options are something that

worry Amazon customers. But even if it didn't, it's a great way to separate your ad from other similar products (and get higher rankings with an increased conversion rate).

One easy way to achieve this is through Amazon's Distribution to offer frustration-free packaging. That is because Amazon uses fewer packaging and products which are entirely recyclable without losing quality protection.

Main Points To Remember To Reference Your Products On Amazon Properly:

Amazon's primary target is full CPC (revenue per customer).

For rank goods, the Amazon ranking algorithm uses delivery efficiency, significance and customer loyalty.

Use as many keywords as possible to fill up as much of the feature list listing as possible.

Optimize customer service using FBA (Fulfillment by Amazon).

Find opportunities to promote customer input, and do whatever you can to please them, such as AMZcockpit.

Above all: More sales = better rankings = more sales.

There you have it! You now know exactly what Amazon rankings are looking for to ensure their customers are satisfied.